THE GOLDEN EAGLE

King of Birds

Also published by Melven Press

Seton Gordon: The Immortal Isles.

The author at 90. (*Adam Watson*)

THE
GOLDEN EAGLE
King of Birds

by

SETON PAUL GORDON, C.B.E.

with a foreword by

Desmond Nethersole-Thompson

MELVEN

PRESS

PERTH 1980

ISBN 0 906664 04 7

Acknowledgements are due to the following without whose advice
and assistance this reprint would not have been possible:
Desmond Nethersole-Thompson, James Brown, Lea MacNally,
Eric Palmar, Lady Jean Rankin and Adam Watson

First published in 1955 by Collins

The Melven Press,
176, High Street,
Perth, Scotland

Printed and bound in Great Britain by
REDWOOD BURN LIMITED,
Trowbridge and Esher

TO AUDREY

whose help has made this
book possible

CONTENTS

ILLUSTRATIONS

xi

ERRATUM

Caption on page 70 and above
for "year" read "week".

INTRODUCTION

WITH the exception of some years during the first World War, I have lived all my life in, or in reach of, the country of the golden eagle. I have thus been able to follow the fortunes of these great birds for more than half a century.

Since my earliest days of bird watching the golden eagle has been my favourite, because of its size and nobility of appearance and, perhaps even more, because of its unrivalled powers of flight. "Lethargic" and "ignoble" are terms which have been applied to the golden eagle, but the men who used them showed that they had only superficial knowledge of this fine bird, the very spirit of the hills and high corries of the Highlands of Scotland. The eagle is a complete individualist: that is one reason why it appeals to me, and why I enjoy watching it.

It is a long time ago—April, 1904—since I photographed my first golden eagle's eyrie. The nest was in a Scots fir, and was built far out on a strong lateral branch, rather more than half-way up the tree. The site was in a deer forest of Upper Deeside, and a private road passed near the eyrie, although not in sight of it. The deer-stalker on that beat of the forest was Charles Macintosh, a first-class salmon fisherman and deer-stalker. The eagles usually nested in this eyrie every second year, the alternative site being on a rock not far away. When I heard that the eagle was sitting I set out with a friend to photograph the eggs. This was in the days of the Kearton brothers, who were then doing work of great value in arousing a love of nature, especially of birds, in the young. I recall my boyish admiration for Richard Kearton, and how I took him, later in the same year, through the night past this eyrie in order to reach a ptarmigan on her nest by sunrise.

At this time I was the owner of a motor bicycle with a trailer, so my friend and I were able to transport the large half-plate camera which I then used, along the estate road to the neighbourhood of the eagle's tree. The first branch of this tree begins twelve feet from ground level, but the stalker had brought with him a short ladder. When I had climbed the ladder, he lifted it (with me on it) and held it against his chest, and thus I was able to reach the first branch. It was an exciting moment when at length I arrived at the eyrie and looked into the great nest with its crown of living fir branches. On a lining of great wood-rush (*Luzula sylvatica*) two large round eggs were resting. They were blotched and spotted with rusty red, one of the eggs being more heavily marked than the other, as I have since found to be the unvaried rule. I had before this watched golden eagles on Mount Keen and Morven, but this was my first sight of an occupied eyrie.

This tree-nesting eagle sat very closely: she did not appear to realise the approach of danger, or perhaps she hoped by remaining quietly on the eyrie to escape notice. When we arrived at the foot of the tree there had been no sign of the golden eagle. The stalker then hit the tree smartly with a stick. At once a head was thrust over the side of the eyrie and two flashing eyes regarded us furiously. The eagle then rose, slowly and with dignity, took a few steps to the edge of the nest-platform, and launched out on her broad wings, flying heavily until she had cleared the neighbouring tree-tops, when she began to spiral upwards and soon disappeared from view.

A year or two later, the eaglet belonging to a neighbouring pair of golden eagles in this forest fell from the eyrie, built near the top of a rock, and the eagles made a new nest round it as it lay at the foot of the rock, unharmed by its fall. I often visited this eaglet, and it came to have no fear of me, and would take food from my hand, even a banana skin! I had unfortunately to abandon my visits in order to go to Oxford, to sit my examinations for Responsions.

About the same time, I made several expeditions to the neighbourhood of Mount Keen, a high, conical hill rising on the border-march between the counties of Aberdeen and Angus. There were fir trees not far from Mount Keen where a pair of golden eagles nested. My companion on these occasions was Admiral Sir Arthur Farquhar, a good ornithologist as well as a distinguished naval officer. He was a friend of Colonel Willoughby Verner, who about this time published his book, *My Life among the Wild Birds of Spain,* in which, among other matters, he mentions his observations of the golden eagle in that country. Later, when I was working for my degree at Oxford, I spent two memorable week-ends in the Highlands, on one of these week-ends studying the golden eagle, on the other the snow-bunting. On both occasions my companion was a fellow undergraduate, Sir Malcolm Barclay-Harvey, who later was to be Governor of South Australia. The eagle's eyrie at which we watched was built in a Scots fir growing at an elevation of approximately 1,900 feet above sea level, immediately beneath one of the eastern Cairngorm Mountains. This tree is between two and three hundred years old, and has changed scarcely at all during the past half century. The eyrie is less than half-way up the tree. We reached the neighbourhood of the eyrie an hour after midnight, and waited beneath a neighbouring fir until daylight. The bold song of a missel thrush awoke me from an uneasy sleep at 1-55 a.m. It was not until an hour later that the first chaffinch sang, and by this time the mother eagle was visible, standing on the edge of the nest. There was one eaglet in the eyrie. The early morning air was cold, yet the eagle was not brooding the eaglet, but was standing over it, her wings slightly raised. Many years later, my wife, during an all-night watch from a hide at another eyrie, observed the same thing—that the eaglet, however cold and unhappy it may be, is guarded, but not covered, by the parent bird during the night hours.

When the sun rose at four o'clock (this was before the day of Summer Time) the glen was bathed in dark red light. The golden eagle also was transformed into a bird of ruby-red, and the white down of the eaglet was tinged with pink. The next day we were back at Oxford University. At that time (I took my degree in 1911) there was no Edward Grey Institute, and no British Trust for Ornithology at Oxford, and bird interest was shared by only a small band of enthusiasts.

In my early years of bird study I contented myself with nest photography and photography done by stalking the birds. After 1915, when I married Audrey Pease, whom I first met at Oxford, where she also took an Honours Degree in Natural Science, we began photography from hides. We have since then watched many a pair of golden eagles from hiding tents placed near tree and rock eyries. We have had hard days and nights together, suffering from cold and wet in hides after long, tiring walks over the hills, sometimes in fine weather, sometimes in wind and rain, or in snow.

The golden eagle remains my favourite bird, and from my home in the Isle of Skye I spend many days watching a pair of eagles which after ten years of acquaintance have become like old friends. In the writing of this, the book of the eagle, I have had the valuable help and expert criticism of my wife. Since the second world war, domestic and farm duties have prevented her from taking part in as much bird watching as she would like, but she still finds time to listen to, and often to solve, golden eagle problems. She has read through the manuscript of this book many times, and her help and suggestions, and also her watches and observations at eyries, make the work partly hers. We have shared the building of hides, and have taken watch and watch about. The processing of my own photographic illustrations has been her task and it is no exaggeration to say that without her help and encouragement this book would not have been written.

Correspondents from many countries have given me valuable information. I thank them all, especially the following:

Hans Johansen, Zoological Museum, Copenhagen, Denmark; C. J. Tillisch, Copenhagen, Denmark; Professor Holger Holgersen, Stavanger, Norway; K. Curry-Lindahl, Stockholm, Sweden; Carl Stemmler, Schaffhausen, Switzerland; Professor G. J. van Oordt, University of Utrecht, Holland; Dr. Rokitansky, Vienna, Austria; Professor Augusto Toschi, Italy; Noel Mayaud, France; Sir Alvary Gascoigne, late Ambassador to the U.S.S.R.; Roy Bedichek, Texas, U.S.A.; Maurice Broun, Hawk Mountain, U.S.A.; Walter Spoffard, New York, U.S.A.; Chandler S. Robbins, Laurel, Maryland, U.S.A.; Alva G. Nye, Hawk Hill, Virginia, U.S.A.; Professor W. Rowan, Alberta, Canada.

In Scotland, among those who have given valuable help are:

Sir Ronald Campbell, K.C.M.G. a former ambassador in Cairo; Thomas Adam, Sutherland Estates Office, Golspie; Stainton Crosthwaite, Glasgow; Alexander Gibson, Lochbuie; Niall Rankin of Treshnish; Desmond Nethersole-Thompson, Aviemore; Adam Watson, Turriff.

All these, and others, I gratefully thank, and also James Fisher, resident editor of the *New Naturalist* series and author of many bird books, for his helpful suggestions and contributions. That distinguished linguist, Miss May Baillie, Lochloy, Nairn, has translated for me some of the letters received from foreign lands. Some of the incidents described in this book, particularly in connection with the golden eagle's food, have been related in my *Days with the Golden Eagle (1927);* they will bear recounting, the more so as this book has been out of print for many years.

FOREWORD

FOR the first 30 years of this century, after the great work of Harvie-Brown and his companions, Seton Gordon was the only ornithologist working full time in the Scottish Highlands.

Reared on Deeside, he first photographed the eyrie of a golden eagle in 1904; and later, in the same summer, he led Richard Kearton, the pioneer nature photographer, to a ptarmigan's nest in the high Cairngorms.

Seton Gordon was an almost compulsive writer, publishing his first articles when he was 14 or 15 years old. He later went to Oxford, where he graduated with Honours in Natural Science, with aspects of montane botany as a special subject. He then took a Diploma in Rural Economy and subsequently studied Forestry in Russia, France and Germany. Soon after his graduation he married Audrey Pease, a talented ornithologist, who for many years was his companion and collaborator in the field. Now Gordon embarked on the precarious career of nature photographer and freelance writer. His first book *Birds of the Loch and Mountain* was published in 1907. Over twenty more books were to follow. At the same time he developed his remarkable skill as a writer of articles on many other Highland subjects besides birds. He was also a splendid lecturer. Almost to the end, he had the gift of enthusing his listeners, whether they were members of a learned society or of a village gathering.

In 1921 he was chosen as official photographer to the famous Oxford University Expedition to Spitsbergen. There he was in good company. The leader was Francis Jourdain – Pastor Pugnax to many of his contemporaries – the greatest authority on the breeding biology of Palearctic birds. On this expedition Julian Huxley, then possibly at his peak as an ornithologist, made a remarkable study of the courtship and displays of red-throated divers, and A. H. Paget-Wilkes concentrated on the breeding behaviour of the turnstone.

For some years the Gordons lived in Aviemore, but in the late 1920s they settled permanently at Upper Duntulm in Skye. Always, however, he was on the move through his beloved Highlands and Islands. He particularly loved the Inner Isles which he knew so well when he was Admiralty Patrol Officer in 1914–1916. In later years he also travelled to many parts of Europe in search of birds and copy. He visited some of the remarkable bird reserves in Holland. In Switzerland he lamented the persecution of the golden eagle. He also went to Norway, with J. C. Harrison, the bird artist, who collaborated with him in *Days with the Golden Eagle*.

Always a writer of charm and sensitivity, Seton had the gift of painting wonderful word pictures which quickly set his readers alight. I can never forget first reading *Hill Birds of Scotland* in the Linen Hall Library in Belfast, when I was only 12 years old. Then, and later, I warmed particularly to the chapters on golden eagle, dotterel and snow bunting. You could almost feel the wet clammy mist swirling like smoke in the high corries, and imagine yourself on those great broad-backed Grampian hills of Scotland where the rare and mysterious dotterel brooded its eggs almost at your feet. Best of all, he described the old pine forests and corries in the hills where golden eagles built their huge eyries. Seton's *Hill Birds of Scotland* (1915), John Walpole-Bond's *Field Studies of Some Rarer British Birds* (1914) and Willoughby Verner's *My Life Among the Wild Birds of Spain* (1909) were the books that lit the spark for me. I now began to identify with these quite different kinds of writers and ornithologists.

Out of the blue, in May 1936, came my first letter from Seton Gordon. I was then living in Spey Valley. He asked me to look out for a cock snow bunting which he had heard singing in a corrie in the Cairngorms. A few days later a friend and I were camping on that particular hill, so I was able to report back that we had not seen the snow bunting there but had watched it, or another, in glorious song-flight on a different ben a few miles away.

In June 1941, when my first wife Carrie and I were watching dotterel and golden plover in the west Cairngorms, we saw a distant figure slowly toiling up towards the tops. It was a tall man, wearing a bonnet, a tweed jacket and kilt, and when he saw us against the skyline he drew out a long telescope to spy us. There could be little doubt about the identity of the hillman. This was my first meeting with Seton. I particularly remember the softness of his voice and his warmth and friendliness. I also recall his slow, steady and almost tireless hill stride. We had several memorable days together in the field. Thereafter we sometimes met and regularly corresponded about eagles, dotterel and snow buntings. A little quirk of his was to send postcards, written in his most distinctive handwriting. Here at home the children always instantly recognised them.

Seton and Audrey Gordon used their cameras to document and supplement the fascinating observations recorded in their hides. Some of their photographs are remarkable by any standard. In 1925 Seton photographed the nest-relief of a pair of greenshanks at a nest near Loch Morlich. We have a signed print framed on our wall. This is still the finest action photograph of exchanging greenshanks ever taken. Another outstanding photograph shows a hen dotterel laying an egg. Many of his golden eagle photographs are magnificent. In all of them you notice how relaxed and untroubled his beloved eagles look.

A few dedicated naturalists are so absorbed by the animals they are studying that they are always identified with them – David Lack with robin and swift; Edgar Chance with the cuckoo; David Stephen with the roe deer; Adam Watson with red grouse and ptarmigan; and my own family with the greenshank. To all of us, Seton Gordon will always be remembered for his outstanding work and research on the golden eagle.

The Gordons made many stimulating observations and contributions to our knowledge of Highland birds, particularly dotterel, black-throated diver and red-necked phalarope. But their principal contribution to ornithology is contained in *Days with the Golden Eagle* (1927) and in this book, which was first published in 1955. Seton's love of golden eagles was such that he never tired of watching the same or different pairs, day after day, week after week, and indeed often year after year.

The Gordons watched golden eagles in many parts of Scotland, but they made their most continuous observations at different eyries in Spey Valley, Sutherland, and in Skye. Their account of the Spey Valley eyrie has always enthralled me. In *Days with the Golden Eagle* Seton describes how he first found that nest. 'It was one of those rare April days when the sun shines with a summer warmth and the air is soft and mild. There was no breeze in the old pine forest and the ancient, heavy-crowned trees seemed to hold their branches eagerly towards the strong sun. All at once high in the blue vault of heaven, I saw the form of a golden eagle sailing serenely above the forest. From the fringe of the woodlands a few grouse rose, terrified at their approach, and scattered wildly. She heeded them not, but as she half-turned in her flight the sun shone full upon the golden plumage of her neck, and she became a veritable eagle of burnished gold. For a time she sailed thus above the forest, then suddenly steered eastward . . . and closing her great wings shot like a thunderbolt to the trees of a steep hill-face about a mile from where I stood.'

The observations made from the hide beside this eyrie will always be a delight to any eagle-watcher. I knew this wood well and in the 1930s often looked in passing at that massive, but slowly disintegrating eyrie, in the old pine high up on the hill. In my years the eagles never again used that nest; but in 1934–35 a female eagle, young and white-tailed, built and sometimes brooded an eyrie in another part of the wood, without ever laying eggs in it. In 1936, still with white on her tail, she laid her first egg. How well I remember creeping slowly up the steep hillside just after dawn on an early April morning and for a few wonderful minutes watching the eagle brooding with drops of dew still glistening on the hackles of her head.

Apart from the golden eagles and their eyries, this was a marvellous Strath. In 1933 and 1937 three pairs of greenshanks courted and nested in the forest bogs and clearings; and Scottish pine crossbills often, and siskins and crested tits regularly, reared their young in nests in the forest.

In the eleven weeks during which their hide stood at the eyrie, the Gordons watched the home-life of these eagles for 167 hours spread over 31 days; a wonderful example of stamina and dedication. Here they had many notable experiences. On 28 June Audrey Gordon watched the male eagle, panting in the heat and almost exhausted, carry up a roedeer fawn to the eyrie. Besides the more customary prey of red grouse, ptarmigan and mountain hares, the eagles brought in two more roe deer fawns and three red squirrels. How did the eagles manage to catch these agile little mammals?

From that eyrie the two observers watched and photographed an almost mortal struggle between the eaglets. The much heavier bullying female eaglet, which they called Cain, at one stage almost continuously attacked Abel, her smaller brother, which only survived with pain and difficulty. Pompous boffins now describe the struggle between brother and sister eaglets in the eyrie as 'The Cain and Abel syndrome'. The down torn from the back of his neck and his back by the aggressor sometimes adhered to her bill and she had difficulty in removing it. Yet she continued her fierce attacks. Many a time she chased him round and round the eyrie, but preferred to attack while he slept and to aim vicious blows at head or neck or back. This was truly female chauvinism at its worst!

In this marathon feat of observation, continued until late July, both eaglets and observers suffered severely from attacks by midges and biting flies. 'After a single bite from one of them my whole leg swelled up.'

The Gordons watched and listened to all that was going on around them. Redstarts had a nest close to the eyrie; and chaffinch, goldcrest, coal and crested tits, ring ouzel, mistle thrush, song thrush, stonechat and cuckoo, red grouse, woodcock and greenshank were all recorded by the watchers in the hide.

Another of Seton's favourite pairs of eagles had eyries on a rock in a wild deer forest in Sutherland, where my family and I also study waders. Here, over a period of 5 years, the Gordons watched from hides for at least 500 hours. He writes vividly of the food and neighbours of these eagles in habitats so different from those in the Spey Valley pine forests. The parents fed red grouse and rabbits to their chicks, mixing this diet with stranger meat. One day in July the male carried in a large black vole; another time one of them took a stoat to the eyrie. These eagles were grand parents and most lovely to watch. Once she fed the eaglet on the carcase of a red grouse. 'Her behaviour then became almost human, for she arranged tiny heather twigs over the eaglet, working very gently and carefully; then she stepped back to admire the effect.' Another time he noted that the mother eagle was apparently rummaging for earthworms in the floor of the nest.

When an egg failed to hatch the female eagle listened for a sign of life in it and periodically brooded it. The shell fragments of the other egg disappeared, evidently eaten or carried away. In a year when both eggs hatched, the larger – presumably the female – eaglet dropped down to the eyrie where her brother was lying, 'and gently tweaked the feathers of his tail. He responded by nibbling at her throat.'

In the wild flowlands of Sutherland the neighbours of these eagles included greenshank, curlew, snipe, common sandpiper, dunlin, lapwing and golden plover; and nearer to the eyrie were meadow pipits, willow warblers, blackbirds, ring ouzels and wrens. Black-throated divers, wigeon and goosanders also graced lochs nearby.

Seton writes: 'No two pairs of golden eagles behave alike.' This is well demonstrated in the three most intriguing chapters in this book – 'Eight years observations at a Golden Eagle's Eyrie.' The story of this pair in Skye is unique. He knew the two eagles when they were young, with large patches of white on their tails, and long before they had started to breed. Thenceforward, throughout eight years, he watched them in all seasons. What an amazing account this is. And what a wealth of love and dedication he shares with us all. Anyone who has not yet read this story is almost to be envied.

Through his 26x telescope he discovered that these eagles sometimes started to build or repair their eyries early in November, and continued to do this throughout the winter. He lovingly describes their mating and sexual displays. The discovery that this pair of eagles regularly changed duties during incubation is of much interest to all eagle-watchers, who for many years had believed that the female was entirely responsible for incubation. At an eyrie in Argyll in 1938 I was most excited to find that the large eagle which we had watched one day was later replaced on the nest by a smaller bird which had a missing pinion feather. But that was only a fragmentary observation. In Skye, Seton's eagles sometimes changed places at the nest almost hourly during incubation and just after the eaglets had hatched. Once the male eagle visited the brooding hen three times in a single hour.

He gives many fine descriptions of the change-over pattern and ritual. 'As she sails out over the cliff and sets off to hunt, or to find relaxation in soaring and diving, he escorts her a little way, then swings round and dives swiftly back to the eyrie. Now comes the moment when his extreme care of the eggs is seen. He walks forward gingerly to the nesting cup and, once in position, lowers himself slowly over the precious egg which takes six weeks of brooding to hatch.'

He made many other discoveries. The young eagle of a previous year possibly sometimes visits the territory and flies with its parents in early spring. We also learn that in early August the young eagle is able to catch mice and thus supplements the supply of rabbits which the parents continue to carry in until the end of September or later. Twice Seton watched his beloved eagles killing lambs; incidents he describes quite dispassionately and with absolute integrity.

Seton knew the golden eagle in all seasons and he never lost his sense of wonder. 'How can I regard the eagles as anything but my friends. I cannot regard them with the cold scientific eye and consider their hormones, their glandular reactions or their behaviour complexes.'

He had little interest in the *trivia* and *minutiae* of contemporary ornithology, with its endless graphs, tables and statistics. He never even found time to analyse the remarkable

observations contained in his notebooks. For Seton was a busy
man with a living to earn and a family to educate. A detailed
analysis of his data would have added no extra sparkle to his
writing and brought little grist to the mill. But all over the
world students of the golden eagle have greatly profited from
his knowledge and dedication. In Volume 4 of the great
Handbuch der Vögel Mitteleuropas I found well over 30 references
to his eagle studies.

Seton corresponded with all those who were out and about
in eagle country – naturalists, keepers, stalkers and shepherds,
landowners and factors. This book is thus the richer for many
notes that otherwise would never have been recorded.

He had a wide circle of acquaintances. These included two
of the tragic figures of the World Wars, Edward Grey, Foreign
Secretary in Asquith's Government in 1914, and Neville
Chamberlain, Prime Minister at the start of World War 2.
Both these men were keen bird watchers and ardent fly fisher-
men. Seton's famous photograph of Edward Grey's favourite
robin perching on his hat, is now on the wall of the Edward
Grey Institute at Oxford. I also recall how proudly he showed
me his telescope, which the Duke of Windsor, then Prince of
Wales, had inscribed and given to him. He had previously
used field glasses but immediately discarded these for the
telescope with which he became as skilful as a professional
deer stalker.

Many regarded Seton Gordon as a Highland character and
almost as an eccentric. In any part and in any company he
was certainly easily and instantly recognised in his kilt, bonnet
and jacket. But eccentric he was not. He was a courteous,
kindly, cultured man of great ability and sensitivity. Although
not a Highlander born, he loved our Highlands, the Highland
people and the Highland way of life. Gaelic was not his native
tongue, but he was keenly interested in Highland legends and

history and in the old language and its place names. He was a good piper, an excellent judge of piping, and a member of the Scottish Pipers' Society. A skilled fly fisherman, he caught salmon on many of the great rivers of the Highlands. And as a young man he was awarded his golf blue in 1911 when he represented Oxford against Cambridge.

Seton used to drive an old Wolseley car, looking all around him and keeping well to the middle of our narrow single-track Highland roads. Once he drove from Merkland to Loch More in front of two furious Sutherland police constables who continuously blared the horn of the patrol car. Oblivious to all excitement, Seton disappeared into the drive of Loch More Lodge and the constables did not follow!

When I last met him he was with his wife, Elizabeth, in Inverness. His eye was as bright as ever and he was warm and enthusiastic. We spoke about greenshanks, snow buntings and dotterel and, inevitably, about eagles.

In his long life Seton Gordon saw many changes. When he left us, in March 1977, in his 91st year, our Scottish birds were in good heart. The osprey and goshawk were back. Golden eagles had nested in the English north country and snowy owls had bred in Shetland. Wood sandpipers and Temminck's stints regularly sang above a few Highland marshes and flowlands; and fieldfares and redwings had prospected, pioneered and reared young in a few remote and rather secret places.

DESMOND NETHERSOLE-THOMPSON
Ardgay
1979

CHAPTER I

The Golden Eagle in the British Isles

THE golden eagle is now the only British eagle. It may be distinguished from the white-tailed or sea-eagle (*Haliaeëtus albicilla*) by its longer and squarer tail, and by having the tarsus feathered to the toes. The golden eagle's bill is black; the bill of the sea-eagle is yellow. The curve of the tip of the upper mandible of the golden eagle is less vertical than that of the sea-eagle. These points of difference are supplementary to the most obvious one—the pure white tail of the adult sea-eagle, very noticeable when the bird is on the wing.

The golden eagle no longer nests either in England or in Wales. In 1953 it bred in Northern Ireland, for the first time since 1910. It has not bred in the rest of Ireland for many years. Earlier naturalists did not differentiate between golden eagle and sea-eagle. In 1183 Giraldus Cambrensis tells us that in Ireland, "eagles are as numerous as kites in other countries." This may well have continued to be the case until the seventeenth century, for in his *Pinax* of 1666, which contains what has been described as the first printed list of British birds, Christopher Merret records that the golden eagle "migrates to us from Ireland where it abounds," and Merret's correspondent, the great Norfolk naturalist Sir Thomas Browne, obtained an Irish eagle alive and kept it for a couple of years. In England an Act of Parliament was passed in 1457 against these birds. In about 1538 John Leland describes an eagle's nest at Castle Dinas Bran, near Llangollen in Denbighshire. In the seventeenth

7

Map of the breeding distribution of the Golden Eagle, *Aquila chrysaëtos,* compiled by James Fisher. Broken line: eagles present in the breeding season, but breeding irregular or unproved. The form *obscurior* is united with *kamtschatika,* and *fulva* with *chrysaëtos* (see Appendix, p. 231). Some authorities would retain *fulva* for the British population, and the population breeding from S. E. France to Persia

8

century eagles still nested on Snowdon,* as noted by Ray and Willughby, who visited Snowdonia in 1658 (Ray) and 1662 (both). An old Welsh name for the Snowdon massif is the Eagle Rocks. Ray also found an eagle's eyrie in wooded country near the Derwent in the Peak Country of Derbyshire in 1668 (see Raven, 1942).

In the ten years 1776-1786, seventy eagles were killed in the parishes of Braemar, Crathie, Glen Muich and Tullich in Aberdeenshire. and from 1831 to 1834, 171 adult birds and fifty-three young and eggs were destroyed. About this time, and even later, the eagle was persecuted relentlessly, and it is indeed remarkable that the species should have survived.

William MacGillivray, writing in 1842, mentions that he has studied the golden eagle chiefly in the Outer Hebrides and that, although it was by no means rare, it was less common than the sea eagle. He said that "vast numbers" had been destroyed because of the extension of sheep farming in the Highlands. MacGillivray was probably thinking of the days of his own visits which ended in 1830; in 1841 his son John appears only to have known of a single eyrie in the Outer Hebrides. But a little later Robert Gray wrote, "On all the Outer Hebrides the golden eagle is still a well-known bird, and from Barra Head to the Butt of Lewis various eyries existed in the breeding season of 1867. In the islands of Lewis and Harris they are best known . . . on North Uist there were two eyries last year . . . on Benbecula, where eagles are frequently seen, there are no eyries; but on the next island—South Uist—there is one every year on Mount Hecla." Harvie-Brown in 1870 found eight eyries of golden eagles in Harris, and one in North Uist. In 1887, H. A. Macpherson knew of eyries in North Uist. In Arran it was exterminated in or about 1850, but reappeared

*H. E. Forrest notes that golden eagles were "still found about Snowdon" in *c.* 1800.

9

about 1904 and, being now protected, has continued to nest there. Recent reports of sea-eagles nesting in the Hebrides are due to certain pairs of golden eagles nesting on sheer sea cliffs, in sites which a sea-eagle might be expected to choose, sometimes on the actual cliffs where sea-eagles formerly nested.

In the posthumous edition of his book *The Moor and the Loch*, published in 1888, John Colquhoun of Luss tells us that, in the Blackmount Forest, he was able to see, from the shore of Loch Baa, both golden eagle and sea-eagle above their nesting territories. The golden eagle nested on a rock west of the loch, the sea-eagle on the large island on Loch Baa. The golden eagle hunted on the high hills, the sea-eagle over the low, boggy ground. Their hunting grounds being distinct, the two birds rarely met, but there were occasional clashes, in which the golden eagle always got the better of the sea-eagle. Colquhoun lived in Victorian days, when a bird watcher did his best to secure a rare bird as a trophy: he attempted to shoot the sea-eagles of Loch Baa in Argyll, but was apparently unsuccessful. His story is valuable, because it shows that the sea-eagle bred inland as well as on the coast. The Loch Baa eyrie was on a birch tree. As Colquhoun was being rowed out to the island, the sea-eagle left her eyrie and perched on a neighbouring tree, "her white tail shining like the silver moon." The hunter landed, his companions made a "hide" for him (surely one of the first "hides" on record), a small aperture was made for his gun barrel, and for six hours he remained in his "hide," his gun covering the eyrie. During this long watch, the sea eagles usually floated at an immense height, but sometimes dived to the neighbourhood of the eyrie, beating their great wings which, he tells us, made a hoarse, growling noise like the paddles of a steamer heard at a distance on a calm day. On one occasion the eagle did indeed return to her eyrie, yet Colquhoun did not fire, and the reader has the feeling that he was half-reluctant to destroy her. At all events, after this long watch in the "hide" he did not return until the following year, and we are not told what happened then.

It would not be difficult to make an up-to-date golden eagle census for Scotland, but I am glad this has not been made for, if published, it would undoubtedly be harmful to the species. Sheep farmer and grouse preserver on reading the report on the numbers of their "enemy number one" would exclaim, "Just what I have always maintained; there are far too many eagles in the country; we must see that their numbers are quietly and unofficially reduced."

In Scotland, taking the country as a whole, the golden eagle population is (1954) approximately stationary. In certain districts the species has increased, in others it has decreased. In the western Cairngorm area in Inverness-shire there is a considerable decrease. That experienced observer, Desmond Nethersole-Thompson, tells me that in 1953 there were only two regular breeding pairs in the area, compared with five pairs in 1934. In Aberdeenshire, on the southern flanks of the Cairngorms, the decrease is not so noticeable, and here some of the deer forest owners protect the eagle carefully. Although slightly scarcer here than it was when I knew the district first, *c.* 1905, the golden eagle must have increased considerably between 1850 and the beginning of the twentieth century, for William MacGillivray, whose *magnum opus, Natural History of Deeside,* was published posthumously in 1855 by command of Queen Victoria, records that a few years before that date the species was very rarely seen in the Braemar area, and he was doubtful if there was a single breeding pair. He writes, "In the course of six weeks' excursions among the mountains I saw only two individuals—after all it might have been only one individual, twice seen." Shepherds and gamekeepers, he says, had almost destroyed the species. The golden eagle is still unpopular in Aberdeenshire, for the county is proud of its grouse moors, and its large grouse bags. All credit to those who protect the bird here.

In the Hebrides, I see a distinct increase as compared with the stock in 1934, but there has been a distinct decrease in the six years 1947-1953. Here there is less game-preserving than in the Central Highlands, but poisoned bait is sometimes set for foxes and the eagle may take the bait. In the West Highlands, opposite Skye, it was reported that a dead eagle was found beside a poisoned hind.

The golden eagle's status in Scotland is now roughly as follows. It has never been proved to nest in Shetland, although this island group was a stronghold of the sea-eagle. In Orkney there was one eyrie, on the high island of Hoy: this was used until about 1844. In Caithness the species breeds sparingly but here, again, grouse-moors and golden eagles do not go well together. In Sutherland the species has been given protection by two great landed proprietors: in this county it is holding its own and is perhaps increasing in the west. In Ross-shire pole-traps were illegally set for eagles in recent years, on grouse ground towards the east of the county. In the high, and rugged, lands towards the western fringe of Ross-shire the eagle is more secure, and the numbers remain more or less stationary. Inverness and Argyll have fewer golden eagles than they had forty years ago, but the species is widely distributed. The county of Angus has more golden eagles than might be expected and here a number of landowners preserve the bird. In Aberdeenshire, taking the county as a whole, there has been a slight decrease. Perthshire is not eagle-minded, and here there has been a decided decrease. In Dunbartonshire, where there is a large area of wild country, the species is now not less in numbers than forty years ago, but from Stirlingshire it has disappeared, except perhaps for one pair. South of the Highland Line, the golden eagle has returned to its ancestral strongholds, or some of them, in the counties of Ayr and Kirkcudbright: it may have spread to them from the Island of Arran, where the species has been protected for some time. There is no reason why, if not molested, the golden eagle should not return to the high hills of the Lake District and of North Wales, from which strongholds it has long been exterminated. I am told that immature golden eagles have been shot in the Lake District in recent years. Most of the Western Isles of Scotland have a small golden eagle population. The species breeds on Lewis and Harris, probably on North Uist, South Uist and on Vatersay. The Isle of Skye has a number of pairs. A few eagles nest on the Isle of Mull, and a few on Jura, but on Islay the species is almost extinct. On Bute it is seen passing, but does not nest: on Arran there are perhaps two nesting pairs.

The Hebridean golden eagle is a rather smaller, and noticeably darker bird than the golden eagle of the Scottish mainland. This was first noted by Robert Gray more than a century ago in his book *Birds of the West of Scotland*. One Hebridean haunt of the golden eagle is a deep glen in the island of Harris. A high rock, often dark and grim in driving rain, rises sheer from a loch, lonely and unfrequented, and on a small ledge high on this rock the eyrie is placed. The glen is little more than a hundred feet above the Atlantic yet the impression given is of much greater height, for the scenery is grand and Alpine in character. The eagles, as they rise in spirals high above their nesting rock, must in clear weather see the cone of Boreray of St. Kilda on the far Atlantic horizon; they must see the ocean swell break in white spray against the rocky shore of Gasker, nursery of the grey seal. In early summer they must see the snowfields on the Cuillin of Skye across the Minch, faint and nebulous in the far distance. They must often see herds of red deer grazing on the green, grassy slopes beneath them, and must note the white forms of the black-faced sheep which also find pasture here. In early June the rowan trees which grow beside the eagles' loch perfume the air, vibrant with the calls of greenshank. The eagles of this remote and unfrequented glen hunt along the slopes of the neighbouring hills. One day, when some friends and I were standing, after a stiff climb, at the entrance to a mountain cave where a noted freebooter formerly lived, one of the eagles swung round the shoulder of the hill, at the edge of the mist which hid all the higher slopes. The bird, looking vast and formidable, was almost upon us when it sighted us. Never have I seen an eagle so flustered. With strong and rapid wing-thrusts it flew at its best speed across the deep glen and out of sight in less time than it takes to narrate the incident.

Another eyrie, on the Scottish mainland in Sutherland, was beside a salmon river, at the edge of a birch wood which is a favourite haunt of that rare animal, the pine-marten. Curiously enough, the marten is no longer found in the pine forests of Scotland, but lingers in the birch woods of the north-west coast, and also out in the open country, in this part of the Scottish Highlands. Rabbits, hares, and grouse are all scarce in the country of this pair of golden eagles, and it is possible that the birds at times prey on the martens, but these animals, being mainly nocturnal, would not be so easy a prey as the stoat, which is often taken by the eagle to its eyrie as food for the young. An observer in the summer of 1951 saw a golden eagle swallow at the eyrie the hinder part of a stoat without difficulty —the young were not invited to share the meal.

One of the most spectacular eyries of the golden eagle was built some years ago on a high sea-cliff in the Isle of Skye. I found this nest late in the evening of a brilliant July day, and the low sun, shining in the clear air over a pale blue ocean, the

Eagle flying out from nesting cliff. (*C. E. Palmar*)

short green grass at the top of the cliff, the cliff face pleasant in the sun's rays, and the two eaglets in their inaccessible eyrie five hundred feet below me, formed a picture rare and delightful. As I approached the cliff from above, the male eagle soared from the rock, carrying a young rabbit; a little later the female also rose, then slanted to alight upon what was evidently an old eyrie, whereupon she was mobbed by a pair of ravens. One of the ravens, standing on a projecting ledge above the eagle, peered down intently at her, craning its neck the better to see its large enemy. The raven dived suddenly close past the eagle, then returned to its former perch, its mate obviously exhorting it to make another attack. In a recess in the rock, near the top of the cliff, was yet another unoccupied eyrie of the eagles. Seeing two eyries, neither of them in use, I was about to turn away when I noticed the occupied nest half-way down the thousand-foot cliff. In the eyrie were two eaglets, which were evidently a late brood. Although the date was 14 July, they were not fully feathered and could not have flown until August —the neck of one bird was still in white down. It is possible that the herring gull whose feathers lay on a ledge had been killed and plucked by one of the parent eagles, which were probably the pair seen from the sea by Gavin Maxwell and recorded in his book, *Harpoon at a Venture*. I have myself seen them when sailing near that wild coast, either perched on the rock or soaring buoyantly on the sea-breeze, moving high above the herring gulls and apparently ignoring them.

Another nesting site of the eagle is a dozen or more miles from that just described. Here the eyrie is also on a sea cliff, facing south. The cliff face is broken, and the eyrie is on a broad ledge, 150 feet above the water, from which the eaglets see fulmars pass on buoyant wing. As I was watching this eyrie on a June day I saw a small party of gannets fly past the eyrie. It must be rare to see at the same time in the field of one's glass a couple of sturdy eaglets in their eyrie and a flight of ocean-going gannets. Neither the gannet nor the fulmar are birds usually associated with the golden eagle. On this cliff a pair of peregrine falcons nest at some distance from the eagles and a pair of ravens make their home near. Across the Minch the Outer Hebrides, from North Uist to Barra Head, are seen, isles of splendour as the summer sun dips beneath them. In this eyrie the eaglets hear the deep music of the ocean swell and see ships pass beneath them: the smoke from a tramp steamer may drift across their nest. They see in calm weather herring-gulls and gannets in a white cloud plunge or dive repeatedly into the green water after a shoal of mackerel or herring and continue to feed until, gorged, they settle on the oily water. At a little distance from the eyrie whales spout, porpoises break the water's surface as they hurry past, and the tall fins of basking sharks sail indolently this way and that. At the edge of this cliff, which extends for miles along the coast, there are great rabbit colonies, and it is on them that the eagles feed themselves and their young. Inland from the cliff the hill is under sheep, yet the shepherd on whose ground the eagles nest has never seen a lamb in the eyrie.

When a pair of golden eagles uses a tree as a nesting site it is almost always in natural forest, where the trees are widely spaced; the outposts of the forests are sometimes used. The only exception I know to this rule is on Upper Deeside, where an eagle nests each year near the edge of a thick, planted wood of Scots fir and larch. In this instance there is no second eyrie and the nest has been used each year since circa 1911. The site is one a grey crow might choose, but the eagle is sufficiently near the edge of the wood to have a good outlook. In May 1952 I sat on the roadside in the glen and through my glass could see the brooding eagle's head, with its hackles of golden brown. Her mate was soaring high above her, and she once looked up at him. Snowy hills rose in the background but in the glen beneath the plantation the rugged and old birches were filmed in green, and among them was a larch which held its soft young needles to the sunlight. This pair of eagles live mainly upon rabbits which are plentiful in the glen. The great frost of 1947 almost wiped out the rabbit population, and the eagles must have gone hungry often; the rabbits have now increased and flourish once more.

It will thus be seen that in Scotland the golden eagle has varied nesting sites and territories. In the Central Highlands these are usually in forest areas, with the eyrie in a Scots fir, rarely in a birch, once in a willow. If the eagles' home is above tree level, the nest is in a rock. In the Hebrides the eyrie may be built in a sea cliff, or on an inland rock, never in a tree. The eyrie may be almost at sea level in the west; in the Central Highlands it may be 3,000 feet above the sea. The eagle's territory is almost entirely a Highland one, but in western districts it is gradually spreading southwards.

Although as a rule the golden eagle lives in secluded places, there are times when it may be seen from a main road or a railway. In the Isle of Skye *Aquila chrysaëtos* was seen in full chase after a cock grouse by a stalker who was a passenger in a bus travelling along the road from Sligachan to Portree; pursuer and pursued passed only a few yards from the bus. One very wet and misty evening in mid-September I had crossed Kylerhea ferry in my car and as I climbed the steep 900 foot ascent leading to Broadford in Skye, I was soon in the mist-cap. Each hill stream was a white torrent and the rain was falling with extreme violence. When I had crossed the watershed at Bealach Udal, the Inhospitable Pass, and was travelling down the small glen on the far side, an eagle, looking huge in the mist, sprang from a small birch tree beside the road, where it had evidently taken up its roosting quarters for the night.

The Golden Eagle: King of Birds

The eagle crossed the burn, flying low, and beyond the farther bank pitched heavily in the heather: no doubt it quickly returned to the shelter of the birch after I had passed. On one occasion, when I was in the train as it crossed the Drumochter Pass between Kingussie in Inverness-shire and Blair Atholl in Perthshire, I saw a golden eagle chasing grouse: I once saw the same thing from the train on the Oban-Stirling railway as it descended Glen Ogle.

The habit of buzzards of perching on telegraph poles in the West Highlands and Islands of Scotland is, I think, a modern one. The bird does not trouble to rise when a motor passes, although a pedestrian alarms it. Buzzard and golden eagle are often confused by the tourist, and I am used to receiving reports of golden eagles perched on telegraph poles. I have yet to see a golden eagle using this stance, although the bird might possibly do so on a lonely Highland road bearing little traffic. I am informed that three golden eagles have been electrocuted on Hydro-Electric poles since electric schemes began in the Highlands of Scotland.

No two pairs of golden eagles behave alike. Some are residents, others are migrants, although in Britain migration is only partial. In some parts of the United States the golden eagle is a true migrant, both young and old sometimes travelling thousands of miles.

The golden eagle is almost always a bird of silence although very occasionally it may utter a high, far-carrying yelp. It never by calling advertises the presence of its nest like the peregrine falcon. Once and once only have I known a golden eagle call when disturbed from her eyrie—she was the owner of the fifteen-foot-high eyrie in a Scots fir elsewhere referred to. On this particular occasion she did not fly, as usual, out of sight, but alighted on the top of a neighbouring fir tree. After a time she approached her nesting tree by flying from fir-top to fir-top.

18

When quite near the eyrie she uttered a series of liquid, babbling notes. This volume of deep sound was very unlike the usual high-pitched yelp of the golden eagle. She was then approximately one hundred yards from her nesting tree and her behaviour in venturing so close before danger had gone was exceptional.

There is still much to learn about the brooding weeks of a pair of golden eagles. I have mentioned elsewhere that at the eyrie I have watched during eight seasons the male takes an equal share of brooding from the day the first egg is laid, yet I think that is the exception. More watching, from a safe distance, of eyries during the hatching season is necessary, and this I recommend as valuable work for future observers. I believe that at most eyries the eagle receives little help from her mate.

There is work, too for the eagle observer of the future in recording whether it is usual for the golden eagle to pair before being fully mature. At present, it is thought that the bird is mature at the age of four and a half years, but there is room for more observations on this point.

I write in this book of the golden eagle's relationship with man. To put it briefly, this bird is not harmful where there is a sufficient supply of the natural food of the species. On a well-stocked grouse moor, a pair of eagles make no appreciable difference in the number of grouse on the ground: the weaker grouse are killed. Grouse disease is never prevalent in eagle country. It must be remembered that rabbits, the golden eagle's chief food, are injurious to crops and young plantations, and here the eagle is man's friend. Again, the grey or hooded crow is the shepherd's enemy, and the golden eagle habitually preys on this bird. In Scotland, the number of lamb-killing eagles is small—less than five per cent.

As I have mentioned at the beginning of this chapter, naturalists in earlier days did not discriminate between the different species of eagle. For one thing, they were handicapped in having no binocular nor telescope. They could not study a bird closely unless they killed it. No one thought of watching a bird from a hide. Some of us remember the days of the first hides, and recall that Richard and Cherry Kearton used the stiffened skin of an ox, and of a sheep, and also a sham tree-trunk, for their close observations and their remarkable photographs. An enormous anthology of the eagle in literature, history, and heraldry could be compiled, and no doubt would be most interesting to the general reader, but not really to the ornithologist because the stories would refer to any large bird of prey and not specifically to the golden eagle, which has been recognised as a distinct species for less than three hundred years.

The ancient Greeks wrote of the eagle, but we do not know what the species was—nor did they perhaps know themselves. Indeed in most of the early quotations we cannot say whether the bird is an eagle or a vulture. The lines from Homer seem to point to an eagle—a vulture would not pounce on a hare.

In the Bible are many beautiful references to the eagle, but eminent biblical authorities now say that the bird referred to is the griffon-vulture. It is thought, too, that the eagle-headed sculptures of the Assyrians represent the griffon-vulture. There are old stories of the eagle in Celtic mythology—in Eire, in Wales and in Scotland. In most of the tales the longevity of the eagle is stressed. It is believed the Welsh traditions date from the tenth and eleventh centuries. At that time the eagle was numerous in Wales, and in the tales Snowdon is named Eagle Mountain. Writing in the twelfth century Giraldus Cambrensis avers that the eagle of Eagle Mountain is prophetic of war and that "she perches on the Fatal Stone every fifth holiday, in order to satiate her hunger with the bodies of the slain . . . and has almost perforated the stone by cleaning and sharpening her bill."

The Golden Eagle in the British Isles

In Scotland there is a strong tradition in the Hebridean Isle of Lewis that the youth of the golden eagle is renewed when the bird deliberately breaks off the curved end of the upper mandible on a large stone. The curve has now become so pronounced that the eagle can no longer tear off its food from its prey, and has become old and thin. On one occasion I lectured at a country school in Lewis. I mentioned the eagle but said nothing of this curious tradition, yet almost all the scholars described it in essays which they wrote afterwards.

Eagles were so destructive in Britain in the fifteenth century that the Act of Parliament, passed in 1457 against them, referred no doubt to both golden eagle and sea-eagle: it was not until two hundred and nineteen years later that Ray separated the two species, in the first (Latin) edition of Willughby's *Ornithology*.

A great poet, who is also a naturalist, may in time write a poem worthy of the golden eagle.

The Highland chief, as a mark of his rank, carries in his bonnet three flight feathers of the golden eagle on occasions of ceremony; the Highland chieftain two, and the Highland gentleman one. In 1951 a great clan gathering was staged in Edinburgh. A number of the chiefs then wore eagle feathers in their bonnets, but I noticed that some of them were tail feathers, and not the flight feathers which should correctly have been carried. Although the wind reached the force of a gale, not one feather came adrift on that great day.

CHAPTER II

The Golden Eagle in Winter

IT IS usual for the golden eagle to remain paired throughout the year, and perhaps for life, and no birds that I know show more devotion and consideration towards each other. This devotion continues after the nesting season and through the dark months of winter. The pair of golden eagles whose life, over eight years, I record in Chapters X, XI and XII appear devoted not only to one another but to their home. Each evening during winter they come in from hunting, sometimes together, sometimes from different directions, at dusk to their rock, sailing in to roost as the light ebbs. The weather is often stormy, and the eagles have, it seems, fore-knowledge of the wind that will blow during the night, choosing the roosting ledge which will give them shelter. The only time they left their rock for more than a few days, from the year they first colonised it until they lost their young in May, 1952, was during the long-sustained frost of February, 1947. Len Howard's remarkable book *Birds as Individuals* gives insight into the personalties of the tit family, and their love affairs. The golden eagle does not allow so intimate a human approach as the tits, yet I have seen sufficient of this pair of golden eagles to realise that they are exceptional birds.

The power of a golden eagle to fast for the space of a week (a habit long known to falconers) must be to its advantage during wild winter weather when the mist covers the hills and driving snow harries the high ground. The eagle must then remain on some sheltered ledge, or in shelter of a tree, during the short hours of daylight, for hunting is impossible in these conditions. On a day when I saw a raven forced to the ground by the strength of the wind, I think an eagle might have remained air-borne, but I doubt if it could face a gale of 100 miles an hour, a wind force which was on two occasions experienced in the Hebrides during the winter of 1951-52, and at least once in the following winter.

All pairs of nesting golden eagles in Scotland do not remain actually on their territory during the winter months, but they do not as a rule wander far. Food supply and weather conditions largely determine their movements. Abroad, the golden eagles of northern Sweden partially migrate, but many remain in the snowy fastnesses of the north throughout the winter where they feed on the carcases of reindeer. The Swedish authority Dr. Kai Curry-Lindahl of Stockholm, tells me that it is the adult golden eagles which remain: the young birds drift south, to Southern Sweden and Denmark. The movement of the young golden eagles bred in the Scottish Highlands has not been determined, with any accuracy. A friend of mine, familiar with the golden eagle, said he saw one of these birds in the vicinity of Chester, high in the sky and moving toward the south-west. Little, too, is known of the movements of the immature birds during their first four years—that is, before they make a home of their own. As I have recorded in another chapter, the young golden eagle on one occasion remained with its parents until November, within a fortnight of the beginning of the repairs to the nest for the following year. On another occasion I saw the family party —father, mother and eaglet—still together at the end of December. I must state however that the adult birds in both these instances were those whose home life is a model to us all, and many young eagles are driven away in October by their parents.

In Norway, as in Sweden, the young golden eagles migrate

south in winter. In the winter of 1950-51, Dr. Holger Holgersen of Stavanger Museum informs me, a young eagle, ringed that year, was recovered at a distance of 145 kilometres from the place where it was ringed.

It is probable that the immature golden eagles from Lapland migrate farther than this. In Southern Sweden, of the 500 golden eagles shot during a number of seasons in Scania, only 14 were adult birds. On the other hand, so Dr. Curry-Lindahl informs me, all the golden eagles sent from the north to the University of Uppsala are adults.

In the United States of America great interest is taken in the migration of the golden eagle. Maurice Broun has given me most interesting notes on the subject. From the observation post on Hawk Mountain, Kempton, Pennsylvania, he saw, during 12 autumns, 651 golden eagles pass on migration. In the "fall" of 1945, when Maurice Broun was engaged on war service, Professor F. J. Trembley recorded 13 golden eagles crossing the hill in one day. Yet, as Maurice Broun writes to me, in April 1952, "in recent years we have seen fewer and fewer birds-of-the-year, among the golden eagles passing down our ridge. The bird simply cannot cope with civilization. I am afraid it is doomed." The golden eagles appear over Hawk Mountain from early October until early December, the majority passing during the first half of November. My correspondent is of the opinion that nearly all these golden eagles are "a remnant of a strictly eastern North American population," and that the birds which frequent Hawk Mountain and adjacent ridges on migration come from some northern breeding area.

Just where this breeding-area is in north-eastern North America is somewhat of a mystery. Golden eagles nest sparingly in the Appalachian chain as far south as North Carolina, some hundreds of miles south of Hawk Mountain; in the continuation of the Appalachian chain north of Pennsylvania they may still nest in New York State, for a friend of Maurice Broun's, whose ability to recognise the golden eagle is unquestionable, told him that he had seen an adult, and a full-grown juvenile learning to fly, "somewhere in the Adirondacks" during the summer of 1946.

The golden eagle still breeds in two or three counties of Maine (Palmer, 1949), where it has at least four eyries. Some of the migratory eagles must breed yet further north than this, for the number of Maine records each year is "certainly in excess of the number of birds from Maine eyries alone." There may be a few still breeding in the maritime provinces of Canada, but certainly the bird has never bred in Newfoundland (Peters and Burleigh, 1951) and has only once been alleged to breed in Newfoundland Labrador (at L. Mishikamau in the interior, see Austin, 1932). There is no evidence that it has ever nested in Quebec, though odd birds have been taken in Ungava, on the south Labrador coast and at Lake St. John. But on the west side of Hudson's Bay N.A. Cormau saw golden eagles several times in 1914 on the Manitoba Shore, and one was shot off a tree-nest not far from Cape Henrietta Maria in Ontario in 1938. Others have been seen here since in summer, and on the west side of James Bay (Manning, 1952).

Maurice Broun states that he sees peregrines, goshawks and red-shouldered hawks mob the golden eagles as they pass over Hawk Mountain. He has only once seen the eagle retaliate. His own graphic description, which I quote, is from his book, *Hawks Aloft: the Story of Hawk Mountain*—

"Imagine, if you can, lying on your back and gazing with me into the zenith through a pair of 7 x 50 glasses. We see in the field of the binocular a large dark bird, and a small hawk, neither clearly identifiable. We wonder how many hawks have been missed, flying at that incredible height above the

The Golden Eagle: King of Birds

Lookout. We switch to the greater reach of the 18-power binocular, and find that the big bird is an adult Golden Eagle, its satellite still indeterminate. The smaller bird is making desultory passes at the eagle. Suddenly the eagle thrusts forward, executes an Immelmann turn as effortlessly as a fly landing on a ceiling, and grabs the smaller hawk, which puts up a feeble, momentary struggle. The eagle, with set wings, hurtles earthward at terrific speed, and, still clutching its prey, disappears into the densely wooded flank of the ridge. The wings of the smaller hawk are fully out-stretched during the meteoric descent, and we note the ruddy breast of the Red-shouldered hawk. It is all over in a matter of seconds !

I was alone, tense and breathless, and, I must confess, somewhat spent from following closely this hair-raising episode. I felt for the doomed Red-shoulder, but, at the same time, I had nothing but admiration for the eagle and its aerial performance. The bird's hunger was greater, apparently, than its capacity to tolerate any impudence or annoyance. I have seen upwards of 200,000 Raptores in passage over the Sanctuary, but this has been the only instance of "big fish eat little fish."

In Scotland, the wandering habits of the young golden eagle during the first autumn and early winter of its life produce a crop of correspondence in the local press on the appearance of that very rare British bird, the white-tailed or sea-eagle. The young golden eagle carries a considerable area of white on the tail, and those who mistake it for the white-tailed eagle invariably have no knowledge of the rarity of the latter bird. In Scotland, even those pairs of adult golden eagles which return to roost in the neighbourhood of the nesting site hunt in winter over a wider area than in summer. On the Cairngorm

Hills they hunt often on the high ground, the home of the ptarmigan (*Lagopus mutus*). When snow covers the high hills, as it usually does in winter and early spring, the ptarmigan in their white plumage are not easy to detect. Sometimes, however, during a mild spell of winds from the south west in December, the snow melts, with the exception of a few wreaths here and there. When a golden eagle is hunting in the neighbourhood, the ptarmigan of the district fly to the nearest snowfield, and remain on it until the eagle has gone, for they apparently realise that once on the snowy surface they are inconspicuous, but that on the dark hillside they can be seen at a distance. I have seen ptarmigan, at times such as these, at a distance of several hundred yards and they seemed, on the snow-free hillside, like small blocks of white quartz among the dark rocks. One November day, two friends and I were crossing the Larig Ghru pass in the Cairngorms. From the high corries above, a flight of ptarmigan appeared, moving at their best speed and obviously terrified. Sailing idly, without effort, after them came a golden eagle, then, swinging aside, the great bird returned into the Garbh Choire of Braeriach. The ptarmigan, on the other hand, continued their fast flight over the shoulder of Ben Mac Dhui, travelling at a height of about 4,500 feet above sea level and about 2,500 feet above where we stood watching them until they disappeared from sight. In winter, as in spring and summer, the eagle in the Scottish Highlands hunts both high and low ground. Adam Watson on one occasion saw in Glen Derry a thrilling pursuit of a cock capercaillie by a pair of golden eagles, the capercaillie, at the last moment, hurling himself into the shelter of thick firs where the eagles did not follow.

Male eagle flying into eyrie with prey (half a rabbit).   (*C. E. Palmar*)

The Golden Eagle: King of Birds

There is considerable doubt concerning the area which a pair of golden eagles need as their territory. F. Fraser Darling in his comprehensive work, *Natural History in the Highlands and Islands* calculates that a pair require ten thousand acres to keep them supplied with food. My own experience is that a number of Scottish pairs have no more than five thousand acres. Desmond Nethersole-Thompson's estimate is about six thousand acres. In winter the territories are more loosely held.

I have mentioned that some pairs of golden eagles habitually roost near the eyrie throughout the winter. The roosting place is on a ledge of rock, if the eyrie is itself on a rock, and on a Scots fir (sometimes a dead tree, bleached almost white) if the eyrie is on a tree. The white droppings and the small, downy feathers in the neighbourhood at once identify the roosting tree to the trained observer.

In winter, I have seen two pairs of golden eagles meet and perform, without enmity, breath-taking aerial manoeuvres, rising into the clouds, falling through them at tremendous speed, then flattening out and sailing into the wind with wings so steady that the birds looked like a squadron of aeroplanes. The young birds of the season may join in those friendly winter parties. On the other hand, when incubation has begun, the bird on watch will sometimes pursue the eagle from a neighbouring eyrie if it should pass over, even at a great height.

My own observations on the early winter repairing of an eyrie show that more evidence is needed in order to prove whether that is the rule or the exception: I am inclined to think it is the exception in Scotland. Because of the severity of the winter in Northern Europe, winter nest-building can be ruled out there, and also in the higher hills of the Scottish Highlands.

An acquaintance of mine was climbing on the Cuillin Hills in the Isle of Skye in early spring. He and a companion were making the difficult ascent of Sgùrr Dearg. There was an exceptional depth of snow on the range, each ridge being deeply covered. A golden eagle rose ahead of them and floated past, looking enormous, only a few feet away. They saw in the snow six pairs of talon marks, made as the eagle had run over the snow before being air-borne. The bird had added to the momentum of the run by wing thrusts, and the marks of its wings in the frozen snow were distinct. The last pair of talon marks had broken the cornice of snow at the edge of the precipice, which fell almost sheer for one thousand feet.

I myself remember seeing, in deep, newly fallen snow late in the season on Braeriach, one of the Cairngorm Hills, the perfect impression of a golden eagle's wings.

A number of observers have recorded what can only be described as games played by a pair of eagles. The game may be played with a grouse or ptarmigan, or some inanimate object. Murdo Ross, deerstalker on Glen Canisp forest in Sutherland, told me in detail, in a letter, of a remarkable scene he and others out stalking saw in the forest. The female eagle of a pair which had their home in that neighbourhood appeared carrying a black object with which she rose to a great height. She dropped what she was carrying, allowed it to fall a little way, then dived after it, dropped at great speed considerably beyond it, abruptly checked her fall, and as she rose a little way with the impetus she had gained during the descent, caught the object in her foot. Several times she repeated this performance. Her mate then appeared and took his part in the game. She as before dropped the object from a great height, but this time did not attempt to overtake it; the male overtook and caught it. The two eagles at last tired of the game and dropped the object, this time for good. Murdo marked where the plaything had fallen and on going to the spot found that it was a hard, dry piece of moss. Donald Fraser, stalker at the Derry in Mar

Forest, told me he had once seen this game played with a dead ptarmigan.

These light-hearted games are indulged in when, in the late autumn and winter months, the serious business of rearing a family is over.

In conclusion one may say that the golden eagle's territory is usually much wider in winter, and is not so strictly defended. In the milder western breeding areas courtship and nest-building may take place in winter, but in the more severe climate of the Central Highlands the problem of food occupies the birds during the short winter day: they know, besides, that at any time a heavy snowfall may nullify their nest building.

CHAPTER III

The Golden Eagle in Falconry

FROM the dawn of history, hawks have been used in falconry. In the fourth century A.D. a Greek named Ctesias was taken prisoner by the Persian king, whose name was Artaxerxes Mnémon. Ctesias has recorded that in his day there existed in Central India a hunting people named Pygmy who killed foxes and hares not with dogs but with eagle, kite, raven and crow. We do not know exactly where this race of hunters lived, but the Norwegian naturalist Collett has suggested that this Pygmy race may have been a Mongolian people from Tibet.

The east has long been the home of hunting with eagles. Dement'ev, (1943) has much to say of this hunting. In the year 1926 the market for golden eagles at Orenburg in south east Russia still persisted. Six years later, there were still fifty hunting golden eagles registered by the Kirghiz.

It is chiefly the Mongol people east of the Volga who practise hunting with eagles. A typical hunting region is the high table-lands of the Tian Shan mountains, on the borders of Kirghiz and Sinkiang. At one time the species of eagle used was not known by European naturalists, but it is now agreed to be the golden eagle, probably of the race *A. chrysaëtos daphanea*. The bird is rather larger and more powerful than the European golden eagle, and is named Berkut or Burkut by the Kirghiz and Cossacks.

When a golden eagle's eyrie is found in the mountains the young eagles when feathered are taken, often at a great hazard

31

because of the high rocks, from the eyrie and their training at once begins. So greatly is the trained golden eagle prized that its owner will not part with it except at a considerable price. A horse, or two camels, was a fair price for a golden eagle up to the beginning of the second world war.

The equipment of the golden eagle falconer must be particularly strong because of the great weight and strength of the bird. The falconer wears a glove of folded leather on his right hand (western falconers use the left hand for the glove and the left arm for the eagle's perch). The falconer is usually mounted, and the eagle is carried on the arm, the strain and weight being relieved by a prop borne on the knees or saddle of the mounted rider—his wrist rests on this prop. A hood of supple leather, covering the eagle's head but not its bill and nostrils, is used. The eagle is recalled by waving the lure, which is usually a stuffed fox's skin complete with tail. The training of the young eagle begins when its master shows it the skin of a hare or a gazelle with a small piece of meat placed in each eye-socket. The eagle at first fears this strange apparition, but gradually becomes bolder, perches on the head, and begins to eat the meat. In the second stage of the golden eagle's training the stuffed animal, attached to a string, is pulled along the ground. The eagle flies after it and seizes it, placing one foot on the back, the other on the head. After a month of this training the hunter releases a young fox, or a young wolf, which is allowed to run 50 or 60 yards before the eagle (which has been kept for 24 hours without food) is released. The golden eagle, with a few powerful thrusts of its wings, followed by a low glide, quickly overtakes its prey, seizes it and kills it. It is not allowed to feed on the animal, but is taken off it and is then fed on pieces of meat which its master carries in a bag—the eagle must learn not to damage the animal it has captured, because of the value of the skins of the foxes it will later kill. In Mongolia the golden eagle is used chiefly for killing the corsac fox, *vulpes corsac*. The fox-hunting season is autumn and the first part of winter. During the season a skilled golden eagle should capture from 30 to 50 foxes, the skins of which are a valuable source of income to its master. The eagle is also flown at wild goat, gazelle and, more rarely, hare. In Turkestan a twelve-year-old golden eagle named Alagym captured 14 wolves in a single day. Although the wolf of Turkestan is less formidable than that of East Europe or of Siberia this was a remarkable feat. Foxes are killed outright, but larger animals, such as the wolf, are caught and held until the human hunter, who is mounted and is armed with a rifle and a knife, arrives and kills the animal. The struggle between wolf and eagle is sometimes so severe that it must be difficult for the hunter to kill the wolf without injuring his eagle. When hunting a wolf, the golden eagle overtakes and swoops down on the fleeing animal, gripping the mask with one foot, in order to prevent the wolf biting, and the back with the other. The great bird then does its best to bring its two feet closer together and thus break the animal's spine, but with a wolf this is seldom possible, and the eagle is content to hold it until the arrival of its master. It is said that if an eagle several times misses its stoop it becomes so angry that it will sometimes fly at a man. On one occasion an eagle swooped at its master because he was wearing a cap of fox fur. The eagle's talons pierced an artery and the man died.

C. J. Tillisch of Copenhagen, a well-known authority on hawking and falconry throughout the ages, tells me that in 1951 he was present at a meeting of falconers at Heimbach near Cologne in Germany. Here he met Göring's former falconer, Fritz Loges, who later served in the same capacity with the British officers at Neuhaus. Loges said that he had trained many golden eagles for Göring, receiving the birds chiefly from Norway and Austria. He said that the golden eagles from

Norway are smaller than those from Austria, and are suitable for hunting hares: the golden eagle from Austria, on the other hand, can tackle foxes. Loges said that in Turkestan it is only the female of the Berkut (the Berkut is perhaps the largest of the many races of golden eagle) which can be used for wolf-hunting. It is necessary for the eagle to be very agile, as well as of great strength, to subdue a wolf. There was, Loges told Tillisch, some years ago a notoriously fierce and strong wolf which made a habit of preying on the sheep flocks of one district of the Kirghiz. The head man of the district, being unable to trap or shoot this wolf, sought the aid of the eagle falconers. On the appointed morning the falconers on horse-back, each with his eagle on the hood, set out for the rendezvous. One of the eagles pursued and struck the great wolf, but before it was able to bind on it with the mask-grip the wolf half-turned, snapped at the eagle and killed it. That was a bad day. The leading falconer had lost his most valuable eagle, and the other falconers could not be persuaded to risk their own birds. The mounted men sorrowfully returned home, and the wolf was left in peace, to continue its raids. The falconer who had lost his eagle trained another bird. He hoped with it to avenge his loss. The day came when the wolf was found and hunted with the second eagle. Again the wolf behaved as before, and a second valuable golden eagle was dead. That falconer was a determined man. In turn he trained, and lost in succession, eleven golden eagles, and all that time the big wolf was working havoc among the sheep. One can imagine his feelings when he rode out with his twelfth golden eagle on his wrist to seek battle once again with the wolf. After a long ride, the huge wolf was seen in the distance. The eagle was liberated and after a stern chase over-took the wolf. This time, before the wolf could strike with its terrible jaws, the eagle had grasped its mask with a grip of iron and held the animal until the falconer, galloping up in breath-

34

Typical eyrie site in central Inverness-shire.   (*Lea MacNally*)

less haste, killed the wolf with his knife. The eagle did not escape without a wound, but recovered and lived to hunt again. There was great rejoicing that the slayer of the sheep had at last been killed. The news of the eagle's victory spread quickly, near and far, and caused a sensation, both among the populace generally and among the falconers. Men came great distances to the "jurte" or house of the bird's owner in order to see the heroic eagle. In the house the visitors could see also the price that had been paid for the victory. On a long silk string were strung the heads of the eleven golden eagles which had been killed by the wolf. More cheerful was the sight of the wolf's pelt, and the gold medal which the falconer had received from the hand of the great Stalin.

A golden eagle used in falconry sometimes escapes, and from such an escape we fortunately know something of the longevity of this bird. In the early part of the nineteenth century, according to reliable contemporary evidence, sportsmen shot a golden eagle in France. Round its neck this bird had a collar of gold. On the collar was engraved the following inscription:

CAUCASUS PATRIA: FULGOR NOMEN: BADINSKI DOMINUS MIHI EST; 1750.

This may be translated; "Caucasus my native land, Lightning my name, Badinski my master, 1750.

The eagle was shot in 1845, and thus at the time it was killed, far from its home, it had reached the age of 95 years, even if it had been a young bird when the collar had been placed round its neck . . . I see no reason to doubt this evidence, which was printed in the *Aberdeen Free Press* in the year 1845. After studying the golden eagle for fifty years and more, I am convinced that the eagle's natural life can be more than a century. Traps, guns, and poison usually claim a golden eagle before its life-span is completed. The old Highland adage bears out the eagle's longevity; Yarrell (1871, *British Birds,* vol. 1) mentions that a golden eagle is reputed to have lived in confinement for 104 years in Vienna.

Possibly this record quoted by Yarrell is the same as that of the golden eagle belonging to the celebrated Prince Eugène François, Duke of Savoy and Piedmont, who had a famous menagerie at Belvedere outside Vienna. According to Fitzinger (1853) a female golden eagle was taken on the strength in 1729, transferred from Vienna in 1871 to Schönbrunn, where it died in 1809 after about 80 years in captivity. The late Major Flower (1938) the principal authority on avian longevity, was "prepared to accept Fitzinger's statement" on Prince Eugène's long-lived eagles and vultures to begin with, but was subsequently warned by Prof. O. Antonius of the Schönbrunn Zoo that "such was the glamour and glory attached to the name Eugène, there might have been "understudies" who took the places of the originals when they finished their mortal careers."

We find, according to Flower, that the twenty longest-lived known golden eagles average 15 years (4 of the 20 being alive at the time of recording). The longest-lived records known to Flower were 19 years (Estonia) and 20 years (Germany). If we set aside Prince Eugène's eagle, as we have from the above average, we find that the longest-lived individual to have lived in captivity did so for 46 years.

Our ambassador to Persia, His Excellency Sir G. H. Middleton, has kindly found out for me the present use of the golden eagle in falconry in that country. Hunting with the eagle is apparently still practised in remote mountainous areas in South Persia, amongst the Bakhtiari, Boir Ahmadi, and Qashqai tribes. The eagles are flown against the great bustard (*Otis tarda*), and also less frequently against shikar lambs (ibex and mouilon).

Sir G. H. Middleton also tells me that a curious use is made of eagles and hawks in the Gulf Littoral in Persia. Here they are flown against tortoises for sport. The birds lift the tortoises and bear them aloft to a great height, when they are released. The impact when they reach the ground breaks their shells and no doubt the tortoise itself is usually killed. The eagle then descends, and devours the meat.*

*The golden eagle is not ruled out, but possibly this refers to the Lammergeier, *Gypaëtus barbatus,* which is known to feed in this way.

CHAPTER IV

The Eyrie and Nesting Habits

IN THE Western Highlands of Scotland, and in the Hebrides, the golden eagle nests on a rock, very rarely on the ground; in the Central Highlands the site may be either a rock or a tree. The tree chosen is usually a Scots fir, but I have known of two eyries in birch trees in Scotland in the Central Highlands, and an exceptional record of an eyrie in a willow (*Salix*) in the Eastern Highlands. In Sweden a low birch (*Betula*) is occasionally the nesting site. In Switzerland, the golden eagle has nested in spruce (*Picea alba*), in Swiss pine (*Pinus cembra*) and in mountain pine (*Pinus montana*). In Switzerland the trees are on ledges of precipices, but in Scotland, and also in Sweden, on gently-sloping ground. Tree-eyries are sometimes blown down, but I have not heard of an eyrie being blown down to the ground when it was occupied. In the Central Scottish Highlands a pair of eagles may nest one season on a rock and the next in a tree, but one pair which I have known for many years have never nested on a rock. In the Central Highlands a tree is usually chosen if the spring is a severe one, with much snow. In a very severe spring, a pair of golden eagles may find all their rock-sites (they may have as many as four or five) buried in snow. If no sites in trees are available, they may be forced to nest at lower levels. This happened in the spring of 1947.

It is the exception for the same eyrie to be used two years running. The break in the tenancy is, I think, made in order that the nest after its use may be cleaned and purified by the rains and winds, frosts and snows, of two winters.

Desmond Nethersole-Thompson watched a pair of golden eagles choosing the new nesting site. He told me that the female brooded on three different eyries on a long cliff-face, the male soaring above her and pitching on ledges while she visited one eyrie after another. Later, both eagles rose high into the air, then dived and zoomed in spectacular manner for several minutes. I myself witnessed what appeared to be the choice of the new site, one November afternoon, the male then taking the initiative (See Ch. XII, p.193). A pair of golden eagles are almost always the owners of at least two eyries. A pair in the Central Scottish Highlands provide the only exception to this rule which I know. Here the nesting site is unusual—in a thick, closely planted wood—and the same eyrie has been used since around the year 1910, when the deerstalker of the ground brought me news of the exceptional nesting place. Although the wood is a close one, the eyrie is near the edge of it, and the eagle has a good outlook as she broods.

In Scotland a pair of rock-nesting eagles may build their nest so near the foot of the cliff that it may be reached from below. This has happened even on a sea cliff.

Very occasionally a pair of golden eagles will build their nest on the ground below a cliff. A stalker on Loch Torridon told me that he had once found an eyrie in that unusual position. In the same district an eagle's eyrie during a winter storm fell from its ledge to the foot of the cliff 100 feet below. In the early spring the eagles repaired the fallen eyrie where it lay instead of building a new nest on a ledge of the cliff.

It is usual for the golden eagle to build on rocks with a north, north east, or east aspect. In early spring, when the site is decided on, a warmer south aspect might seem more suitable. The reason why that aspect is rarely chosen is, I think, because the direct rays of the sun in summer are so powerful that the eaglet would suffer much distress if the eyrie faced south. It is indeed true to say that the parent eagle shields her eaglet from the sun when in the downy stage, but does not show the same anxiety to shelter it from cold. It is seldom that a rock eyrie faces west: in a disused west-facing eyrie, a pair of peregrine falcons in 1930 hatched their young.

A raven is careful to build its nest below a protecting "overhang" of rock but a golden eagle usually favours a more exposed ledge. There is one Hebridean eyrie I know, where the site is actually on the ground, on the steep face of a narrow glen. The eyrie is completely protected from the weather by the overhanging rock.

I know a number of sites of golden eagles' eyries in sea cliffs, where in former days the sea-eagle nested.

The size of a golden eagle's eyrie varies greatly. The tree eyrie near which my wife and I spent 167 hours in a hide during one season (Ch. IX, p. 141) was approximately six feet deep from nesting cup to foundations and at least four feet across the top. By far the deepest eyrie I have seen is on a Scots fir above a glen in the Central Highlands of Scotland. This eyrie, to my personal knowledge, has been in use during a period of 45 years. It has gradualy increased in size until (1954) it is approximately fifteen feet deep. The top of the eyrie is now actually the highest part of the tree. Looking at this eyrie from the ground, the observer sees how one nest after another has been built on the foundations of the last, and that each eyrie retains its individuality in the whole structure. The brooding eagle must now be prepared to face much exposure. The weight of this great eyrie must be a burden to the old fir, yet it remains erect and sturdy at the age of perhaps 300 years while others around it have been overthrown by winter gales.

The Eyrie and Nesting Habits

A rock eyrie in Scotland never approximates the largest tree eyries in size.

The foundations of most golden eagles' eyries consist of large sticks and branches. These are almost always dead; they are too large for the eagle to break off the tree. Where sticks are not available, the eyrie may be built throughout of heather, or occasionally of dried bracken. On the strong platform of sticks are placed branches, sometimes of considerable size. The platform of the eyrie, and the sides of the nesting cup, are of smaller branches, or of heather. The antlers of small stags were used in the construction of an eagle's nest on a rock in Caithness.

Another eyrie in a rock was built mainly of birch branches and twigs, with a foundation of larger, birch sticks. A golden eagle, nesting at an elevation of over 3,000 feet on the Cairngorm Hills, brought to the eyrie a large branch which she must have carried the best part of ten miles. The small green fir shoots and branches with their green needles which form the top of a fir-tree eyrie are wrenched off some neighbouring tree by the eagle's bill; they are never taken from the ground. When looked at from above, eyries in fir-trees are seen to have an interwoven platform of fir branches fresh and green as those of the living trees which grow around them. In the Highlands of Scotland the cup of the eyrie is almost always lined with the great wood-rush. Murdo Matheson, deerstalker, gamekeeper, and bird observer in Glen Garry of the west for more than half a century, and the discoverer of probably the last osprey's nest in Britain, told me that he had watched, through his stalking telescope, golden eagles in winter tearing out plants of wood-rush from the ground. His observations led him to think that the eagles left these uprooted plants to dry, and that they built them into their eyrie in early spring.

The golden eagle has so strong a liking for the great wood-rush that she will carry it in her bill to the eyrie after the eaglet is

41

hatched. This I have seen and photographed, and Niall Rankin has recorded with his camera, in this book, a similar incident.

In California, a golden eagle may line the eyrie with eucalyptus leaves carried a considerable distance: in the humid coast belt there an eyrie was very thickly lined with rabbit fur.

In the Western Highlands of Scotland there are few eyries in trees, and branches of Scots fir, the eagle's favourite nesting material, are not usually available. Here the golden eagle builds the foundations of the eyrie mainly of sticks of the mountain ash (*Sorbus aucuparia*) which support the nest made, perhaps, of heather reinforced by juniper, the nesting cup being generally lined with wood-rush. On one occasion I saw a nesting cup lined with moorland rushes. I found frequently the growing shoots of bearberry (*Arctostaphylos uva-ursi*) and wild raspberry (*Rubus*) in an eyrie.

The courtship of the golden eagle may begin in early winter, and may continue at intervals for four months. The act of mating may take place during any month from January until May. Most of the golden eagle's courtship is aerial, and consists of superb aerobatics, both male and female taking an equal part. The male may swing over the female with wings raised to an angle of 45 degrees, or he may stoop at and chase her. Desmond Nethersole-Thompson once saw both eagles roll over on their backs, extending their legs upward; this he thinks may have been a symbolic food pass.

The actual mating may take place in deep snow. On 28 January 1950, I was approaching the territory of a pair of golden eagles. It was a perfect winter day, the snow lying deep and evenly-spread on the moor, the sky almost cloudless, the air very clear. Both eagles were soaring near the rock on which their two eyries are placed. One of the eagles had a mind to alight on the top of the cliff but the snow, drifted on the ridge to a depth of several feet, was too heavy. The eagle, still air-borne, was now attacked by a pair of ravens; after the ravens had left him (it was the male bird) he did succeed in making a landing. The snow was so deep and soft that when he again rose he had to struggle in order to become air-borne. He flew a little way, then again alighted in the snow. Here, after a few seconds, he began to beat his wings as though he were mating the female; yet there was no sign of a second bird. When the eagle, two minutes later, took wing, I was surprised to see his mate rise, a few seconds afterwards, from the same spot. The deep cup she had made in the snow when she had earlier alighted had entirely hidden her from my sight, and the male had indeed been mating her when his wings had been violently agitated. Thus the eagles began the honeymoon, beneath a deep blue sky, in a world of white. This was almost exactly six weeks before the egg was laid.

The golden eagle remains with its mate throughout the year; the union is probably a life-long one. Courtship is little dependent on weather conditions. With most birds, the nesting season occupies only a fraction of their year, but I have known a pair of golden eagles begin eyrie repairs as early as November, only a few days after their eaglet had left them. Their nesting cycle was thus a year.

The year following that in which I had witnessed the mating, I was in the eagle's country on 16 February. The day was calm and overcast, and there was no snow on the hills, although there had been, so far, little hint of spring. The male eagle was perched on the top of the nesting rock. He later rose, sailing indolently in spirals eastward as he gradually gained height. He now began to glide against the breeze that evidently was blowing at this altitude. After travelling without wing movement the best part of a mile, he alighted on the grassy slope near the top of a hill and I saw that his mate was standing where he had come to earth. Almost at once he sprang on to her back and mated or attempted to mate her, with wings moving quickly. The pair then stood close together, quite still, for many minutes. When they rose it was the female who displayed, by falling with closed wings and each time quickly regaining her former height: this display took place surprisingly near the ground. Again alighting, the pair then remained almost motionless close together for an even longer period than before. When at last they rose, one after another, they were hidden for a time from my view by the shoulder of an intervening hill: a few seconds before they reappeared a dozen ravens and a greater black-backed gull were seen, flying wildly and in evidently alarm. The ravens had perhaps, been feeding, on a dead sheep and had been suddenly disturbed by the eagles. The eagles ignored the fleeing birds, and alighted on the top of a hill pass, where they stood like a pair of love birds, side by side, their feathers touching. A few days later, it was again the female who did the rising and falling stunt, in and out of the clouds. She once passed near the male, who shot out his legs, presumably in playful greeting.

Golden eagles may perform the act of mating long after the eggs have been laid. One year, on 30 April, I was in golden eagle territory. A raven was mobbing the male eagle, and after a time the female, perhaps disturbed by all the croaking of the angry raven, left her eyrie. She had then been incubating at least a month. There ensued exciting aerobatics, the pair of ravens diving at the eagles with incessant croakings, the eagles answering with an occasional yelp. The eagles later alighted together on a knoll, the female larger and darker, the smaller male more bleached in plumage. Their golden heads and yellow feet could be seen in the field of my glass. The eagles then rose, sailed one behind the other right over me, looking like small aeroplanes, and the female did stunt flights, swooping with wings almost closed and legs held down. Her aerial rush

Newly hatched
eaglet.
(*Lea MacNally*)

was plainly heard. Again both eagles alighted on the cliff-top. The female may have softly called to him, for the male suddenly flew over to her, alighted on her back, and mating took place, the male moving, rather slowly, his outspread wings in order to maintain his position. The act of mating accomplished, the female rose, passed swiftly across the face of the cliff, not far from the bottom. When she neared the eyrie, built in a cave-like recess, she shot upward, alighted skilfully, and disappeared on to her eggs. Mating at the end of a long period of incubation is noteworthy.

Observers have reported that they have seen golden eagles assume weird positions when mating, but I have seen nothing unusual in the attitudes of the birds, and am sceptical of these reports.

As I have already mentioned, nest-building or nest-repair does not end with the laying of the eggs. During the twelve weeks the eaglets remain in the eyrie the parents periodically bring living shoots of trees and shrubs. It is unexpected to find in the eyrie of a great bird of prey the flowering shoot of a mountain ash, the perfume of the flowers mingling with the smell of the prey. The green feathery branch of a larch (*Larix*) found in the early summer of 1952 at an eyrie at 3,000 feet, must have been carried up vertically at least 1,200 feet, for no larch grows in Scotland as high as 2,000 feet above sea level. This habit of carrying living branches to the eyrie is probably world-wide, and is not confined to Europe. E. S. Cameron in America describes a Montana eyrie, and states that "the whole external circumference of the nest rim was interwoven with an ornamental binding of green pine tops."

The golden eagle's egg is small for the size of the bird. In shape it is rounded, the shell being thick and granulated. The ground colour is creamy-white. Blotches or spots of amber-brown may be evenly distributed, or may be concentrated at one end of the egg. In a clutch of two, one egg is more heavily marked than the other. Unspotted eggs are sometimes laid. Witherby's *Handbook of British Birds* states that the average size of 100 golden eagles' eggs from Scotland is 77.02 x 59.48 mm. Max. x 88.9 x 66 mm. Min. 70.3 x 56, and 77.6 x 51 mm.

The golden eagle's clutch consists usually of two eggs, but there are many instances of one egg completing the clutch. Three eggs are only occasionally laid in Scotland but in the southern states of America this is not apparently unusual. In America there is in an egg collection one authenticated clutch of four eggs, which Herbert Brandt tells me in a letter was taken in the San Francisco area. There is also one Scottish record of four eggs. Yarrell mentions this clutch, taken at a tree eyrie in Scotland: he quotes an article by Captain Powlett-Orde in *The Ibis* to this effect. Desmond Nethersole-Thompson tells me that in three records he has made of clutches of two eggs, the interval between the laying of the first and the second egg was 96–120 hours. That five days should on occasion elapse before the laying of the second egg is noteworthy. Murdo Matheson, deerstalker and author, wrote to me that in 82 golden eagles' eyries he examined he saw a clutch of three, eight times: on 15 occasions only one egg was present. He never saw three young reared. When first I heard, thereafter, that one pair of Scottish golden eagles was in the habit of rearing three young each year, I formed the impression that the birds were buzzards and had therefore been wrongly identified. A photograph sent me of the eyrie with three feathered eaglets at once dispelled these doubts. The eyrie, which I later visited, is on a rock of no great height, almost immediately above a hill loch: it can be reached by a moderate climber without difficulty. On a grass-covered boulder near, the eagles were in the habit of disembowelling the rabbits and hares which they carried in for their young. The eagles have now left the site, or it may be that the male has found a new mate. For some seasons in succession the rock was without its eagles. The rock is now tenanted again, but the clutches of eggs number only two. It is likely that the prolific female was trapped or shot.

I was fortunate in visiting the eyrie during the last nesting season of the original female, and in seeing three downy eaglets in the nest. The pair of golden eagles reared 24 young in 8 years. The ninth year only two were reared. When I visited the nest that year, one of the three eaglets was lying lifeless in the eyrie. One of the surviving eaglets, from its exceptional size probably a young female, was the most aggressive eaglet I have seen, and although still in down, without hesitation advanced to attack. I have little doubt that it had killed the lifeless eaglet.

In the eyrie were 6 hares and 2 grouse. My friend who showed me this nest said that one day he had found no fewer than 6 grey crows in the eyrie; they were all skilfully plucked.

This was in the glen where, earlier, a pair of golden eagles had pursued and attacked a peregrine falcon which was carrying food to its eyrie. The peregrine for a time had succeeded in retaining hold of its prey, but in the end was forced by the severity of the attacks to drop it. The observer hurried to the spot where the prey had been dropped and found not a grouse, as he had expected, but a grey crow.

In Chapter XIII (p.203) *et sequentes,* I describe the late autumn and early winter building of a pair of golden eagles, the birds almost daily adding to the nest from mid-November until mid-December. This, I think is unusual, but in 1952 December building was noted in Mar Forest, and even in the glens of the high-lying Central Highlands January building is not exceptional, in open weather. On 24 January 1953, I watched the male eagle make three flights with heather to an eyrie in ten minutes. Since eggs are not laid in Scotland until March, it follows that nest-building may continue during several months.

There are exceptions to this leisurely nest-building. Donald Falconer, a careful observer in Sutherland, told me that in 1949 a pair of golden eagles drove a pair of ravens from their nest when the raven brood were almost ready to fly. The ravens, as it happened, were using the only suitable ledge on the rock. Why did this pair of eagles delay so long in the choice of a nesting site? They may have been a youthful pair, nesting for the first time, or may have been robbed of their first clutch. I have not known a golden eagle lay a second time, but Desmond Nethersole-Thompson, who has much experience in the nesting habits of Scottish golden eagles, has known of two second clutches—both in Sutherland. Donald Falconer's eagles, after they had routed the ravens, began, about 20 April, to alter and enlarge the ravens' nest. Two eaglets were hatched, and were still in the eyrie on 24 August.

When a heavy snowfall occurs just before laying time, the eagle may brood the eyrie in order to keep the nesting cup free of snow, the male standing on guard near. Later, when she has laid, the male may roost near her, as Niall Rankin in 1952 proved when he paid a surprise visit to a rock eyrie at midnight in May.

On one occasion I had the good fortune to see a golden eagle keeping her empty eyrie snow-free. She was a late layer, and the date was 17 April. The site of that Aberdeenshire eyrie is high and exposed; it is over 2000 feet above the sea and March layings would probably be drifted up. On this mid-April day half a foot of fresh snow lay on the roadside in the glen, and before I reached the eyrie I was struggling through snow which averaged 30 inches in depth. The male eagle was perched above the rock, and took wing when I approached: when I came in sight of the eyrie the female at once rose from it and flew away. The eyrie was deeply covered with snow, but the actual cup of the nest, on which the eagle had been brooding, was snow-free

48

and the only dark speck in all that snowy landscape. It was difficult to approach the eyrie, for each ledge above it was deeply snow-covered.

Judge my surprise, when at length I could look down into the nest, to find it empty. The eagle had been keeping her eyrie free of snow and may have been about to lay her first egg. When next I visited the eyrie there were two eggs in it. This was on 22 April, and there was still much snow remaining, although it was now slightly broken up by the sun's heat.

The only sound to break the silence of that snowy country was the croaking of ptarmigan.

Where a golden eagle's nesting site is comparatively sheltered and snow-free, the eggs in Scotland may be laid before mid-March. The earliest date on which I myself have seen the eagle brooding was 9 March. That afternoon I witnessed the "change-over," the male taking the female's place on the eyrie (see Ch. XII, p. 186). On 7 March, I had seen only one bird in the neighbourhood of the eyrie, and it is possible that the egg was being laid on that date. The month of February had been mild, with high winds from south and south west.

In the great continent of America, the northern-nesting golden eagles have not yet arrived at their nesting sites when those of their species already have young in the southern states. In California, for instance, egg-laying has been recorded on 9 February, and in Arctic America there are instances of eggs being found on 27 May and as late as 29 June. Even in Europe, Carl Stemmler in Switzerland has seen eggs in an eyrie as late as 12 June. In Scotland I have never seen unhatched eggs after May.

In the Scottish Highlands the earliest record I know of the hatching of the eaglet is 15 April, the observer here being Adam Watson, whom I had earlier directed to the eagle's nesting tree.

49

The same observer saw the eaglet take its first flight on 5 July —a fledgling period of twelve weeks all but three days. That eagle must have laid early in the first week in March and I think this is the earliest record from Scotland. Another eagle in this district, also a tree-nester, is almost as early. In the West Highlands the period of incubation was established in 1952 by Alexander Gibson, a careful observer. He found the first egg laid on 22 March and the first young hatched on 4 May—43 days. Desmond Nethersole-Thompson notes an incubation period of 43–44 days for the second egg laid.

Golden eagles are conservative birds and will not readily forsake a nesting site for good even if they are disturbed, but they will not again use an eyrie which has been proved unsafe. In Ch. IX p. 148, I have described how the weight of one of the feathered eaglets, combined with the remains of a roe-deer calf, caused one side of the eyrie to break away, throwing the eaglet to the ground. Although the second eaglet remained safe and the eyrie was a long-established one, the eagles have never used it since. Another eyrie, this time on a rock, was abandoned because it took fire. The spring was a dry one and when the deerstalker told me that he intended to set fire to the long heather growing on the slope beneath the eagles' rock I told him the eyrie might well be set alight, because a heather-grown crack ran up the rock to the nest. The stalker laughed at my fears, but I was unconvinced, and late in the day, when the fire had almost burned itself out, I visited the place. The only smoke which now rose was a thin column from the eyrie itself. I realised then that my fears had been well-grounded and on climbing to the eyrie found the two eggs scorched and blackened. Although the eyrie was not entirely destroyed, the eagles did not repair it in the seasons which followed.

It is not easy to observe closely the home life of a pair of eagles before the eggs hatch. The eagle may desert her eggs if

Eagle at eyrie. The eaglet has just been fed and is satiated. (*Niall Rankin*)

suddenly disturbed, especially from above, or if the eyrie is frequently visited. It is never safe to put up a hide at an eyrie before the eggs hatch. Niall Rankin was awaiting the hatching of the eaglets before erecting his hide. Another photographer was shown the nest, at once set up a hide, and the eagles deserted.

When hatched, the young golden eagle is covered with white down with pale-grey tips. Later, creamy-white down, of a thicker texture, replaces the first covering. The feathers begin to appear through the down at the age of approximately 21 days. The back is full-feathered before the feathers of the neck are grown. From its hour of hatching, the eaglet cheeps shrilly and continuously for long periods, even when it is being brooded. Its cheeping becomes more plaintive if it should be left exposed to the air. Even during the first week, the eaglet may be left unattended by either parent if the day should be calm and warm; under these conditions it seems quite happy by itself for an hour and more. Brooding ceases, except in rain or snow, when the eaglet is three weeks old, all events during the hours of daylight.

I have always thought that, where two eggs hatch, the sex of the eaglets is different—brother and sister—because of the marked difference in size from the earliest days. This might be verified if a trained chick-sexer visited a number of eyries. The bullying, and sometimes killing, of one eaglet by the other is a feature of the early weeks of the young birds. My own observations I record in Ch. IX, p. 142. Both Niall Rankin and J. H. Stainton Crosthwaite have seen from hides the killing of one eaglet by the other. The latter observer had reason to believe that one eaglet killed the other for four years running, or turned it out of the eyrie, to die on the ground below.

The eaglet, even when fledged, does not recognise its parent in the air, and calls excitedly to a passing gull or raven. When its own parent arrives with prey, cheeping is increased to a pitch of frenzied excitement.

Where the nesting rock is low and broken the eaglet may walk out of the eyrie before it is full-fledged and wander on foot some little distance, usually returning to the nest at night. This happened at the eyrie observed and photographed by H. B. MacPherson in 1909. Looking at Harry MacPherson's photographs, taken nearly half a century ago, which illustrate his book *Home Life of the Golden Eagle,* I am impressed afresh by their excellence, even by present-day standards.

At the age of approximately a month the eaglet begins to feed itself, although it is still chiefly fed by the parent for a considerable time after this.

The eaglet is particular in its sanitary habits. Before it "evacuates" it backs, unsteadily in its youthful days, to the edge of the nest and ejects its semi-liquid faeces over the side and well-clear of the eyrie, with astonishing power and precision. It indeed ejects further than the adult bird: thus the eyrie never becomes "white-washed" and foul with droppings. like the nest of the raven.

It seems that when an eyrie is unduly disturbed the parent eagle occasionally moves her young to a new site. Robert MacAulay, for many years stalker at Stack Lodge in the Reay Forest, told me that his father, on approaching an eyrie, saw the eagle fly off carrying an object in its talons. A dead eaglet lay beneath the eyrie, which was empty. A week later the observer returned, and then found a living eaglet in down in the eyrie. He was sure that the eagle had carried off her remaining eaglet, and had later brought it back. Robert MacAulay himself saw two eaglets suddenly appear in an unoccupied eyrie early in June, and had no doubt that the eagle had brought them from another nest, where she had perhaps been disturbed. In 1951, at an Upper Deeside eyrie, much the same thing happened. Here the stalker on whose ground the eyrie was situated told me that there had been two eggs in this nest. In mid-May, when he visited the nest, he found in it pieces of egg-shell, but no young birds. A little later he found two eaglets about a fortnight old on a ledge 300 yards away, with a rudimentary eyrie made round them. He said they could not possibly have reached the new site by themselves. The nest had been a good deal disturbed by visitors.

Each pair of golden eagles varies in their time of bringing food to the young. The eagle is not an early riser, and at the eyries at which my wife and I have watched, the young have not been fed before seven in the morning—usually rather later. Prey was never brought late in the evening. At these eyries, all the food was brought in by the male, and deposited on the nest. A correspondent, J. C. Leitch, watched a golden eagle's eyrie in 1952 in Kintyre and found that the male did the hunting, but the prey was sometimes transferred to the female in the air. The transfer of the food seemed to be made by the female snatching it from the talons of the male. This habit one associates with the harriers and not with the golden eagle. On the occasions when the female did not meet the male and take, in the air, the food he had brought, the male left it always on the same rock, where his mate immediately collected it.

When the eaglet becomes feathered the parents begin to be bored by it. They now visit the eyrie less frequently, and should the eaglet be slow in making its first flight they seem deliberately to starve it. Wing exercises at this stage form an important part of the eaglet's life. The young bird flaps its wings so long and vigorously that it seems it must unwillingly fly itself out of the nest, despite the firm grip it takes of the edge of the eyrie with its feet. The first flight, when at last it is made, must be the most thrilling moment of the young eagle's life. I have not

seen this at close quarters from a hide, but H. B. MacPherson*
vividly describes it. Let me quote his word-picture of the scene:

> And then a wild, weird cry rang echoing down the glen.
> For the first time I had heard the yelp of the adult eagle,
> the voice of the Queen of Birds calling to her young. Thrice
> was the note repeated, then silence reigned again for awhile.
> The eaglet cheeped continuously until, as though seized by
> some irresistible impulse, he flapped to the very edge of the
> abyss, and turned his head from side to side, listening to her
> call. And now he, too, changed his cry, his voice seemed to
> break, and the adult yelp, though in a lower and feebler key,
> burst from his throat. The eagles called to each other; yelp
> answered yelp as they held strange converse in this wild
> mountain solitude. The young eagle gazed around him as
> though taking a last farewell of his birth-place, spread out
> his giant wings and vanished for ever from my sight.

A golden eagle's eyrie sometimes has strange visitors. Stainton
Crosthwaite records in his film a pied wagtail, watched with
great interest by the eaglets, catching flies in an eyrie. The
wagtail a little later actually alighted on the back of one of
the eaglets.

The fledgling period of the young golden eagle varies: it
remains (unless disturbed) in the eyrie for several days, sometimes more than a week, after it appears to be fully feathered.
In 1951 an eaglet, hatched on or around 23 April, was still in
the eyrie on 13 July, and at a distance of a mile could be heard
calling for food. It had then been in the nest for 12 weeks all

*These striking lines were written by the direct descendant of James
MacPherson whose translations of the poems of Ossian have aroused
vehement controversy among Celtic scholars of succeeding generations,
although none has denied the beauty and dignity of language in these
translations.

but three days. Between 13 July and 18 July close mist hid the eyrie. On 18 July the bird had flown. Stainton Crosthwaite was once fortunate to see both eaglets leave the eyrie together on their first flight. The birds were still flying strongly when they disappeared round a hill over a mile away.

The responsibilities of the parents are by no means over when the eaglet has left the nest. Prey is still carried to it, and the eaglet may remain in the neighbourhood of the eyrie for some weeks, at times even months. Its parents indeed take more interest in it after it is air-borne than during its last weeks in the nest, and prey is brought it even when in mastery of flight it is indistinguishable from its parents. One season an eaglet remained with its parents until the end of December, perhaps longer.

During the spring and summer of 1952 Niall Rankin made a series of valuable observations on the weight of a golden eaglet in an eyrie in the northern Highlands of Scotland, and he has been good enough to give me the results of his observations for my book. There were at first two eaglets in the eyrie, but the larger pecked the smaller to death.

WEIGHTS OF SURVIVING EAGLET

May 10.	16 ozs. (other eaglet was 12 ozs.)	
May 17.	2 lbs. 0½ ozs.	
May 19.	2 lbs. 2½ ozs.	
May 21.	2 lbs. 14½ ozs.	Gain of 12 ozs. in 48 hours.
May 22.	3 lbs. 5 ozs.	
May 23.	3 lbs. 12 ozs.	
May 24.	4 lbs. 3 ozs.	
May 25.	4 lbs. 11 ozs.	
May 26.	5 lbs. 2 ozs.	

Eagle's nest and eggs. A rock eyrie in the West Highlands.   (*C. E. Palmar*)

WEIGHTS OF SURVIVING EAGLET (CONT.)

June 9.	7 lbs. 2 ozs.	
June 10.	7 lbs. 0 ozs.	Loss of 2 ozs. in 24 hours.
June 11.	6 lbs. 11 ozs.	Loss of 5 ozs. in 24 hours.
June 12.	7 lbs. 4 ozs.	GAIN of 9 ozs. in 24 hours.
June 16.	7 lbs. 10 ozs.	
June 19.	8 lbs. 3 ozs.	It never again reached this weight.
June 20.	7 lbs. 11 ozs.	Loss of 8 ozs. in 24 hours.
June 21.	7 lbs. 11 ozs.	
June 22.	7 lbs. 5 ozs.	Another loss in weight.
July 4.	7 lbs. 14 ozs.	
July 5.	7 lbs. 11 ozs.	
July 7.	7 lbs. 12 ozs.	
July 14.	Eaglet away from eyrie.	

The considerable loss in weight during the time when the feathers were growing is remarkable. It looks as if it was due to the development of the feathers and the amount of energy required to grow them.

The eaglet left the eyrie when in the neighbourhood of seven and three quarter pounds in weight.

What happens to the young golden eagle after it has been driven off by its parents, or has gone of its own free-will since food is no longer brought it? There is a curious lack of information about its habits until, at the age of four years, it is mature and mates.

In the countries of the Arctic the young eagles migrate south in winter, but those of the Scottish Highlands are resident, except on rare occasions. In some instances they remain partly on the territory of their parents, where they are tolerated although not encouraged. Throughout the summer of 1952 a 1951 eaglet remained in the neighbourhood of the rock where it was reared: its parents, having failed to rear young in 1952, left the district in June and did not return until October.

Immature eagles are from time to time shot or trapped in

England, but these are almost always immature sea-eagles, on migration from Scandinavia.

My own impression is that the young Scottish golden eagles wander over the Highlands of that country during their first winter. When shot or trapped, as they undoubtedly often are, nothing is said about it, because of public opinion and the fear of prosecution. In the British Isles, few young golden eagles have been ringed or banded, and I do not think there has been one instance here of the recapure of a banded eagle.

In a golden eagle family the ties are not readily broken.

One afternoon late in July, warm and sunny, I crossed a hill from the summit ridge of which I was in sight of an eyrie. On short, springy turf, close-grazed by rabbits and sheep, a young golden eagle was feeding on a rabbit. A few feet from it, one of the parents was perched on a rock, the other stood on the roots of a small tree growing at the edge of the cliff. After a time the eaglet tired of its struggles with the rabbit carcase and began wing exercises, running from place to place and beating its wings violently. The conspicuous white area on the under side of each wing was seen. When one of the parents began to feed on the remains of the rabbit the eaglet, yelping excitedly, danced round it, but was ignored. The family party then proceeded to enjoy the warm sun and the eaglet lay sun-bathing on the turf, its wings outspread and resting on the ground.

On one occasion I had the memorable experience of being in sight of two pairs of golden eagles, each at their own nesting station, at the same time, for the two eyries are not more than three miles apart, and I was on high ground between them. It was June, and early that morning as I climbed the hill I had seen the rising sun turn the green grass in the corrie to deep, glowing red. When I reached the hill top the sun was high and the light brilliant. Here I watched one pair of eagles and their downy eaglet far below me and then, spying the neighbouring hill where I knew another pair of eagles had their eyrie containing a feathered eaglet, I saw the dark form of one of the birds near it, moving through the blue, radiant sky. The eagle then alighted on his rock, and I saw that his mate was already there. They stood side by side, dark even in full sunlight against the bright green of the grassy slope below them.

Most of my observing has been done at rock eyries, but the description of the country of a tree-nesting pair may be interesting.

The glen where these eagles nest is one of the most unfrequented in the Central Scottish Highlands. The Scots firs which grow here are several hundred years old; the bleached skeleton of one of them is that of a tree of exceptional size. A few birches, also of great age, are in the glen. In May these renew their youth and clothe themselves with fragrant leaves. Indeed the leaves of very old birches have a more aromatic and delicate scent than those of younger birches. Two world wars have left the trees unharmed, for there is no road or track through the glen—else the trees had probably been felled. A clear stream flows through the glen, and it is in an old fir close to it that one of the eagles' eyries (they have at least three) is built. Here the brooding eagle has the brotherhood of water birds as her companions. She sees goosanders fly past, fast and straight, as they travel to and from their nesting hole in some ancient fir, the breast of the drake snow-white against the dark forest. She sees the dipper feeding in the clear water of the stream, turning over small pebbles with its bill, and eating the aquatic larvae which shelter below them. Near the close of her long brooding period of six weeks she may hear the husky call of the first cuckoo and the soft song of the first willow-warbler, and may see the sandpiper's arrival. She may listen to the redstart's short song and see the flash of his brick-red tail as he flits through the firs. She may see the northward flight of the wild geese, and of the wild swans also, as the snow fields on the great hill above the eyrie gradually lessen in size.

Her "next-door" golden eagle neighbour also nests in a Scots fir. The tree, one of beauty and dignity, may have flourished even at the time of the Jacobite rising of 1745. Here the eagle looks westward in her eyrie, built on a stout branch rather more than half-way up the tree. She is an acrobatic bird, alighting on the tree at a lower level than the eyrie, then springing upwards, monkey-like, from branch to branch until she has climbed to the nest. As she broods, near the hatching of her young, she sees a tree-pipit neighbour descend, singing his high-pitched song, to the topmost branches of a Scots fir. She hears oystercatchers in the glen below utter their shrill courting music, and they may at times fly over her in their courtship flight, which is accompanied by appropriate flutings. A ring-ouzel sometimes sings from a neighbouring fir; in his song are the notes of a blackbird interspersed with the long, sad song of the ring-ouzel.

One of the highest nesting-places of Scottish golden eagles is a conical hill where their eyries—there are several of them—approach a favourite haunt of ptarmigan, and the eagle as she broods must hear often the croaking of these white-winged birds. One of the eyries belonging to this pair of eagles is a nest of rare beauty and symmetry; another, near it, is so old that it has almost reverted to earth and dust. Along the top of the cliff the rocky ground is carpeted with the little azalea *Loiseleuria procumbens;* the pink flowers open when the eaglets are very young. On the dark May day when last I saw that eyrie the deep red azalea flower-buds added small touches of exquisite colour to the sombre scene. In the neighbourhood of the eyrie is one of the highest hills in the Scottish Highlands. Here, on a calm sunny day, the eagle off-duty may perch for hours—true king or queen of the hills and the glens.

The Golden Eagle: King of Birds

In most European countries the golden eagle nests considerably higher than in Scotland. For instance, Carl Stemmler tells me that the highest eyrie he knows in Switzerland is 7,200 feet above the sea, in the Rosegtal. In 1953 I saw one above Zermatt at approximately this height. He says the majority are between 4,700 feet and 6,000 feet. All these heights exceed Ben Nevis, highest hill in the British Isles, and although Switzerland lies far south of the Scottish Highlands, this greater altitude results in the Swiss eagles laying later than those in Scotland.

Since the golden eagle in Britain, and indeed throughout Europe and Asia, is reckoned to be a solitary bird, the Valley of Eagles in the Rocky Mountains in Alberta, Canada, must be unique if it is indeed the nesting place of a colony of these great birds. Professor Rowan, Professor of Zoology in the Department University of Alberta, on 6 August 1952, went up by pack horse to visit this high valley, going in from Entrance, a station on the C.N.R. Professor Rowan tells me that the valley is named on the map, Eagles' Nest Pass, but has been named by the Indians, Valley of the Eagles, since time immemorial. The valley is inaccessible for the greater part of each year because of snow. Attempts have been made to visit the valley in June, but they have never succeeded because then the valley is still blocked by the winter snows. The eagles' nesting site is a vast rock-face, rising about 1000 feet perpendicularly from the floor of the valley, which is so narrow that no satisfactory view of the cliffs is possible from the farther side. The eagles' eyries are in caverns into which enormous masses of sticks have been stuffed. My correspondent saw a number of golden eagles flying in and out of the valley, but his visit was too late in the season for him to verify the reports of communal nesting. He tells me that the local ranger some years ago went through the pass in August, and counted 21 golden eagles on, or around, the nesting rock, and was convinced the eagles were nesting in a colony. Professor Rowan ends his letter to me as follows:

> The golden eagle, so far as I know, is always solitary in Canada, but then we consider the osprey the same, yet there are colonies of ospreys, both in the State of New York and in Yellowstone Park, Wyoming. So I suppose the eagles in the Valley of Eagles might represent a colony, unlikely as one must consider such a thing.

SUMMARY: EYRIES AND NESTING HABITS

The Eyrie may be on a rock, inland or on the coast, or on a tree. Very occasionally on the ground below a rock. When built on a rock it faces usually north, north east, or east.

Most eagles have several eyries, which they use in rotation. In Scotland, an eyrie may exceptionally reach a depth of fifteen feet. Living fir shoots are much favoured in nest-construction, as is the great wood-rush for the lining of the nesting cup. Both eagles carry nesting material. The eyrie is sometimes built before the end of December. Courtship may also take place before the end of the year. Mating may take place six weeks before laying, and after the female has been brooding at least a month.

Nest-repair or decoration continues during incubation and right on to the feathering of the eaglet.

The usual clutch is two eggs: three in Scotland is exceptional. There is one instance of four in Scotland, and one instance in America. Eagle may brood eyrie during snow before egg is laid. In some instances, the male takes an equal share in brooding the egg or eggs. The male occasionally broods the eaglet. The female does most of the feeding and the male most of the hunting, but there is no hard and fast rule.

The laying season varies in different countries—in Scotland

the laying month is usually March. Incubation period is around 42 days. One eaglet may kill the other when they are at the downy stage.

A golden eagle may move its young to another eyrie if unduly disturbed.

The male eagle may pass prey to the female, harrier-fashion, in the air.

The fledgling period is around twelve weeks. Records of shorter fledgling periods are rarely of value, as the eaglet has usually been disturbed and made to fly before it would do so if left to itself.

Eaglets actually lose weight during the growing of their feathers.

There is much variation in the length of time young birds remain near their parents after leaving the eyrie.

CHAPTER V

Food of the Golden Eagle

THE golden eagle in its various geographical races is distributed over almost the whole northern world and preys upon many different creatures. In the Highlands of Scotland, it is my experience that the eagle's chief food is the mountain-hare and the rabbit. Stainton Crosthwaite saw thirty-six rabbits taken to one eyrie in a week.* Next to the hare and the rabbit, I should put the red grouse on the golden eagle's menu. On occasion eagles will take lambs, deer calves, and other moderately large mammals. Lambs are not their normal food; a pair of lamb-killing eagles, as I have often stated, may be compared to a man-eating lion or tiger. The hunting by eagles of some of their larger game is so famous, and has been the subject of so many observations, and so many legends, that I have devoted the next chapter to this subject. The present chapter deals mainly with the golden eagle's normal diet, and ends with a list of all the food taken, of which I have reliable records. My friend James Fisher has checked this list, and has been able to add to it from his own extensive library.

I have either seen, or received reports of, the following prey at golden eagles' eyries in Scotland:

*Myxomatosis, that deadly rabbit disease, has already (1955) closely approached the haunts of Golden Eagle in Scotland.

63

FISH: salmon, pike.

REPTILE: adder.

BIRDS: heron, grey-lag and perhaps other wild geese, domestic duck, capercaillie, black grouse, red grouse, ptarmigan, domestic fowl, lapwing, golden plover, gull, raven, hooded crow, rook, jackdaw, magpie.

MAMMALS: mole, common shrew, man (!), dog, fox, stoat, weasel, badger, domestic cat, wild cat, red deer, roe-deer, goat, sheep, hare, mountain-hare, rabbit, red squirrel, field-mouse, brown rat, bank-vole and water-vole.

Many of these records are very interesting and worth describing in some detail, particularly those of the creatures which are truly the regular food of the golden eagle.

The occasions on which fish have been seen at a golden eagle's nest are rare: salmon and pike have been identified. An accurate observer records the capture of a salmon in a shallow stream. The eagle carried the salmon to the bank but could not free its talons. Next day the observer returned and found that the bird had evidently freed itself. The marks of its deeply-embedded claws in the salmon were obvious.

D. Mackintosh, central Inverness-shire, once saw a salmon in an eagle's eyrie. There were a few bites out of the salmon's shoulder, pointing to the fact that an otter had killed the fish and left it on the river bank. John MacLeod tells me that once at the mouth of Loch Kishorn he saw a golden eagle swoop down and take a fish from a cormorant on the water. This of course sounds as though it were the work of the sea- and not the golden eagle, but MacLeod was convinced that the bird he saw was a golden eagle.

Scotland's most typical reptile is very occasionally taken:

The blue or mountain hare is the preferred prey of the eagle.

Grouse are another natural prey.   (*both Lea MacNally*)

Food of the Golden Eagle

Grigor Grant, Highland character and deerstalker, once found an adder still alive in a golden eagle's eyrie.

*   *   *

Walter MacKay, gamekeeper at Scourie in Sutherland, saw an eagle give chase to a gaggle of grey-lag geese and bind to one of them, falling with it to the ground, at some distance from him.

On 25 October 1953 Desmond Nethersole-Thompson's son, Dawn, watched a golden eagle chase and break up a skein of grey-lag geese above Rothiemurchus forest. The eagle chased the geese for about a mile, driving his wings with great power. Singling out one goose when he had overtaken the gaggle, the eagle swung up and over his quarry and struck it down. The eagle followed the goose as it fell into Glen Eanaich and the observer had no doubt the goose was dead.

Four days later the Nethersole-Thompson family heard the excited crying of geese as they passed over their house. They ran outside and saw that a golden eagle, probably the same bird, was chasing the geese. As the birds were disappearing towards Glenmore, the watchers saw that the eagle was stooping at a goose, but the result of that attack could not be followed.

It is a rather remarkable fact that in the letters I have received from many correspondents on the subject of eagles and game-birds few of the observers have ever seen an eagle actually take a grouse on the wing or on the ground. Now, when it is considered that the eagle does habitually prey upon grouse, that seems to me to be a very curious thing.

James Davidson, Inverness-shire, tells me that never during his forty years' experience of eagles and grouse has he seen an eagle take a grouse on the wing, and only once has he seen an eagle make a determined attempt to do so. On that occasion the eagle chased the grouse for half a mile, and would have

65

caught its prey in another couple of yards had the grouse not bumped into a six-foot wire-netting run which Davidson had for puppies near his door. The grouse was killed by the blow; the eagle missed the netting by inches.

Two Sutherland stalkers, J. Brydon and Andrew MacKay, have given me accounts of how they saw a grouse taken by an eagle on the wing. Brydon writes: "The eagle came flying slowly, and what one would term tacked the top side of the hill first, then turned back and did the same thing say about half-way down. It put up three grouse, which kept together for some time but separated as the eagle got nearer to them. The eagle singled out a grouse and made after it, and in a few seconds made up on the grouse. After a few twists in the air, the eagle sometimes under the grouse and other times above it, the grouse shot straight for the ground. The eagle then like lightning swooped straight down past the grouse, turned back, met the falling grouse, shot out its left leg, and caught the grouse roughly fifty yards from the ground."

Andrew MacKay writes: "I was on high ground on the side of a corrie spying about and nine grouse passed hard on the wing. In a short time another two came and the eagle almost in line with them. When they went down the corrie the eagle was a little in front of the grouse, and as the grouse turned the eagle took one of them about ten feet from the ground."

Only two stalkers of the many I have met or corresponded with have seen a ptarmigan taken on the wing by an eagle.

John Ferguson tells me he has seen this more than once in the high corries of the western Cairngorms. He said that a breeze was necessary for the eagle to succeed, and that in windy weather when a covey of ptarmigan rose and flew across from one side of the corrie to the other the eagle would easily overhaul them, and without any fuss take one of the birds in its foot and fly off with it.

Food of the Golden Eagle

Donald MacIver, Isle of Skye, tells me that he once saw an eagle seize and carry off an old blackcock in the air.

Although I have watched the golden eagle on very many occasions I have never seen it take a grouse or ptarmigan, but one autumn day, when in a lonely glen in the Forest of Mar, I saw an eagle pass overhead carrying a grouse. The bird was still alive, and from time to time flapped one wing helplessly. The eagle for a while circled around, then alighted upon the hillside and proceeded to make a meal of its unfortunate victim.

The following story from Murdoch Macdonald, central Ross-shire, is, I think, unique:

"One very fine day, when I was in the act of setting a fox-trap, about the end of October, I observed two eagles coming in my direction pursuing a grouse. They were quite half a mile away when I noticed them. One eagle would be about forty yards behind the other from the time I saw them till the finish of the chase. The grouse was going at a great pace, but I could see the eagle was steadily gaining. When they were about three hundred yards away from and opposite me—the eagle was hardly moving her wings but was cutting along like a knife, and when she was within a yard of the grouse she suddenly drew in her wings, the tips of her wings close to her body, and shot forward like a ball—I distinctly heard the thump when she struck the grouse. There was a cloud of feathers and it dropped. What I wondered at was that she never stopped or altered her course, but the following eagle picked the grouse up and carried on after his mate, and disappeared over the edge of the hill. I am quite positive this eagle struck the grouse with her breast or shoulder—I mean by shoulder the front joint of the wing when not extended."

67

The Golden Eagle: King of Birds

This is believed by some observers to be the manner in which the peregrine falcon kills its prey on the wing. On the ground the eagle usually kills its prey with its talons, and as my other correspondents who saw an eagle take grouse on the wing are positive that the bird was seized in the eagle's talons and not struck down, the above story is of exceptional interest.

I have reason to believe that during May and early June the golden eagle searches likely heather for sitting hen grouse, and grabs them on the nest. My friend Jack Harrison the bird artist was once lying, well-concealed, watching an eagle's eyrie when he saw the female eagle drop into the heather near him, and rise with a grouse held in one foot. The incident occurred not more than 150 yards from the eyrie, and was the exception to the rule that birds of prey do not hunt near their nests.

That the golden eagle does take red grouse on the wing, the following thrilling aerial chase and capture, watched by my son-in-law Simon MacDonald-Lockhart of the Lee, is ample, and further, proof.

On 27 August 1952 he was stalking on Beinn Bhreac, at the head of Loch Treig in Corrour Forest, owned by Sir John Stirling-Maxwell. It was blowing very hard from the west, hard enough to make walking on the exposed ridge of "The Saddle" on Beinn Bhreac quite difficult. In Simon's own words:

"Richard Mackinnon the stalker and I had spied some stags. We then left the ponyman and were climbing by a small burn on the north face of the Saddle, about 2000 feet above sea level, when we both happened to look up. I rather think some sound must have attracted our attention, although I cannot remember hearing anything. At all events, the ponyman, who is deaf, and who was only 200 to 300 yards down the hill from us, saw nothing of what followed.

Food of the Golden Eagle

Down the wind came four or five grouse, hurtling on the gale, far faster than any driven grouse I have ever seen. They looked like black balls tearing through the air. Up behind them sailed a golden eagle, and with effortless ease snatched one of the grouse out of the air and turned downhill, and into the wind, carrying the prey in its talons. The whole thing can hardly have taken five or ten seconds.

The incident took place a little higher than we were standing as we watched, and at a distance of 300 to 400 yards from us—and about 200 to 300 feet above the ponyman's head. The visibility was quite good, despite wind and rain.*

The eagle disappeared down the hill below us quite leisurely and seemed, when we last saw it, as if about to alight and pluck, and perhaps eat, the bird.

What impressed me most was the speed at which the grouse were travelling, and the ease and accuracy with which the eagle overtook them and snatched one of them. When first I saw the eagle it was travelling roughly horizontally and turned upwards as it seized the grouse I imagine that this was the end of a stoop from some considerable height."

As the records show, all the Passerine birds recorded as the food of the golden eagle in Scotland are Corvids—five species of them. The eagle does not often tackle the raven, who can easily out-manoeuvre it, and often mobs it, in the air. But the following incident is not without interest. Peter Stewart, of Perthshire, the stalker, once saw a raven summarily executed by an eagle. Some ravens were feeding in the snow on a dead sheep. An eagle appeared and, as the ravens were rising from the ground, swooped down and seized a large raven with its talons. The eagle alighted, dropped the raven beside the carcase and

---

*The high wind, while it made the event more spectacular, might not influence the result of the pursuit.

commenced to feed on the sheep. The raven was quite dead, having been pierced through the body.

Turning to the more lowly mammals, the finding of moles by a Sutherland stalker at an eagle's eyrie must be an unusual incident, for the mole is rarely above ground. I have several times seen a stoat as prey in a golden eagle's eyrie, but the hind-quarters of the creature only. John MacLeod, keeper in the Isle of Skye, once came upon an eagle eating one; it was newly killed, for its blood was quite warm. But sometimes a stoat can be too much for an eagle—witness an incident that was observed some years ago near Cape Wrath in the north-west of Sutherland. A golden eagle was seen to rise higher and higher in a rather strange manner, and then fall to the ground as though it had been shot. The observer hurried to the place and was just in time to see a stoat appear from beneath the eagle and run away. There was a deep wound in the eagle's throat and the bird was dead. The eagle must have lifted the stoat into the air, and the stoat must have fastened its teeth in the eagle's throat, severing arteries and causing death in the air.

Undoubtedly the chief food of the eagle in Scotland is the mountain or blue hare, or the rabbit in some districts. I have never seen an entire adult blue hare in a golden eagle's nest, but only the hind-quarters. The head is presumably eaten by the captor before the carcase is carried to the nest. On the other hand, leverets are brought entire, and also rabbits. Golden eagles sometimes take rabbits out of snares, either dead or alive.

In 1952 a pair of golden eagles had their eyrie near the Mull of Kintyre. J. C. Leitch, on whose ground the birds nested, told me that the eagles fed their young, to the best of his knowledge, entirely on blue hares, carrying them bodily, but slit open, to the eyrie. He said that the eagle sailed along the face of the cliff, carrying the hare without difficulty. One day

A young fox taken as prey with a five to six year old eaglet. (*Lea MacNally*)

he watched the male bird come in with a hare. The female rose to meet her mate, took the hare from the male in mid-air, and went down with it to the eyrie.

This observer told me that on several occasions the eagle after leaving the nest was seen flying out to sea, as if to hunt on the coast of Northern Ireland. The Kintyre Eagles perhaps hunted in Northern Ireland, and later they, or their family, in all probability colonised a country where the species had been extinct for more than forty years.

A pair of golden eagles will guard their hunting territory against strangers, yet I think that there are, besides these private preserves, what may be called communal hunting grounds. One of them is the high plateau of Ben MacDhui and near it (as the eagle flies) the plateau of Braeriach, both on the Cairngorm Hills of Scotland. The ground here is more than 4,000 feet above sea level and the snow lies too late in spring to allow the eagles to use the cliffs as a nesting site. Here, I have the impression that the eagles of Deeside, Strathavon, and Strathspey sometimes meet in fine weather in spring and summer. One sunny April day of 1953 I was watching an eagle brooding her eggs on an old Scots fir in an Upper Deeside glen. Her mate came over and when above the eyrie rose in the up-draught beneath a cumulus cloud to a height of at least 5,000 feet. He then set off in that graceful and swift glide I have come to know so well and disappeared towards the Cairngorms, passing high above the nesting territory of another pair of eagles on his flight to the common hunting ground.

The golden eagle, like other birds of prey, has the habit of ejecting through its mouth the fur and bones of its prey in the form of pellets or castings. These castings are sometimes of remarkable size and thickness. One which I found on the Isle of Skye on 8 June 1952 measured 100 x 55 mm. Dr. A. C. Stephen, Keeper of the Natural History Department of the Royal Scottish

Museum, made a careful examination of this and another casting I sent him. He reported that the casting consisted entirely of remains of the Scottish mountain-hare (*Lepus timidus*). The result of this investigation deserves publicity because the pair of eagles responsible for the castings nest on sheep ground, yet there were no remains of lambs in the pellets.

*   *   *

The findings of most foreign observers confirm that, while the eagle takes the opportunity of capturing many curious animals as prey, it depends everywhere to a very large extent on ground rodents, partcularly hares, marmots and their relatives.

In Sweden, Curry-Lindahl gives me much information on the golden eagle's prey in that country. Calves of the reindeer are sometimes taken, also fox, stoat, lemming, hare, vole, black grouse, capercaillie, ptarmigan, various species of geese, and once a rough-legged buzzard. He also records song-thrush, fieldfare, redwing and meadow-pipit. From Estonia comes a remarkable record of an adult crane brought as prey to an eagle's eyrie, the observer being Dr. Johannes Lepiksaar. The following list of golden eagles' prey in Estonia is recorded by Zastrov—hedgehog, marten, polecat, domestic dog, fox, roe-deer, two species of hare, field-vole, capercaillie, black grouse, hazel-grouse, tawny owl, domestic fowl.

In Norway, Løvenskiöld gives as eagle prey, reindeer calf, lamb, hare, rat, vole, lemming, squirrel, small dog, raven, grey crow, magpie, wild goose, wild duck, lapwing, golden plover, gull, also meadow-pipit and song-thrush.

From Finland, Hörtling (1929) records grasshoppers as golden eagles' prey!

It is well known that in a "lemming year" birds (the snowy owl for example) lay unusually large clutches of eggs. In the "lemming year" of 1891, Løvenskiöld tells us that in a Norwegian golden eagle's eyrie were found, on 19 July, five eaglets. Three of them were almost fledged and two were very young. The lemmings which provided so abundant a food supply may account for this unique double-clutch.

In America, Arthur Cleveland Bent quotes the presence in a golden eagle's eyrie in California of numerous ground-squirrels, also cotton-tailed rabbit, crow, meadow-lark, and gopher-snake. Bent also gives porcupine as the eagle's prey. One eagle died as the result of attacking a porcupine. The bird was literally covered underneath with quills, and there were a number of quills embedded in the roof of its mouth. The eagle was very thin, and many of the porcupine quills had penetrated deep into the flesh, causing pus to form. In British Columbia, on 3 August 1913, Edward Preble found an adult goshawk in a golden eagle's eyrie.

E. S. Cameron (1905) mentions sharp-tailed grouse, jack-rabbit, cotton-tail rabbit, mountain-rat, meadow-pipit, and snake as prey. He states that the golden eagle captures rattle-snakes. It "feints several times at the snake to make it uncoil, and seizes it just behind the head with one foot, while gripping it further back with the other. The snake is then taken to a tree or rock, and the head torn off and, according to one observer, immediately devoured, before the body is deposited in the eyrie."

In districts of Canada where prairie-dogs are numerous the golden eagle is of great assistance to human settlers by preying on these pests. The bird kills also raccoons, woodchucks, marmots, opossums, and skunks. Among birds, turkey and great blue heron are taken, also short-eared owl and red-tailed hawk.

Telford Hindley Work watched two Californian eyries built in giant sycamores: one of the eyries was fifty-five feet from the ground. On 19 March, two eaglets in the first eyrie were rather less than a week old; in the second eyrie the eaglets were hatched later, and were estimated at ten days old on 2 April. That day there were twenty-two freshly killed ground-squirrels in the eyrie. The observer emphasises the good the golden eagle does in killing ground-squirrels which, he says, destroy valuable crops and in some districts carry bubonic plague.

A study of the food habits of nesting golden eagles, in the Coast Ranges of California, has been recently completed by S. Kent Carnie. Between 1947 and 1952 he studied the nests of seventeen pairs, and found that the most important foods brought to young were ground-squirrels and jack-rabbits. Some pairs brought many fawns of black-tailed deer to their young, and mammals collectively made up over three-quarters of the food (by individual frequency). The yellow-billed magpie was the most commonly taken bird.

Nearly all workers on the American golden eagle concur that the larger ground rodents are everywhere the chief prey; but certainly in some areas the young of game-mammals like antelope (in Montana and Texas, for example) and deer (California) may form a significant part of the diet; this does not necessarily mean that the eagle-population must be controlled as a consequence.

The Japanese golden eagle is a rather small race known as *A. chrysaëtos japonica.* Yamashina states that in this country Inuwashi, as the golden eagle is named, has been known to carry to the eyrie fox, deer-calf, rabbit, and squirrel, also dogs and cats which have gone wild. Among birds, pheasant and ptarmigan are eaten; Count Kiyozumi found in an eyrie in the Japanese Alps the leg of a rabbit and the tail of a copper pheasant.

In Kamchatka hares and trapped sable-martens are mentioned by Bergman as prey.

74

Food of the Golden Eagle

To revert to Europe: in Switzerland Carl Stemmler once found two field-mice in the stomach of a golden eagle which was sent him. He has seen in Swiss eyries the following mammals: squirrel (very often), two species of hare, marten, fox, marmot (very often), chamois kid, roe-deer calf, red deer calf. He considers the marmot to be the chief food of the golden eagle in Switzerland. He has often seen an adult raven in the eyrie, and also carrion-crow, rock-partridge, young Alpine chough, ptarmigan, black grouse, capercaillie, young ring-ouzel. In one eyrie Carl Stemmler found the remains of twenty-five marmots. At a late nest he found on 25 June an eaglet only a fortnight old. A squirrel was the only prey in that eyrie. At the eyrie to which my wife and I habitually saw squirrels brought, in the Highlands of Scotland, the eaglets were at least a month old before they were fed on these animals.

In the Himalayas, as in Switzerland, the golden eagle preys on marmots. Lieut. Colonel H. Delme Radcliffe saw a golden eagle carry a large marmot half a mile, flying low. The eagle was shot. Its weight was ten pounds and that of the marmot was one pound more.

*   *   *

LIST OF ANIMALS PREYED UPON BY THE GOLDEN EAGLE

SA: observed in Scotland by the author and his wife.
SO: observed in Scotland by others.

	Where observed	Remarks
INSECT		
Grasshopper	Finland	
FISH		
Salmo salar, salmon	SO	
Esox lucius, pike	SO	
Archoplites interruptus, Sacramento perch	U.S.A.	
Catostomus occidentalis, Sacramento sucker	U.S.A.	

75

	Where observed	*Remarks*
REPTILES		
Tortoise	? Persia	
Pituophis catenifer, gopher-snake	U.S.A.	
Lampropeltis getulus, ring-snake	U.S.A.	
Vipera berus, adder	SO	
Crotalus horridus, rattlesnake	U.S.A.	
Crotalus viridis,		
Pacific rattlesnake	U.S.A.	
BIRDS		
Ardea cinerea, heron	SO	
Ardea herodias, great blue heron	U.S.A.	
Cygnus sp., swan	? Europe	alleged to have
		killed
Anser anser, grey-lag goose	SO	attacks at least
Wild geese	SO, Norway	
	Sweden, U.S.A.	
Anas platyrhynchos, domestic duck	SO	
Anas platyrhynchos, mallard	U.S.A.	
Wild ducks	Norway, U.S.A.	
Cathartes aura, turkey-vulture	U.S.A.	
Accipiter gentilis, goshawk	Canada	
Buteo jamaicensis, red-tailed hawk	U.S.A.	
Buteo lagopus,		
rough-legged buzzard	Sweden	
Falco sparverius,		
American sparrow-hawk	U.S.A.	
Tetrao urogallus, capercaillie	SO, Sweden,	
	Switzerland,	
	Estonia	
Lyrurus tetrix, black grouse	SO, Sweden,	
	Switzerland,	
	Estonia	
Dendragapus obscurus,		
dusky grouse	Canada	
Lagopus scoticus, red grouse	SA	
Lagopus mutus, ptarmigan	SA, Sweden,	
	Switzerland,	
	Japan, U.S.A.	
Tetrastes bonasia, hazel-grouse	Estonia	
Pedioecetes phasianellus,		
sharp-tailed grouse	U.S.A.	

76

Food of the Golden Eagle

	Where observed	Remarks
Centrocercus urophasianus, sage-hen	U.S.A.	
Lophortyx californica, valley-quail	U.S.A.	
Quail spp.	U.S.A.	
Alectoris graeca, rock-partridge	Switzerland	
Gallus gallus, domestic fowl	SO, Estonia, U.S.A.	adult and chickens
Phasianus colchicus, pheasant	Japan	
Meleagris gallopavo, turkey	U.S.A.	
Grus grus, crane	Estonia	adult !
Vanellus vanellus, lapwing	SO, Estonia, Norway	
Charadrius apricarius, Eurasian golden plover	SO, Norway	
Charadrius dominicus, American golden plover	U.S.A.	
Other plovers	U.S.A.	
Numenius arquata, curlew	? Europe	
Tringa nebularia, greenshank	SO	
Larus spp. gulls	SO, Norway	
Columba fasciata, band-tailed pigeon	U.S.A.	
Geococcyx californianus, road-runner	U.S.A.	
Tyto alba, barn-owl	U.S.A.	
Bubo virginianus, horned owl	U.S.A.	
Strix aluco, tawny owl	Estonia	
Asio flammeus, short-eared owl	U.S.A.	
Megaceryle alcyon, belted kingfisher	U.S.A.	
Colaptes cafer, red-shafted flicker	U.S.A.	
Asyndesmus lewis, Lewis woodpecker	U.S.A.	
Alauda arvensis, skylark	? Europe	
Corvus corax, raven	SO, Switzerland, Norway	
Corvus brachyrhynchos, American crow	U.S.A.	
Corvus corone, carrion-crow	Switzerland	
Corvus cornix, hooded crow	SA, Norway	
Corvus frugilegus, rook	SO	
Corvus monedula, jackdaw	SA	
Pica pica, magpie	SO, Norway	

77

	Where observed	Remarks
Pica nuttalli, yellow-billed magpie	U.S.A.	
Coracia graculus, alpine chough	Switzerland	young
Cyanocitta stelleri, Steller jay	U.S.A.	
Aphelocoma coerulescens, scrub-jay	U.S.A.	
Turdus pilaris, fieldfare	Sweden	
Turdus ericetorum, song-thrush	Sweden, Norway	
Turdus musicus, redwing	Sweden	
Turdus torquatus, ring-ouzel	Switzerland	young
Other thrushes	U.S.A.	
Anthus pratensis, meadow-pipit	Sweden, Norway, SO	
Sturnella magna, meadowlark	U.S.A.	
Sturnella neglecta, western meadowlark	U.S.A.	
MAMMALS		
Didelphis marsupialis, opossum	U.S.A.	
Talpa europaea, mole	SO	
Scapanus latimanus, California mole	U.S.A.	
Erinaceus europaeus, hedgehog	Estonia	
Sorex araneus, common shrew	SA	
Homo sapiens, man	? SO, Europe, N. America	alleged carrying off of babies, unproved
Canis lupus, wolf	Turkestan	
Canis familiaris, dog	SO, Estonia, Norway, Japan, U.S.A.	
Vulpes vulpes, fox	SO, Sweden, Estonia, U.S.A.	trapped adults and cubs
Urocyon cinereoargentatus, gray fox	U.S.A.	
Procyon lotor, raccoon	U.S.A.	
Martes martes, pine-marten	Switzerland, Estonia	
Martes zibellina, sable	Kamchatka	trapped adults
Martes americana, American marten	Canada	
Mustela erminea, stoat	SA, Sweden, U.S.A.	
Mustela nivalis, weasel	SA	
Mustela frenata, longtail weasel	U.S.A.	

78

Food of the Golden Eagle

	Where observed	Remarks
Mustela putorius, polecat	Estonia	
Meles meles, badger	SO	young
Mephitis mephitis, striped skunk	U.S.A.	
Felis catus, cat	SO, Switzerland, Japan, U.S.A.	
Felis silvestris, wild cat	SO	
Equus caballus, horse	Ireland	attempt at 'driving' (p. 100)
Sus scrofa, pig	U.S.A.	young
Cervus nippon, Japanese deer	Japan	
Cervus elaphus, red deer	SO, Switzerland, Estonia	calves; may drive adults over cliffs
Capreolus capreolus, roe-deer	SA, Estonia Switzerland	calves
Odocoileus hemionus, mule (black-tailed) deer	U.S.A.	fawns
Odocoileus virginianus, whitetail deer	U.S.A.	
Rangifer tarandus, reindeer	Sweden, Norway	calves
Bos taurus, domestic cattle	U.S.A.	calf; has attacked adults
Antilocapra americana, pronghorn antelope	U.S.A.	adults(?) and fawns
Rupricapra rupricapra, chamois	Switzerland	kid
Capra hircus, goat	SO, Spain, U.S.A.	adults and kids
Ovis canadensis, bighorn (incl. Dall's sheep)	U.S.A., Canada	lamb
Ovis aries, sheep	SA, Norway, U.S.A.	lambs
Lepus europaeus, European hare	SA, Sweden, Norway, Estonia	
Lepus timidus, mountain-hare	SA, Estonia, Kamchatka	
Lepus californicus and ? other sp., jackrabbit	U.S.A.	
Lepus americanus, varying hare	Canada	
Sylvilagus auduboni, and ? other sp., cottontail	U.S.A.	
Oryctolagus cuniculus, rabbit	SA, Japan	
Ochotona, sp., pika	Tibet	

	Where observed	*Remarks*
Sciurus vulgaris, red squirrel	SA, Switzerland, Norway, Estonia, Japan	
Sciurus griseus, western gray squirrel	U.S.A.	
Sciurus niger, fox-squirrel	U.S.A.	
Eutamias spp. chipmunks	U.S.A.	
Cynomys sp., prairie-dog	U.S.A.	
Citellus beecheyi and other spp., ground-squirrels	U.S.A.	
Marmota marmota, alpine marmot	Switzerland, U.S.A., Canada	
Marmota monax, woodchuck	U.S.A.	
Thomomys bottae and ? other spp., pocket-gopher	U.S.A.	
Erethizon dorsatum, porcupine	U.S.A.	
Apodemus sylvaticus, field-mouse	SA, Switzerland, Norway	
Rattus norvegicus, brown rat	SO, U.S.A.	
Neotoma fuscipes, dusky-footed woodrat	U.S.A.	
Lemmus lemmus, lemming	Sweden, Norway	
Clethrionomys glareolus, bank-vole	SA, Norway, Sweden, Estonia	
Arvicola terrestris, water-vole	SA	
Microtus californicus, Californian vole	U.S.A.	
Microtus spp., field-voles etc.	Europe, N. America	

As will be seen from the systematic list of prey, in the countries inhabited by all the races of golden eagle, the prey is somewhat similar. One may say that the heaviest prey habitually taken in the adult stage is the marmot. Of immature animals red deer calves, roe-deer calves, the kids of goats, and the lambs of black-faced sheep are probably the heaviest prey. At the other end of the scale, the smallest and lightest prey ever recorded is the grasshopper. The most extraordinary prey is undoubtedly the porcupine. One can say that the most natural food in all countries is some species of *Lepus*.

General Sir Philip Christison has told me of an epic encounter on the heights of Mam Ratagan in the west of Inverness-shire between a golden eagle and a wild cat. The general was near the top of the pass on a mid-winter morning. The ground was snow-covered. With him was a fox-hunter of the old school, his pack of cairn terriers slung over his back in a sack. On the snow a wild cat was "spied "eating a white hare. Scarcely had the two human onlookers taken cover to watch the cat at its meal when the air was filled with a deep sound—the stoop of a golden eagle from a great height. The eagle alighted in the snow near the wild cat, which spat at it and held its ground. The eagle craned its neck this way and that towards its formidable adversary, while it thought out its course of action. Suddenly rising into the air to no great height, it swooped down, lifted the cat, and carried it away. When passing above some stony ground at a height of several hundred feet the cat was seen to fall. The onlookers, hurrying to the spot, found the cat dead and mangled. The eagle meanwhile, apparently unharmed, disappeared from view, but was found next day, partly disembowelled, and with severe injuries to one leg: it soon succumbed. The cat when lifted, or on passage through the air, must have inflicted the wounds with its claws or teeth.

CHAPTER VI

Hunting Habits of the Golden Eagle

THE highly exceptional incidents of eagles attacking man have been much exaggerated. I can relate only two. A man leaving the water after bathing in a Hebridean loch was attacked by a golden eagle. He hurriedly returned to the water. A second time the eagle attacked him, but when close to him apparently realised that its quarry was its formidable enemy man, and at once sheered off. This eagle had evidently no previous experience of what *Homo sapiens* looked like in *puris naturalibus* !

James Fraser, a deerstalker in west Inverness-shire, was once attacked. The incident was remarkable—and painful. Fraser writes:

"I was sitting on the hill with my dog Polly when I heard an unusual noise above me. Suddenly an old cock grouse dropped between the dog and myself. The dog searched for and found the bird, but instead of retrieving it licked it all over, then allowed it to go its own way. I thought no more of this affair. Later in the day I was spying my ground when I was swooped upon by the eagle which must have dropped the grouse at my feet. The bird caught me by the ankle with its talons, sinking them deep into the flesh. My dog was soon upon the bird, and with my other foot I managed to kill the eagle, much to my pleasure. Before I could clear the talons from my ankle I had to cut them with my knife. Whether the bird meant to attack me or my dog is a mystery, but I have a feeling that the dog working with the grouse aroused the anger of the eagle for depriving him of his prey."

I will now quote a third instance of golden eagle versus man, but here I am doubtful if the eagle's attack was deliberate. Let the reader judge for himself. My correspondent writes:

"I came on the eagle on the flat at the bottom of a narrow gully with steep sides. It was a calm winter day, with six inches of soft snow. The eagle made no effort to go, so I went down the slope to see what was wrong with him. When I got to within a couple of yards I stood to see what the eagle was going to do. It had a good look at me, then walked towards the slope, up which it went with difficulty on account of the soft snow. When it got up twelve to fifteen yards it turned and looked straight in my face, then spread its wings and flew straight for my face. I had a strong walking stick, and just as the eagle reached me I jumped to one side and 'let drive' at it as hard as I could, and by a fluke got it on the top of the head. It went down all of a heap in the snow, with wings and tail all over its head. I thought I had killed it, but on looking closely I saw that it was breathing heavily, and by and by up came the head out of the snow, and in a short time the eagle got on its legs, pulled its wings together, and walked across the gully and up the opposite slope a few yards. It had a good look round, then spread its massive wings and flew away down the gully as if nothing had happened, and in a few minutes was soaring in the sky hundreds of feet up."

My own feeling is that in this instance the eagle was not

deliberately attacking the man, but had misjudged the height of its take-off and could not avoid him. My correspondent showed unusual leniency in allowing the eagle to escape.

Highland deerstalkers sometimes tell me of attacks made by the golden eagle on their dogs, and when I was on the Ben MacDhui plateau I myself watched a golden eagle half swoop towards my collie Dileas, who was some distance ahead of me. That Highland personality and gamekeeper, the late Murdo Matheson of Invergarry, saw an eagle stoop at a setter. The eagle came down to within twenty yards of the dog.

Another attack was made, in a neighbouring district, on the terriers of a fox-hunter. So determined was the eagle that one of the fox-hunters had to shout at the bird, and then to shoot at it, in order to prevent it from carrying away one of their dogs. The fox-hunter told me that he thought the eagle was attracted by a muster-coloured Dandy Dinmont terrier, which was very conspicuous. Archibald MacQueen, who told me (Chap. VI) p. 99 about the eagles eating the stags left out over the week-end, said that the stalker was on one occasion on the hill accompanied by a small black terrier. The terrier was running at a little distance behind the stalker when a golden eagle stooped at it, lifting it into the air. The stalker fired his gun, and the eagle dropped the dog, which was so badly injured that it did not recover.

Donald MacIver, keeper in the Isle of Skye, once found a very small collie dog, almost as small as a Cairn terrier, in an eagle's nest. It is possible that the dog was caught in a trap, or dead when taken by the eagle.

Once, on the plateau of Beinn A'an, I saw the fur and skin of a fox scattered over the ground, and I have little doubt that an eagle, coming upon a fox (perhaps a young animal) unawares, had killed it and made a meal of it there and then.

I have received a number of interesting accounts of fights,

or "sparring matches," between fox and eagle. Old John Ferguson, a native of Badenoch and a stalker of many years' experience, told me that on one occasion he approached unobserved an eagle's eyrie in a rock. He noticed that a fox was half-way down the rock, attracted by the ptarmigan in the eyrie (Ferguson could see their white wings). Overhead the two parent eagles were soaring.

The fox saw that he could not reach the "larder," and evidently did not think the spot a healthy one with the old eagles so close. He climbed the rock and trotted off across the moor, and as he went he held his brush straight up in the air. Ferguson thinks he did this in order that, as he put it, "better his tail should be attacked than he himself."

On another occasion Ferguson was out stalking with a gentleman. They were near the top of a hill when the stalker saw what he thought was the antler of a stag in "velvet" crossing the skyline. Ferguson was afraid that they had disturbed the deer which he knew were ahead of them, and kept very still. But the fancied stag in "velvet" was only a fox. An eagle was soaring close above him, and this fox also was holding his brush straight in the air, since the eagle was too near for his liking. The supposed antler in "velvet" was the fox's brush!

One day, when Ferguson was visiting his traps in Glen Feshie, he came to where he had set a trap on either side of a "bait," and found a golden eagle in one trap and a fox in the other. Ferguson tells me that the best method of trapping a fox is by setting two traps, because if a fox is at all suspicious of a "bait" he waits until he sees that something is caught. For example, when he sees a hooded crow struggling in a trap the wily old fox thinks to himself, "Now that the trap has caught somebody it cannot catch *me*," and then walks up and eats his fill. Thus it is necessary for the trapper to match cunning with cunning. On this occasion Ferguson believes the fox must have seen the eagle trapped, and, chuckling, to himself came in on the other side—and was caught too!

The eagle was alive, but very weak because of its long imprisonment in the trap. The trap had been set for a fox, and Ferguson told me he was more than sorry to find an eagle in it. He carried the bird home, and kept it for some time in a shed, hoping it would recover. In a few days it became so tame that it would allow the stalker to open its bill and push small pieces of venison down its throat; unfortunately it did not long survive.

Sometimes fox and eagle feed together off a dead deer, and a stalker told me that once during a bad snowstorm he spied a fox and eagle eating a carrion deer and, stalking them, shot the fox. The late Major Ellice of Invergarry told me that he once saw a fox and an eagle, one on each side of a small "nobber," watching a dead hare. Peter Stewart, Perthshire, once saw an eagle giving chase to a fox. Time after time the eagle swooped down and, in passing, slashed at the fox with its wing. The fox showed no fight, but flopped down flat on the ground each time to escape the blow. The pursuit continued for nearly a mile, when the fox got to ground in some deep moss hags. Then the eagle flew back and, alighting where the fox had first appeared, commenced to feed on the carcase of a deer.

David Dempster, West Perthshire, tells me that he once saw an interesting trial of strength between eagle and fox. He was out stalking, and says:

"We got up to the beasts, and found that our stag lay down. So we decided to wait until he got up. When we were waiting an eagle came and sat upon a big flat rock about fifty yards from us. We could see by the bird's movements that he was in a bad temper, and annoyed by something lower down the hill, as he kept twisting and turning his head and craning

his neck. A fox came into sight about thirty yards lower down and came stalking up a hollow towards the eagle. He kept rather to the right of the eagle until he got above him, then he moved slowly towards the eagle, just like a dog 'drawing' on birds. When about a yard from the eagle the fox stood with tail straight out, one leg up, like a dog on grouse, and the eagle faced him with neck stretched forward. In this position they faced each other for some little time, then the fox drew himself up, arched his back, and made a spring for the eagle, who was ready for him and, as I thought, met the fox half-way, slashing at the fox with wings and talons. The fox had to run, the eagle slashing him as he went. It was all over in a very short time, the fox running downhill while his friend sailed about quite proud of himself, as we thought. My gentleman did not get a shot at that stag, as the deer cleared out while the scrap was going on, but it was well worth losing a shot for that wonderful sight we had seen. I can still see that picture, although it is just thirty years since it happened."

Duncan MacRae, Sutherland, once saw a fox galloping up a hill near him. When he was about eighty yards off, an eagle suddenly came up behind him, caught him, lifted him about a yard off the ground, then dropped him. The fox turned round to keep the eagle off, and the two stared at each other, the fox with his mouth open showing his teeth and the eagle with his neck out and his feathers ruffled. The fox then tried to make off, but the eagle soon caught him and lifted him about a dozen feet off the ground this time. Again he dropped the fox, and again on the ground the same staring match took place. The

Eagle returning to nest with a twig.   (*C. E. Palmar*)

fox then made off and the eagle pursued, but did not lift him this time. The fox was a big dog-fox, and must have proved a heavy weight for the eagle.

James Davidson, keeper in Inverness-shire, writes:

"I saw an eagle attack a fox one day on the hill. The fox got up on its hind legs open-mouthed and bit and snapped all round, and while the eagle was rising to make another stoop the fox made off as hard as he could gallop. When the eagle stooped again he stood up on his hind legs as before and snapped and bit at him, and before the eagle could stoop again the fox had reached some haggy ground where the eagle could not get at him."

Alex. MacDonald, west Inverness-shire, writes:

"I once saw an eagle chase a fox, and every time the eagle would try to catch the fox he would turn on her. Before the eagle finished chasing the fox she caught him by the hind quarters and lifted him about ten or fifteen yards in the air: the fox turned and caught the eagle by the breast and she was obliged to let him go."

From Murdoch MacDonald, central Ross-shire, comes the following story:

"A keeper friend of mine was watching a fox den, and he had a fox cub tied to a stake below the cairn to entice the old fox to come so that he could shoot her. Suddenly he heard the bleat of a lamb above him, and when he looked up he saw an eagle with a lamb in its talons. It passed directly above the cub, and hesitated as though looking at it. He knew where the eyrie was about a mile away, and watched the eagle go straight to it, and in a few minutes it was back again for the fox cub." "The next act I won't mention," concludes this interesting tale.

Donald Crerar, late head stalker on Ardverikie Forest and a direct descendant of the Crerar mentioned in Scrope's classic work on Deer Stalking, has given me the following vivid narrative of a fight between a golden eagle and a wild cat:

With Sir John Ramsden's two sons, Crerar was on a fishing expedition in the forest in June 1924. He was on the shore of the loch when he noticed that a golden eagle was swooping, time after time, towards a steep rocky hill-face about 700 yards away. At first no particular attention was paid to the bird, but as it continued to swoop Crerar put the glass on it and followed its dive. He saw an animal sitting on a rounded stone upon a ledge of rock, and it was at this animal that the eagle kept stooping.

At first Crerar thought the beast was a red deer fawn, and then he thought that it must be a fox that had been rolling itself in peat, because its coat seemed to be darker than the coat of a fox should have been. But when at last the animal sprang into the air, striking at the eagle with its paws, Crerar saw that it was a wild cat. Time after time the eagle swooped down upon the cat, with its talons ready to grasp it and its strong legs outstretched. Once, as it came very near, the wild cat again sprang into the air, striking at the eagle with its claws. The spring was such a great one that Crerar distinctly saw the whole of the cat momentarily suspended in mid-air.

This must have alarmed the eagle, as it did not venture quite so near again. Altogether the eagle swooped at the wild cat thirty or forty times, but the cat sprang up at the eagle twice only. At last the wild cat disappeared into a cranny amongst the stones and the eagle sailed away.

A few days later Crerar climbed to the ledge of rock and found that the wild cat had her den there. It was curious that the wild cat should have thus exposed herself to the attacks of the eagle, because, so far as Crerar could see, the kittens were not out in the open.

The golden eagle is fond of tame cats, and no doubt it would be only too glad to make a meal off a wild cat did it not respect those sharp claws.

Murdoch MacDonald, head stalker on a well-known Ross-shire deer forest, found traces of a more sanguinary fight between eagle and wild cat. He writes:

"It happened not more than half a mile from my own house two years ago. There had been a heavy fall of snow through the night and in the early morning, and when I went out I found a wild cat's track quite near the house, so I got my gun and terrier and followed it. The track went along a steep slope where there was no other mark in the snow. I noticed where I thought the cat must have caught a grouse or something, as there were feathers and apparently the marks of a struggle in the snow. But when I reached the spot and examined the feathers I knew they were the head- and neck-feathers of an eagle. Then I saw that instead of the cat having caught something, as I had first thought, he had been caught himself. I could distinctly see the marks of the eagle's wings on the snow where it had come down on the cat, but seemingly the cat had been too quick, and must have caught the eagle by the head, for both had rolled down the steep slope for about thirty yards, where there was a little dip in the slope. There they had had a further struggle, for there were more feathers and a few drops of blood. When the combatants separated the cat must have been dazed, for he kept going round and round in circles in the snow before he got his bearings. But he went another half-mile before I got him in a cairn."

An interesting sequel to this fight was the finding on Blaven, in Skye, of a dead eagle a short time later. A lifeless eagle lying out on the hill is a rare thing to see, and this eagle had been severely injured about the neck and had apparently succumbed to its injuries. It would seem probable, therefore, that this was the same bird that had been mauled by the wild cat on the mainland some distance away.

In a golden eagle's eyrie in the Outer Hebrides domestic cats which had gone wild formed the chief prey brought by the eagles to their young. The shepherd on the ground stated that the cats were sometimes alive when brought to the nest but were paralysed, probably because their backs had been broken when seized. Such cats are taken usually on the hillside when hunting, but Robert MacMorran, an accurate observer who for many years sheep-farmed on the Isle of Mull, told me that on two occasions an eagle attacked one of his cats close to the farm house, but was unsuccessful. This record is unusual, because the golden eagle rarely comes near an occupied house, even if it be the only house in a lonely glen. In other countries also the golden eagle preys on cats. At Planken, in the Municipality of Leichtenstein a golden eagle during severe weather in the winter of 1952-53 swooped down and carried off a domestic cat close to the village. The eagle dropped the cat, but its back was broken.

It is, of course, well-known that the eagles kill and eat red deer calves. Not all eagles do this, and those that do probably kill them only when opportunity permits them to vary their more staple diet of hares, rabbits and grouse. Sometimes the eagles make their opportunities, for there is good evidence that two or three eagles may cooperate in a deer-drive, and corner their prey, or drive it over a cliff. Occasionally they may even tackle hinds, and, exceptionally, young or sickly stags.

The deer-hunting eagles do not fear to tackle a herd of deer, though they are by no means always successful; indeed they almost always fail to separate a calf from an isolated hind, who may stand on her hind feet and strike out with her fore feet in defence of her young. But try they do.

Major Ellice of Invergarry wrote to me:

"In the late autumn of 1926 I was walking in line on the extreme right, trying to get one or two grouse—four guns—a vile day with snow showers. A deer calf suddenly came quite close to me, and followed me so close that I could put out my hand to him to try to entice him to be friendly, After walking for about half a mile (the calf always keeping his place on the right flank) we caught up with a herd of deer on the face of a hill south of us. The calf also spotted them and trotted off to the herd. An eagle at once appeared from nowhere and attacked the calf, but fortunately the herd was too big and the calf joined up."

Duncan MacRae, Sutherlandshire, saw an eagle tackle a well-grown deer calf in the month of February, fixing his talons in the animal's back and flapping his wings in its eyes. The calf galloped downhill to the herd, and the herd at once drove off the aggressor.

Donald Mackintosh, central Ross-shire, writes that he has seen an eagle chasing deer and alighting on the shoulders of a six-quarter-old hind, but an older hind, probably the mother of the young hind, galloped up to her rescue.

Hunting Habits of the Golden Eagle

The Hon. Alastair Fraser wrote as follows to me:

"About 1898 of '99, in Glendoe Forest, I saw the following incident. The stalker and I heard a rattle of stones from across the glen, and saw a hind and calf picking their way across a steep scree of loose shaly rock. We then saw that an eagle was attacking them. The bird repeatedly swooped down on the pair, but never as far as we could see attempted to strike them. Each time the bird came close the hind stood stock still and the calf disappeared under her belly. The moment the danger was passed the hind walked gingerly on, the calf following close behind. These tactics were repeated a dozen times to the best of my recollection. As soon as the hind got on to solid ground the pair cantered off and the eagle left them. It seemed to us that had the hind lost her head, the calf at any rate would have lost its footing even if she had not. As far as I can recollect there was a fall of over 100 feet (at the angle of rest for this shaly stuff), and a fall must have resulted in broken legs. The stalker told me that a man could not cross the line the deer took, or at any rate he would not try. As far as I recollect we watched the deer for about 100 yards across it. When we first saw them they were, I think, about the middle of the scree. How or why the hind and calf got themselves into this difficult position we could not tell."

Lochiel told me that his head stalker saw a pair of eagles pursuing and swooping at a herd of hinds and calves. Eventually the eagles separated a hind and a calf from the main herd and, buffeting the calf with their wings, drove it over the precipice toward which they had been endeavouring to herd the deer. The calf was killed by the fall and the eagles proceeded to devour it.

93

The Golden Eagle: King of Birds

Major Ellice of Invergarry wrote:

"One day while spying I saw a large herd of stags and hinds driven straight past us at the gallop by an eagle. The eagle was trying to detach a deer calf—quite a large one—from the herd. I had a couple of shots at the deer as they galloped past at about 200 yards, but missed them. The eagle never left his quarry, and when he was about a mile from us he succeeded in driving the calf away from the herd. He continued to swoop down upon it, and gradually drove it into a deep burn, where I suppose he finished it off." He continues: "Curiously enough, as we rose to go on with our stalk, a hare which had been lying within two yards of us, and unperceived, jumped up and rolled over dead. I suppose he died of fright."

Finlay Macintosh, head-stalker in an Inverness-shire deer forest, in September 1925 saw three eagles attack a red deer calf. He writes:

"I had just stalked and shot a stag out of a small mixed lot of stags and hinds, and was keeping the herd under observation with a view to getting another stag later on, when an eagle stooped on and struck a calf a terrific blow with her body. As far as I could see the eagle did not attempt to fix her talons or bill in the calf; she simply swooped down at a terrific pace, her wings folded and legs close up to her body. Scarcely had she ascended when another eagle attacked in the same manner, and then a third. All three birds adopted the same method of attack, and confined their attentions to the same animal. As it was September the calf was pretty well grown, and avoided a good many blows by wheeling sharply in little circles just as one of the big birds approached;

94

but attack followed attack so quickly that he very soon got exhausted, and then one of the eagles fixed her talons in his withers and, flapping her huge wings savagely, bore the calf to the ground.

"At this stage the other two eagles alighted some few yards from the one that had just killed the calf, and did not seem to be in any hurry to join the feast. Meantime the herd had moved on a considerable distance, and never paid any attention to the tragedy that was happening to one of their number. Had the deer not been fired at some time before they would have closed in, and prevented the eagles driving one of their number out of the herd."

Charles Mackintosh, for many years second stalker on the Balmoral Forest, once saw an eagle killing a red deer calf in the month of July with beak and talons, while the luckless calf screamed like a baby. Andrew MacKay, a Sutherland stalker, saw an eagle lift a red deer calf high in the air and then let it drop. The bird did not go near it again.

James MacDonald, Inverness-shire, also saw an eagle lift a deer calf off the ground, but the bird did not get away with its quarry because the mother hind and a number of other hinds "practically fought the eagle, and eventually the mother hind stood over the calf with the others gathered around in a group.'

Murdoch MacDonald, central Ross-shire, once found an eagle on a newly killed deer fawn about six weeks old. It was holed behind the shoulder and a good bit of it had been eaten, and as the skin was a pretty one he skinned the calf, and found that it had been killed by the eagle's talons piercing right through its skull!

James MacLean once noticed an eagle flying low over a clump of bracken. After swooping several times into the bracken she put out a fawn, which she attacked. The mother hind was lying farther up the hill, and when she heard the fawn bleating she came galloping down and chased the eagle, which was now flying about six feet from the ground. But her efforts to save her young were hopeless, for the eagle lifted the fawn three times off the ground to a height of about forty to fifty feet, and each time let it drop so that it was killed by the fall."

John MacDonald writes:

"I once saw an eagle swoop down on a herd of deer in Corrour Forest. She picked up a calf about three weeks old and carried it to the top of a high boulder about two hundred yards away. The whole herd of hinds followed the eagle. They surrounded the boulder, bleating and making a fearful din. The eagle sat like a statue admiring the whole scene for the matter of ten minutes, then started feeding on her capture."

Sometimes eagles attack the hinds themselves. Seldom does this attack meet with success; but it certainly has at least once.

John MacDonald, head stalker in a west Inverness-shire forest, tells me that he has often seen the eagle scattering deer in all directions. He once saw an eagle chase a hind into a deep gorge, hoping evidently to kill it, but the eagle was disturbed by seeing him. The eagle's method of attack was to swoop past the deer for some distance, and then, turning abruptly, to fly back and strike the animal in the face.

Æneas Cameron, Ross-shire, tells me that he has seen an eagle trying to drive a hind over a rock; she would have succeeded had not the hind got into a burn. Murdoch Macdonald also saw an eagle chasing a hind. "The hind got into a hole below a rock and the eagle perched close above it." He watched it for quite an hour.

"The hind would sometimes come out a little way and look whether the eagle was still there and then go in again. But the eagle was never moving. At last it flew away and went right out of sight. Directly the eagle went out of sight the hind galloped along the side of the hill, but she wasn't 200 yards away when the eagle was back again and attacked it; but the hind got into another cave and the eagle perched again as close to it as it could get. We watched them for another half-hour and left them in that position, so I can't say what the sequel was, but the eagle was quite determined on killing it."

A correspondent who has actually seen an eagle drive a deer over a cliff is Alick Whamond. He writes:

"One January day I saw an eagle swooping down on a hind in very poor condition. It started driving the hind towards the rocks. When the beast tried to turn, the eagle flew at it and struck it with its wings till it got it to go the right way. At last the hind fell over the cliff and the eagle made a good meal of it. The snow had been lying on the ground for a long time, and I think the eagle must have been driven to attack the hind through hunger."

Donald Ross, stalker in a western forest, writes:

"One day, on coming round a bend in a forest path, I was surprised to see about fifteen hinds within 100 yards of me, all gathered together in a bunch with their tongues out. I could hear them breathing from where I stood. I looked up the hillside, and there I saw a young hind galloping away with an eagle fixed on her back. Sometimes the eagle would rise in the air a few feet, then it would fix on again and keep flapping its wings against the hind. They finally disappeared over the edge of a very steep and rocky hill, and I am almost certain that the hind was bound to get killed among the rocks."

Eagles may even follow and attack stags; in Wester Ross Donald Urquhart's brother once saw a bird following a wounded stag, and he himself saw an eagle hover over a stag that had been hit and was lying down. The eagle settled close to the animal, but saw the stalkers approaching and flew away.

On 11 October 1951 a determined attack by a pair of golden eagles on two young stags was witnessed in Loch Choire deer forest in Sutherland by Mr. T. B. Band and the stalker Hugh MacKay. Two stags were observed grazing above the rock face on the north-east side of Ben Armine. The animals were too young to be stalked, and Mr. Band and the stalker continued to climb until they were level with the stags, which had not winded or sighted them. At this point a good stag was sighted, but there were thirty hinds between the stalkers and the stag, and so the men sat down on the heather in order to consider their next move. The lie of the ground made them sit facing the two young stags, which were no more than 150 yards from them and in full view. They had sat no longer than a couple of minutes when a pair of golden eagles came in sight, flying low over the ridge on the far side of the stags. One of the eagles immediately dived on the stag nearest to the rock face and struck at its head with its talons: it also appeared to be striking with its wing at the same time as it hovered momentarily close to the stag's head. The stag broke into a gallop along the edge of the steep rocks and the eagle, rising about 15 feet, swooped again at the stag's face, striking with its talons and beating with its wings in an attempt to turn the stag. Three times the eagle repeated its attack, each time endeavouring to drive the stag over the rock, but did not succeed, and flew off. The stags ran for 150 yards until they came to a burn with fairly deep, narrow sides. They went into the burn and stayed there. The stalkers wished to use the burn for shelter, but the stags kept looking into the sky, where the eagles circled for ten minutes. They were unwilling to leave their cover, and did not move until the two observers were little more than 30 yards from them, and even then went slowly and reluctantly.

Mr. Thomas Adam, Commissioner to the Duke of Sutherland, adds a note that deer carcases have frequently been seen at the foot of these rocks, and it has always been suspected that the animals had been killed as a result of an eagle's attack, but this was the first time the actual attack was witnessed.

Æneas Cameron of Ross-shire once found a pair of eagles killing a one-year-old stag. It was not quite dead when he came upon them, but he says "they had the skin and flesh holed on the ribs." This instance is remarkable, and it looks as if this young stag must have been alone or perhaps unhealthy. This is the only instance I know of a stag almost grown being killed by eagles.

Golden eagles will feed on a deer which must have been shot and left out on the hill overnight. Archibald MacQueen, at one time farm manager at Torridon in the north-west Highlands, told me that three stags were shot late one Saturday night in a remote part of the forest. It was too late to get the stags home that night, and as Sunday in the Highlands is strictly observed, they were left, partly covered with heather, until early Monday morning. When the ponymen reached the stags, no fewer than ten golden eagles rose from the carcases, which had been almost entirely eaten!

I have few records of encounters between roe-deer and eagle.

Mr. Robert Hargreaves, of the Forest of Gaick, told me that he once saw a roebuck attacked by an eagle. The plucky roe showed no signs of fear, but rose on his hind legs and struck out at the surprised eagle with his forelegs, when the eagle made off. On another occasion a roebuck was attacked in Glen Feshie. The buck was feeding at the edge of a birch wood when an eagle suddenly swooped at and struck at the roe, who dodged the blow and bounded for the nearest clump of trees, where he continued to graze unconcernedly. The eagle did not renew the attack.

John Don, Inverness-shire, once saw an eagle on a roe-deer's back, and was sure the eagle would have killed the roe had the animal not succeeded in gaining the shelter of a thick wood.

Roe-deer keep usually to the woods and as they are screened by the trees the eagle sees them less frequently than red deer. My wife (page 146) actually watched the carrying of a roe-deer fawn to an eyrie as food for the eaglets.

Although there are many instances of red deer being attacked, it must be seldom indeed that an eagle makes an attack on a horse.

Sir Ralph Payne-Gallwey in his classic *The Fowler in Ireland* relates a remarkable story which he heard from an old Achill man. It runs as follows:

I rose early one fine morning to see if my horses were all safe: a mare, her foal, and a two-year-old. I found them near the cliffs over the sea. As I came near, in the early dawn, I saw three Eagles darting at them and fastening their claws into the backs first of one then of the other, and driving them towards the precipice. As the animals sheered off from the edge, the Eagles would keep on their landward side and frighten them again to the cliff. I ran, as for my life, but my dog was before me, barking loudly. When the dog got near the horses, and the birds saw me running up, they flew away. The horses were wild with fear, and trembling. Over this cliff, on to the sands below, the villagers often threw down dead animals, such as sheep and horses; on these the Eagles were known to feed, and my horses did they wish to cast down.

A remarkable instance of an eagle attacking a cow in the Outer Hebridean island of Lewis has been sent me by Admiral and Lady Evelyn Drummond of Garynahine, who took down details of the event from witnesses of it. About mid-day on a morning of June, 1952, seven cows and three stirks or bullocks were grazing on the hill of Eitshal, 735 feet high, rising about half a mile north of Achmore. The eagle singled out for attack a white and brown cow, three years of age. The cow was seen running towards the schoolhouse dyke or wall, and the eagle was attacking repeatedly. The cow was so hard-pressed that she fell on her knees, but rose to her feet and continued to run, the eagle again flying in to attack. The eagle continued to pursue until within a stone's throw of the schoolhouse wall. When the cow was examined there was no blood on her, but there were a few scratches. The eagle then flew back, and attacked a white and dark brown cow which was in calf. Three or four attacks were made before Donald MacArthur, who hurried to the cow's assistance, got near and drove the eagle off. There were three witnesses of the attacks. Whether the eagle was merely amusing itself by stooping at the cows, or whether it hoped to kill them, it is impossible to say. So far as my experience goes, the incident is unique. It is possible that the bird when flying over the hill mistook the cows and stirks grazing on the hill for deer.

Last among the eagle's big game is the sheep and, more important, the lamb.

The one record I have of an eagle attacking a full-grown sheep is from Donald Ross, who writes:

The Golden Eagle: King of Birds

"About ten years ago I was out looking for foxes in Sutherlandshire, and on coming in on the top of a very rough, rocky corrie I saw an eagle rise about one hundred yards away.

"I noticed a bunch of wool fall from its talons, and on reaching the spot where the eagle had risen I found a Cheviot gimmer wedged in between two rocks. She was still alive, and the wool was partly torn from her back. There were a few gashes in the top of her shoulders—done by the eagle's beak. If I had not come on the scene I am quite sure the eagle would have had a good meal of her there and then.

"There is hardly any doubt that the eagle had driven the gimmer in between the rocks, as I could see by the state of the ground that she had been fixed there only a short time."

Few of those correspondents to whom I have written have seen an eagle attack or kill a living lamb, and I have only seen this twice myself. The following incidents I have been able to collect in years of eagle-watching, and correspondence with scores of keepers, stalkers and shepherds throughout the eagle's range in the Highlands.

John Grant, from Sluggan, Carr Bridge, Inverness-shire, writes as follows:

"Some years ago I was a shepherd in Inverlaidnan Glen. About the first week of May, in the height of the lambing season, I was an eye-witness of the following: Along with another shepherd, about eight o'clock in the evening, we were attending to a ewe and a young lamb. We looked up and saw an eagle about two hundred yards from us. It circled round two or three times and made a swoop down

Male eagle broods newly hatched eaglet which cheeps under him. Female listens. (*Seton Gordon*)

at a lamb. The mother of the lamb promptly rushed at the eagle and knocked it on its back in the heather. After recovering from the blow the eagle rose and flew away for about thirty yards, and dived down at another lamb and carried it away. The eagle rose in circles to a considerable height and flew along the slope of the hill. It gradually descended again, and when close to the ground lost hold of the lamb, which fell some fifteen or twenty feet into the heather.

"From the time the eagle attacked the first lamb and carried away the second we shouted and made the dogs bark, but the bird was so determined it did not heed us. When we got up to the lamb it was still alive, and able to run a little. It was bleeding on its right side from a nasty wound, and when we took it to its mother she refused to take it. We took the lamb home, but it was dead the next morning. We were sorry to lose it, as we should have liked to rear it after its unusual experience. The lamb was four days old, and a good specimen. I can vouch the above to be a perfect fact."

Robert Fraser writes as follows from Achnahyle, Tomintoul, Banffshire:

"While on the hills a number of years ago I came round a sharp bend and saw an eagle about thirty feet in the air. It dropped something white, and on going to the spot I found a newly lambed black-faced wedder lamb, still alive, with a cut on one side. The ewe was some distance away. I brought the lamb to its mother, and it lived to be a wedder, although permanently disabled. This is the only case I have actually seen."

John G. MacKenzie writes from Dirdhu, Grantown-on-Spey:

"On Sunday, 1st May 1910, my brother came upon an eagle in the act of carrying away a lamb from its mother's side. He shouted, and threw his stick at it. The eagle then dropped the lamb, which was cut on the throat and back. It had to be carried home and nursed for about a week before it was able to follow its mother. On the following Thursday the eagle carried another lamb fully one hundred and fifty yards from its mother's side; on my brother appearing the eagle rose from it. We have no proof that the eagle killed the lamb, but are fully convinced that it did, as we found that *both* sides had been cleaned by the mother. If the lamb had been born dead she would have cleaned only *one* side. Although to the best of my knowledge and belief the above statement is correct, I should be very sorry if it would be the cause of anyone trying to kill such a magnificent bird."

In May 1935, MacKenzie, deerstalker at the time at Cluanaidh in Inverness-shire, saw a golden eagle snatch up a lamb lying near its mother. MacKenzie, shouting loudly, ran after the bird, whose flight was now laboured. The eagle dropped the lamb, but lifted it again and carried it some distance before dropping it a second time. The stalker carried the lamb home and at once weighed it. The lamb weighed nine and three quarter pounds: it was unharmed except for a gash behind one ear.

Duncan Robertson, west Inverness-shire, once saw an eagle rise clumsily, and on going to the spot found a dead lamb, quite warm, and with the marks of the eagle's talons in its neck.

Much the same thing was witnessed by Walter MacKay, a west Sutherland stalker. MacKay also saw an eagle lift a lamb from close beside its mother. The eagle rose with the lamb about two hundred feet, then let it drop. The only marks on the lamb were talon marks on the neck and head; one talon had pierced the brain.

Kenneth MacGregor, an east Sutherland keeper, writes:

"I have seen personally an eagle swoop down on one of my own lambs and carry it three or four yards. When the ewe made a rush at the eagle she let the lamb go, and the ewe stood beside the lamb. When I reached the place the lamb was quite dead, for the eagle had put her claws through the body. This was a Cheviot lamb."

Duncan MacRae, Sutherlandshire, once saw about a dozen dead lambs on the rocks near an eagle's nest, but the lambs may have been dead when she carried them there.

A correspondent writes from the Hebrides:

"A matter of twelve years ago a pair of golden eagles took heavy toll of black-faced lambs on the west side of the island. They worked together, one deliberately attracting the attention of, and irritating, the ewe, which usually charged and, rearing on its hind legs, struck at the eagle. Meantime the other swooped down behind and bore off the lamb. This was repeated practically daily over a considerable period, the eagles regularly succeeding in getting away with a lamb. Here, every year, there are golden eagles, but not every pair appears to think of attacking lambs. I may say that there are no rabbits here. Where there are rabbits the probability is that the eagles would pay no attention to lambs. I have observed the eyrie of golden eagles, with the eaglet only a few days hatched, full of the remains of the carcases of *rats*."

Hugh Stewart, west Inverness-shire, writes:

The Golden Eagle: King of Birds

"I have seen on one occasion an eagle swoop down on a lamb and carry it away. I watched him closely, and when very high up he dropped it for some reason, or it wriggled out of his clutches. Immediately he made another swoop and picked up another lamb. This time he flew a long way with the lamb and got out of view before landing. An observant shepherd told me that the eagle was a great worry to him, but he added that it did no damage after the end of June, when the lambs would be about 30 lb. live weight. I do not think an eagle ever attacks a full-grown sheep. It is my opinion that during the winter months the eagle lives chiefly on carrion, and does most of the destruction while rearing its young."

Another lamb story comes from D. MacRae from the west of Ross-shire:

"I saw the eagle carrying a lamb just at the top of a high hill, I and another keeper being out fox-hunting. She flew straight overhead, and when we came into view suddenly she dropped a half-grown lamb almost at our feet. I would say the lamb would be 14 lb. It was quite warm, as if the eagle had just killed it.

People maintain that they don't eat but what they kill, but this is a mistake. I have seen them eating off a dead carcase to the extent they could not fly. It was a dead calm day."

Ronald M'Coll, Argyllshire, told me that one of his men saw the eagle swooping down on a three weeks' old lamb and carry it off, and that the same bird did this on four occasions; he thinks the lambs would weigh from 12 to 20 lb.

Probably these weights are slightly exaggerated; I believe that, unless in exceptionally good circumstances where an upwind gives it extra lift, an eagle cannot lift much more than its own weight—and a female weighs 9½ to 13 pounds, a male 7½ to 11.

I have myself on two occasions seen a golden eagle take a lamb. The first incident happened on 25 May and was the more remarkable because the lamb was then probably four or five weeks old. A friend who was staying with us at the time was sitting with me at the observation post. A strong east wind was blowing. I pointed out the eagle to my friend, and she noticed that a lamb and ewe were feeding near where the eagle was perched on the top of the cliff. The lamb was old enough to feed on the grass. My friend said to me, "Do you think that lamb is safe from the eagle?" I replied truthfully that I had never seen a golden eagle take a lamb. Scarcely had I said this when the eagle rose and hovered (this is the only time I have ever seen a golden eagle hover) above the lamb. The ewe ran up and angrily drove off the eagle. The lamb a little later had fed some yards away from its mother. The golden eagle returned to the attack. There was a strong up-draught at the top of the cliff and the great bird, taking advantage of the extra buoyancy thus provided, rose quickly almost vertically from its perch, headed into the wind, dropped lightly almost to the ground and snatched the lamb into the air, carrying it to the far side of the ridge and out of our sight. The lamb was grasped by the back: all four legs were hanging limply, like those of a rabbit when it is carried by an eagle. My friend, who had no stalking glass to bring the scene near, said "That looks like a particularly large rabbit." "Yes," I replied, "the largest I have ever seen." I felt that the eagle had let me down. The ewe did not at first realise her loss and continued to feed. When she saw that her lamb had gone she ran here and there but of course could not find it. She was mystified, for she could not understand that it had been lifted into the air and carried off. The weight of that lamb at the age of a month would have been too great for the eagle to lift unless the strong up-draught had given it extra buoyancy.

While I think it is fair to quote in full the evidence against the eagle, it is right to point out that these incriminating letters are only a small minority of the replies I have had, and my own records are the only ones I have in a long life of eagle-watching. Most of my correspondents have never seen an eagle take a lamb, and surely the vividness with which shepherds and stalkers recall a single event of this kind shows what a rarity it must be. If eagles habitually took lambs we should hear very much more about it than we do.

It is curious that from upwards of sixty correspondents, all of whom have lived in the country of the eagle, I have heard of only about a dozen authentic instances of an eagle actually being seen to take living lambs. Yet these men are out on the hills daily and at all times of the year. The evidence that I have been able to collect seems to point to the fact that eagles take to lamb-killing only when food is scarce, and that with some eagles it becomes a habit. But they prey on lambs only during the first four weeks of their lives, while the eagles are rearing their own young. As it has been proved that eagles can actually kill deer even up to the age of a year, it follows that if they liked they could kill even a full-grown sheep, yet with one exception all the keepers and shepherds agree that they attack only young lambs. Why do they not attack older sheep ? It cannot be a question of weight alone, for they could feed on the carcase where they killed it, as they undoubtedly do on large deer calves which they kill.

The conclusion is that sheep and lambs are really an un-natural prey of the eagle, taken only in exceptional circumstances, either because of scarcity of more natural food, or when peculiar conditions make it easy for the eagle to form the habit of preying on lambs. It is to the credit of the eagle that this should be so when one thinks how easy a prey either a sheep or lamb must be in the hill country, where any white object can be seen by the eagle for miles.

It is seldom that one sees more than two eagles together, except, of course, the family parties in August and September. But occasionally it seems as though eagles do join up into small flocks, perhaps hunting parties. On 25 September 1925 no fewer than nine eagles were seen by Duncan Robertson in a west Inverness-shire forest, and F. Macintosh about the same time saw nine in the neighbouring forest. These were evidently the same birds.

The late Major Edward Ellice of Invergarry told me that he once saw eight eagles together, and another correspondent mentions six. It would be interesting to know whether these companies of eagles were migrating. Certainly a pair of eagles will not tolerate a third bird on their "territory," and I have more than once seen such a fierce attack upon an intruder that the feathers flew!

W. J. Shaw, Inverness, writes as follows:

"In the year 1890 my father, then tenant of the farm of Old-toun, Stratherrick, had what I consider a unique experience. One day in April he was having a round of the sheep, and on the plateau just north of the Pass of Inverfarigaig he heard what he thought were the cries of a child in distress. Crossing a small knoll he saw two golden eagles in deadly embrace. As he approached them he thought the undermost bird caught sight of him, but it was held down by its antagonist, which was so absorbed in the struggle that it paid no heed to his approach. He caught the top bird by the wings and placed his foot on the under one. Searching his pockets, he found he had nothing to tie the wings with, ultimately doing so with a bandage removed from an injured hand. Meantime the other bird had by degrees pulled itself free, and after several attempts managed to soar away. At a cottar's house a sack was procured, and, unaware of the risk he ran, my father carried the monarch of the air home on his back.

"Both were male birds, the captured one, a very fine specimen, measuring 7 feet from tip to tip of its wings."

Another stalker, Duncan MacRae, witnessed a fight between two eagles which ended indecisively.

"It was in spring-time, and the two eagles were about two hundred yards up when they 'clinched' and came down 'heads and tails.' I looked out for a bad smash, but when about twenty feet from the ground they let go. They stood on the ground for some time facing each other, staring at one another with necks out and feathers ruffled. Then they rose and each flew away in opposite directions."

A fight to the death between two golden eagles must be a magnificent sight and one that is very rarely seen. John Mac-Donald, a head stalker in Inverness-shire, writes:

"I did not see the fight myself, but my youngest boy did. I came on the scene immediately afterwards and picked up the dead eagle, the other fluttering off amongst the trees. It was scarcely able to rise off the ground, but we failed to capture it. The dead eagle's gullet was torn completely out of the throat. They were both male birds, and I expect the fight originated over a hen eagle, as it happened during the mating season."

In July of the year 1948, a well-known Scottish botanist,

Hunting Habits of the Golden Eagle

R. Mackechnie, was walking with a friend near Inveraliginn in Wester Ross-shire, when he came across the bodies of two golden eagles, the head of one bird firmly gripped in the talons of the other. Some little time later before this discovery was made, a deer-stalker was able to approach closely two golden eagles fighting in the heather; when they flew off, one rose with difficulty. The fight, then broken off, had apparently at a later date continued to the death. That spring there had been two eyries unusually close together in the district.

CHAPTER VII

Flight of the Golden Eagle

IN THE autumn of the year 1944 I was travelling by air
southward across the Cairngorm Mountains. The pilot of
the small Royal Air Force plane, when he saw the cloud canopy
resting on the tops, decided to fly a little to the east of the range,
and we passed near the frowning slopes of Ben A'an. Ahead
of the plane, almost in its track, I saw a golden eagle. We were
flying at a height of approximately 4,000 feet above the sea
and the eagle, when we passed it, was no more than a hundred
feet, perhaps less, above us, as it sailed scanning the ground
far beneath: through the gaps between the wide-spaced
primaries the sky could be seen. As we approached the bird,
I expected it to take violent avoiding action. Instead, it continued its effortless soaring, supremely indifferent to the airplane. Even had the eagle been so intent on watching the
ground for possible prey that it did not observe the plane's
approach, it is impossible that it could have failed to have
heard the engines.

The behaviour of this golden eagle was very different from
that of the pair on Ben Wyvis in Ross-shire, vide. Chap. VIII,
p. 134. The hill was deep in snow at the time and when a stag
stampeded on seeing an aircraft flying over, it stuck fast in a
deep drift with only head and antlers showing. The pilot of the
plane, and a pair of hunting golden eagles, observed the stag's
predicament about the same time. The eagles evidently considered that stag to be their legitimate prey, and treated the

airplane as their rival. They attacked it with power dives, with such determination and persistence that the pilot had considerable difficulty in avoiding them, but he safely passed their territory and when last he saw them they were sailing low backwards and forwards above the stag, as if to attack. The outcome of that grim affair was unknown, except to the eagles.

I believe that under certain conditions the golden eagle is the fastest bird that flies, yet on a calm day there are faster fliers. Anyone who sees the eagle for the first time as it flies from its eyrie on a quiet day forms the impression of a heavy, broad-winged bird progressing through the air with slow, almost laboured wing-thrusts and travelling slowly. Actually, even under these conditions, the eagle is moving much faster than it appears to be. When seen high in the heavens, it is a supreme artist in flight. It is a specialist in soaring and gliding. Much has been written of its soaring powers, but little of its gliding. Yet its gliding is more remarkable than its soaring, which gives it a mastery over the elements. If a golden eagle should decide to travel to any particular place it does not, like other birds, at once set out in that direction. In Ch. XI, p. 176, I describe how the eagle reaches its destination, whether comparatively near or distant, by spiralling to a height from which one continuous glide will take it to the hill, or corrie, or hunting ground it may wish to reach. This glide may be with the wind or against it, and indeed the golden eagle progresses almost as easily against the breeze as with it. This statement may be hard of belief, but it must be emphasised that the glide, when the bird is travelling against the wind, is at a steeper downward angle than when travelling with it, and the wings are held more bent and closer to the body. In this poise, always inspiring to see, the weight of the bird carries it forward at impressive speed.

The Golden Eagle: King of Birds

Utilising its mastery in gliding, the golden eagle arrives at its destination after a journey on which no energy has been expended: one can almost say that distance means nothing to this bird. I am still thrilled when I see a golden eagle, a mere speck to the unaided human eye, set its trim for a glide and move faster and faster, perhaps to join its mate, perhaps to hunt above some rabbit-haunted corrie beyond my view. What is the limit of a golden eagle's hunting flight when searching for food for the eaglets? Without the aid of a pursuit plane (how often have I longed for a helicopter in which to follow the bird at a respectful distance) the length of these flights must remain problematical. I have often watched an eagle make its aerial climb from its eyrie in the Isle of Skye. At times it rises so high before setting out eastward that I have little doubt that the bird's hunting destination is the mainland of Scotland. Eagles nesting in the Hebridean island of Rum habitually feed their eaglets on rabbits. There are no rabbits on Rum, and the eagles must go for them to Skye or to Eigg—perhaps both of these islands. I am sure that the golden eagle frequently passes over country that is foreign to its habits and where it is rarely if ever seen, but before crossing country of this kind it rises to so great a height as to be invisible. On one occasion a friend and I were approaching the cairn of Meall Fuarvonie, a high hill which rises from the north shore of Loch Ness. A golden eagle was sunning itself on the cairn. At our approach the great bird rose grandly into the sunlit air, then set course for the distant Monadh Liath mountains. He passed over Loch Ness at a height of over four thousand feet.

Eagles are very rarely seen over country where even one or two houses are present. I know of places where daily it is possible to see buzzards soaring over country of this nature, for the sight of a Highland crofter's house does not disturb them in the least, although it is rare for them to approach it closely, like the raven and the grey crow. The golden eagle, on the other hand, keeps to the high ground, or it may be to uninhabited Hebridean coasts.

I have mentioned the beauty and the charm of a golden eagle's glide. No less inspiring is its sailing in the teeth of a breeze. Conditions most to its liking are found when a wind blows in upon a cliff. The air stream is deflected upward by the cliff and the eagle becomes poised and almost motionless on this rising air. The wings are held stiffly extended and made as broad as possible. The primary wing feathers are held in an upward curve, and are widely spaced, so that the sky can be seen between each. In a stately manner the bird moves slowly forward, the steering and the stabilising being done entirely by the tail, which is constantly being moved—now held wide open, now almost closed, now shutting and opening like a lady's fan, which indeed it resembles. The Alpine chough uses the tail in the same manner.

Much has been written of the power dive of the golden eagle, and of the tremendous speed of this downward rush. A power dive implies that the bird is not relying entirely on the pull of gravity. The gannet when it checks its flight on sighting a fish often drives its wings hard as it drops to the water. This is a power dive, but I do not think the golden eagle ever makes a power dive in this sense. The eagle when it goes into a dive presses its wings firmly against its sides and falls, literally headlong, faster and faster. The speed of some of these dives must be in excess of one hundred miles an hour.

An unusual feature of the golden eagle's flight is its occasional trick, when soaring, of using one wing, flapped once, to steady itself on an unstable air current; the wing used is usually the right wing. This has also been noted in the white-tailed eagle's flight in Iceland by Ernest Lewis in his book, *In Search of the Gyr-Falcon*.

The Golden Eagle: King of Birds

Living as it does amid the high hills, the golden eagle is often flying through cloud. That its eye can make use of wavelengths beyond the human vision is probable. A Highland deerstalker was on the hill on a day of close mist. Visibility was down to 20 yards. He was resting beside a cliff where a pair of golden eagles had their eyrie. Suddenly he heard the rushing sound of an eagle's wings as the bird passed unseen close to him, travelling, as he could tell from the noise, at great speed. Unless it had special vision it must have dashed itself against the rock. One February day I watched a pair of eagles sailing wing-tip to wing-tip at the edge of the cloud canopy. They entered the cloud, and did not again emerge from it in my sight.

A gathering of golden eagles is always memorable. The most spectacular I have seen was above the Cuillin hills of Skye. That gathering was in early May, when the birds might have been expected to have been too busy to have found time for an aerial tourney.

A friend and I were standing on the ridge above Loch Choire a' Ghrunnda, the highest tarn on the Cuillin, on 2 May. That day was summer-like and, as often happens in Skye, the last week of April had been fine, warm and sunny. Above, and around this high and lonely lochan, at a height of 2,800 feet above the Atlantic the ground in places was dark red because of the flowers of purple mountain saxifrage (*Saxifraga oppositifolia*), first plant of the hills to blossom after the melting of the snows. In my diary for that day I find a note that a bumble bee was sipping the nectar from one of these flowers—an interesting record for that height so early in the season. Around the tarn, flower-buds already showed on the Alpine form of the sea thrift (*Armeria maritima*).

As we stood on the ridge, white fleecy clouds drifting idly high in the blue vault of heaven, we looked across the deep hollow of Loch Coruisk on to mighty Blaven rising beyond it. A golden eagle now appeared, sailing indolently above the abyss. This eagle was a little later joined by four more of its species, apparently two pairs. The eagles came from various directions, and it almost seemed as if the gathering had been arranged in order that the birds might engage in an aerial display. There were uprising eddies of warm air from the corries, and one of these pairs of eagles, rising on these eddies and an easterly wind current, swung in spirals to an immense height. A fair-weather cumulus cloud was hanging perhaps 8,000 feet above the sea. The eagles reached this cloud and sailed, half concealed, in its billowy depths. The female eagle first began the aerial descent. The male dropped swiftly towards her. She, crossing high above the barren cone of Sgùrr Alasdair, dropped plummet-like in two magnificent dives. Then the pair sailed serenely across Sgùrr Sguman, casting shadows on glistening snow-fields that rested on a slope so steep as to be shunned even by the red deer. The display lasted for upward of half an hour, when the two pairs of golden eagles, and the single bird, separated and disappeared in different directions, and the sky was once more lonely.

My first thoughts were that the eagles must have lost their eggs which, during the early days of May, should have been on the point of hatching, or should already have hatched. Yet in fine weather when the eggs are hard-set, and even when the eaglets are newly hatched, the parent bird on duty may leave them for more than an hour at a time—and this meeting of eagles took place during the warmest hours of an unusually warm day.

The eagles vanished, and now a tortoise-shell butterfly floated rather than flew, over the sharp ridge, passing at once from warmth and sunlight to the cold shadow of the corrie and drifting above the hard-frozen snow-fields which lay in shadow on its steep slope. We looked down upon the small island of Soay nearly 3,000 feet below and saw the reflection of the birches in its lochs, and a boat in the land-locked north harbour, shadowed by birches, the haunt of willow-warbler and cuckoo. On Soay then men still dug the ground in the small fields with the old foot-plough or *cas chrom,* for there was not a horse in all the island, which lies beneath the high peaks of the Cuillin, and is sheltered by them from the cold north wind.

The second gathering of golden eagles which I watched was in winter, early in December. On that day snow covered the ground. Deep and powdery, it hid each peaty pool and each hill stream. To the east, high cliffs, dark as night, rose against a sky which each moment became more sombre and threatening. The white shroud of the moor and the unrelieved blackness of the precipice formed a fitting picture for what followed. Lifeless and stern was the view until a golden eagle appeared, moving majestically down-wind on rigid wings. She—for it was apparent from the great wing-spread that it was a female —swept grandly across a hill pass, and on the far side of the pass, above a flat-topped hill, met three more golden eagles. Those three eagles were almost at once joined by a fifth bird, when an impressive aerial display was begun, which for sheer majesty of flight could not have been excelled. The five eagles, poised at a height of perhaps 1,500 feet above the hill-top, arranged themselves in flying formation and moved majestically against the wind. Higher and higher they mounted on motionless wings, until they entered a cloud layer and were awhile hidden, before descending slightly and reappearing beneath the cloud.

After a time one of the eagles began a series of breath-taking dives. Closing its wings, it fell headlong perhaps 500 feet. It then flattened out, and almost at once mounted until it had

Ten week old
eaglet weighing over
9 lbs minutes before
it left the eyrie for
its first flight.
(*Lea MacNally*)

regained its lost height, the wings being driven fast and determinedly. As it prepared for the next dive the most spectacular part of the aerial display took place. The eagle's wings still drove it upwards, but the bird slowly tilted, as a rocket does at the end of its climb before falling to earth. The eagle at first fell slowly but when it had got its head down the velocity of the fall at once increased. But even before the flier began to fall the great wings were closed and the angle of the descent was controlled by the tail.

As dusk was approaching the two parties of golden eagles separated and made off in different directions towards their roosting places.

"Never" is a strong word, but I think it safe to say that the golden eagle hardly ever hovers, although the buzzard, a bird of similar flight, often does so. But I have frequently seen an eagle, while sailing into a breeze with wings wide and outstretched, suddenly bend its wings back and make them small, the primaries no longer being widely spaced. This curious attitude is maintained for perhaps half a minute, the bird keeping its position with the same apparent ease as when in the more orthodox poise. When soaring the eagle may often be seen to move its head and look around it: the impression is given that the bird is calmly surveying the scene beneath it. I have noticed that under certain conditions the eagle resembles a miniature aircraft. On one occasion I actually mistook a golden eagle for an aeroplane. I was on the top of a hill, and saw, approaching me at a rather lower level, what seemed to be an aircraft. I was on the route sometimes taken by the Inverness-Stornoway aeroplane, and for a few seconds thought that the plane was travelling unusually low. As the object approached, I saw that this was a golden eagle, flying on stiff, motionless wings. During the war, when many Flying Fortresses were passing over the Isle of Skye on passage from Iceland to Britain, one of the Observer Corps on duty at a station was about to report the approach of a Flying Fortress when he realised that the supposed aircraft was a golden eagle.

There are very few authenticated records of the speed a golden eagle attains in level flight. Most modern aircraft travel too fast for a pilot to check an eagle's speed by his own. Of special interest, therefore is a letter which appeared in "The Times" of 3 August 1929 from Lieut. Owen Cathcart-Jones of the aircraft carrier H.M.S. *Courageous*. He was flying down the east coast of Greece and when he was in the vicinity of Mount Kissavos, near Larisa, he was astonished to see a golden eagle fly past his aeroplane on a parallel course at a distance of about 80 feet. The bird did not appear to be at all alarmed by the sound of the engine, and as it passed turned its head to look at the aircraft. The speed of the aircraft was 70 knots, the altitude 4,000 feet. The aviator estimated, from the speed at which the eagle passed the aircraft, that the bird was travelling at 90 m.p.h. If in level, unhurried flight a golden eagle travels at a speed of ninety miles an hour, in a slant or in a dive it must often exceed one hundred miles an hour.

Besides the straight, high dive of the golden eagle there is also the corkscrew dive, exciting to watch. The high dive often develops into the corkscrew dive as the eagle nears the cliff on which it is about to alight; the bird before it corkscrews suddenly changes its flying position, so quickly that the eye cannot follow this evolution. All the observer sees is that the eagle is no longer diving head-first, but is falling feet-first, its bright-yellow legs fully extended and held rigidly in the direction of the cliff which is rushing up to meet them. The wings are still closed, but not tightly closed, and the out-stretched leg and spaced talons may act as a brake. The landing is made skilfully and the perch, even if a small one, is rarely overshot.

Down-wind, the golden eagle progresses either, if speed is

important, in a glide, or in a series of wide sweeps and spirals if it is not travelling urgently. Against the wind it moves almost always in a slanting glide, having previously spiralled to the correct elevation. It is less usual for an eagle to fly *across* the wind; a glide, with perhaps a few wing-thrusts to assist it, is often the method then used.

What is the secret of the golden eagle's mastery of flight? It is not a bird of narrow wing like, for instance, the peregrine falcon. The eagle's wings are indeed unusually broad; perhaps because of this it is unexcelled as a glider among land birds. Its weight and size must help it when gliding against the wind. The up-turned primaries must have a special significance in soaring, for they are held always thus, whereas the primaries of the buzzard, a bird which in its flight resembles the eagle, are neither held in an upward curve nor widely spaced. The harriers, beautiful soarers, all of them, hold the primaries wide-spaced, so does another expert, the alpine chough.

From what height does the golden eagle dive? I was one day watching an eyrie. In the field of my glass was a golden eagle which I estimated at an altitude of 5,000 feet. The eagle suddenly went into a dive. For the first two thousand feet of the dive the wings were only half closed; then they were tightly closed, and the bird dropped at a giddy speed. When the eagle had alighted on the top of a cliff the watcher saw what appeared to him as almost an anticlimax. The great bird ran, with short, mincing steps, to a rocky knoll. As it ran, the mind received the impression of a gigantic starling—here was no dignity or majesty, but an appearance almost ludicrous.

The usual background to the golden eagle in flight is high country, in winter often snow-clad. But one summer day, I was " spying " near the top of Foinne Bheinn (Foinaven), a wild hill in the Reay Forest. The view over the Atlantic was so clear that I thought it might be possible to see Sule Stack, about 40 miles to the north. On Sule Stack is a large gannet colony, and the rock is white because of the multitude of white nesting birds and their droppings. After some trouble I made out this stack, rising like some Arctic peak of eternal snow from the blue floor of ocean, and at the same minute a golden eagle sailed into the field of my glass and at a distance of perhaps two miles gave me an exhibition of graceful flying, the gannet stack of Suleskerry being all the time clear and white as a background.

The size of a golden eagle is shown by the great distance at which it has been seen and identified. An experienced Highland stalker and gillie, John George MacKay, whose home is at Achresgill near Kinlochbervie, told me that he and others were gathering sheep on the high slopes of rocky Foinne Bheinn one summer day. John George was spying Ben Hope (the day was very clear) and was watching stags near the top of that hill when he saw a golden eagle glide low over the deer. I have measured the distance between Foinne Bheinn and Ben Hope and it is approximately ten miles. John George owns an excellent stalking glass and is a careful observer.

The aerial displays of the golden eagle are seen usually when the bird is high above the watcher and appears dark against the sky, but there are times when the sun is seen to shine on the gold feathers of the eagle's head with beautiful effect. One evening the sun had already set in the glen when an eagle rose from its perch and sailed in spirals, higher and higher. At last the bird reached the rays of the setting sun and its golden head became afire as it caught the sunset light. At the actual moment of sunset the eagle was transformed into a radiant bird, each wing primary being bathed in a pink glow.

One cold day of spring a friend and I were on the high hills of Glen Feshie in Badenoch. As we walked along a rocky ridge my friend (as he told me afterwards) felt that he must turn aside and look over the edge of the rocks. Immediately below him he then saw a golden eagle, hanging head-downward over the cliff, its foot held in a strong trap which was secured to the top of the rock. We pulled up the eagle. It was light as the proverbial feather, for it must have been suspended there for days without food, and in the track of a bitter north east wind. The foot was almost severed, and we amputated it. The eagle then got away from us, and began to flop its way toward the precipice. My friend shouted to me to catch it before it was dashed to death, but I was too late. The eagle reached the edge of the cliff—and then a wonderful thing happened. The bird, feeling the up-rising wind current, opened its broad wings. In a second he (for it was like a male eagle) was rising vertically, higher and higher, on wings held motionless. The swift transition, it might almost be said, from death to life, was a thing never to be forgotten. When the eagle had reached a height of perhaps a thousand feet above us his mate came out of the rocks, I think from her nest, and rose to meet him. Together they soared awhile, then disappeared from our sight. I have often wondered whether that eagle, with only one foot, was able to hunt and to feed himself until he became used to his handicap. It is possible that his mate may have captured prey for him. This trapping took place in a country in which the golden eagle is protected by law, and is an example of the difficulty of enforcing any Wild Birds' Protection Act.

In conclusion, it may be said that the golden eagle's flight is such that little energy is expended by the bird under any conditions, and often none at all. The farther the journey, the higher the elevation gained before the beginning of the glide. An eagle wishing to reach a destination fifty miles distant or even farther, is able to reach that destination with the expenditure of no energy. The long effortless glide is made possible by the weight of the bird, as well as by its flying skill.

The Golden Eagle: King of Birds

The breadth of the eagle's wings is an important factor in spiralling to gain the requisite height for the beginning of the glide. The eagle is a supreme aerial artist except for one thing, and that is manoeuvrability: here it is no match for birds like the raven which take every opportunity of annoying it.

CHAPTER VIII

The Golden Eagle's Enemies:
at Home and Abroad

BY FAR the most deadly of the golden eagle's enemies is
man. Man apart, it has few enemies, and these are not
serious ones.

In Britain, the eagle finds its human enemies among sheep-
farmers, grouse-preservers and, occasionally, rabbit-trappers.

The tenant of a grouse-moor dislikes the eagle, chiefly on
account of the disturbance it causes by its presence on the moor
during the shooting season. The disturbance caused is much
more important than the number of grouse actually taken,
which has little effect on a well-stocked moor.

Although a golden eagle will at times take grouse on the wing,
it more often takes them on the ground; when an eagle appears
the grouse therefore take wing, and fly, usually at a considerable
height, wildly and erratically, until they are out of sight beneath
the horizon. Before nightfall the birds may return, but the
sport is spoiled on that moor for the day. Yet, as a Highland
keeper pointed out to me, an eagle may drive large numbers
of grouse on to a moor, as well as out of it.

It might be thought that a pair of golden eagles nesting on
a grouse-moor would seriously affect that moor. This is not
always so. I know a Sutherland moor that is partly grouse
ground, partly deer forest. During the seasons when my wife
and I were observing the life of a pair of golden eagles from a

hide the ground was let to a grouse-shooting tenant until September, when the owner of the estate took over the moor and shot the deer. There is here no boundary between the grouse-moor and the deer-forest, and the eagles daily hunted over the whole area.

After the young birds flew in mid-July old and young left the district, and were never seen by the tenant of the grouse ground, who had no difficulty in shooting his season's limit of birds.

There is no doubt that a moor of considerable extent can support a pair of golden eagles. The keeper of a large moor and deer forest in Central Perthshire told me early in 1953 that he had two pairs of eagles nesting on his ground. He said that the eagles kept to the deer forest part of the ground, and did not interfere with the grouse shooting. The grouse, he said, were each year increasing on his ground, after being almost non-existent at the close of the second world war.

That the stock of grouse can increase despite the presence of eagles is worthy of record.

The mentality of the grouse preserver towards the eagle is shown in the following first-hand anecdote. The admiral carried on a battleship which had dropped anchor in a West Highland sea loch attended a cocktail party on shore organised in honour of the officers of the ship. During a conversation with me he told me that his great ambition was to see a golden eagle, and that he was willing to hire a car and travel a considerable distance in order to do this. I was discussing with him the most likely places where an eagle might be seen when a Highland chief who owned much grouse ground joined us and I told him what we had been discussing. "Eagles ?" he replied—"a perfect curse." The expression on the admiral's face as he heard this new view-point was worth seeing.

The Golden Eagle's Enemies

It is fortunate for the golden eagle that there are in the Scottish Highlands many thousands of acres which are not grouse-moor, yet are inhabited by the eagle. Yet here again the golden eagle's enemy is sometimes man. In a deer-forest without sheep the eagle is tolerated, and may even be welcomed, but much land formerly deer-forest is now under sheep, and where there are sheep the eagle is usually, but not always, unpopular.

It was because of its partiality for sheep that the sea-eagle was exterminated in Britain. The golden eagle does on occasion carry off lambs, but the damage it does is very much less than that formerly caused by the sea-eagle. While there are certain lamb-stealing pairs of golden eagles in the Scottish Highlands, they are in the minority, and there are many pairs of eagles which have never taken a lamb. A West Highland sheep-farmer, who had farmed throughout his life in different areas, all of them eagle country, told me that he had never lost a lamb from a golden eagle's attack. Hostility toward the eagle is therefore not by any means universal among sheep farmers: the publicity from time to time given in the press to lamb-raiding eagles is to be regretted, since it is often sensational and exaggerated. As an example, a fantastic story appeared in more than one newspaper in the early summer of 1951, that an eagle had swooped on a flock of sheep in Northumberland and had killed 50 lambs. I doubt if even the most inveterate lamb-killing eagle has accounted for half that number of lambs in a whole season. This sensational story was copied by one newspaper after another, and no doubt was read with satisfaction by those who think that the stock of Scottish-nesting golden eagles should be reduced.

The appearance of a golden eagle in Northumberland is in itself noteworthy. That great naturalist, Bewick, records that a pair of these birds at one time nested on the rocks of The

Cheviot, but it is almost two hundred years since they last bred there.

Lamb-killing by a golden eagle is the result almost always of a scarcity of its natural food. When hares and rabbits, and grouse and ptarmigan, are on its territory, a golden eagle does not kill lambs. At a Hebridean eyrie where six hoodie crows were found neatly plucked, and where rabbits were brought in large numbers no lamb has ever been seen in the nest, although the site has been under observation for more than ten years. It is mainly in the North West Highlands that the eagle has been accused of lamb killing, yet even here the habit is confined to a small proportion of the nesting birds. Along the north west seaboard wild life is scarce. There are few rabbits and very few hares, while the red grouse is almost non-existent. It was here that a golden eagle was seen to carry a full-grown heron to the eyrie—a bird it would not take under ordinary circumstances.

A golden eagle, unlike a fox, does not kill a lamb for the mere pleasure of killing. The lamb is carried to the eyrie, where it may be laid at once on the actual nest, or else may be deposited on a rock-ledge or buttress in the neighbourhood. One lamb will provide a pair of eagles, and their young, with food for several days. The lamb is usually plucked, in the same way that a rabbit is plucked, the eagle skilfully jerking away the wool adhering to its beak and throwing it over its shoulder.

In the North-West Highlands the lambing season begins in mid-April and continues until early May. Almost always at least one snowstorm is experienced, often accompanied by a frost-laden wind which causes considerable drifting. There is considerable mortality among the young lambs during these snowstorms. When the snow has melted an eagle sees the white, conspicuous form of a lamb that has died: if natural food is scarce it cannot be blamed if it carries this unexpected food to the eyrie.

The Golden Eagle's Enemies

It is probable that half the number of lambs taken by the golden eagle are dead and deserted by the mothers or stillborn when they are carried off. It is to the credit of some shepherds that they realise this. Neither ewe nor lamb has any fear of the eagle. I have watched a golden eagle perched on a post on the top of the cliff which held the eyrie, and all the time a ewe and her lamb were feeding contentedly only a few yards from the great bird.

A point which should be remembered in the eagle's favour is that it preys on hoodie crows, one of the worst enemies of the sheep farmer and the grouse-preserver.

In some Scottish counties the golden eagle* is protected by law, but not in all. In remote districts, even where it is nominally protected, it can be killed without the authorities being any the wiser; it is only where the landowner is eagle-minded that the golden eagle receives efficient protection. Man is undoubtedly the eagle's Enemy No. 1.

One Highland landowner (incidentally he came from south of the Border, and had bought his Highland estate) was credited with giving his keepers orders to shoot the eagle on the nest whenever possible, but trapping and poisoning are more usual methods taken against it. A dead hind is treated with strychnine. The eagle eats the deer's flesh and dies. It must be admitted that the poisoned bait is not always set for the eagle, but may be intended for a fox. The survivor of one pair of eagles recently met her fate by taking from a snare a poisoned rabbit on a neighbouring estate. Eagles are sometimes taken in fox traps, and are killed and buried on the spot. The trapped eagle whose discovery I describe in the last chapter was extremely emaciated and may have been imprisoned in the trap set for it for more than a week.

*By the time this book is printed it will have total protection (with specially severe penalties for destruction and egg-taking) under a new Act.

The Golden Eagle: King of Birds

It is good that active friendship toward the golden eagle is the policy of the Royal Society for the Protection of Birds. The legacy left to the Society of Bird Wardens and Watchers, and originally administered by them, was later handed over to the Royal Society for the Protection of Birds, which now pays rewards to those concerned in instances where it is guaranteed by an independent observer that the young eagles have successfully flown from the nest. This does twofold good, for besides the benefits of hard cash, people in the Highlands are made to realize that the eagle is a bird worth protecting, and that its presence gives pleasure to bird-lovers and induces them specially to visit the Highlands in order to see Britain's grandest bird.

Since I have long realized that man is the golden eagle's real enemy, I have written to golden eagle authorities in many countries in order to learn from them whether in their particular country the golden eagle is protected or not, and have received a number of letters of value. In few European countries is the eagle given protection: in some there is a price on its head. The Swedish authority, Dr. K. Curry-Lindahl, tells me that throughout Sweden the golden eagle is protected by law, and that in Finland also it is given legal protection, except in the province of Uleaborg. I gather that, despite the law forbidding it, the eagle is sometimes destroyed by the Lapps because they say that it kills reindeer, both young and old, and also hares, on which the Lapps depend for food. Curry-Lindahl thinks the harm done by the eagles is greatly exaggerated. He says that in winter thousands of reindeer die on the mountains. The carcases of these animals are eaten by golden eagles and are also devoured by bears, wolves, lynxes, gluttons, foxes and other eaters of dead flesh. A golden eagle is not habitually a carrion eater like the vultures, but in the low winter temperatures of Lapland the flesh of a reindeer which has died remains fresh until May or even June. The Lapps, seeing an eagle rise from a dead reindeer, infer that it has killed it. Curry-Lindahl says that the Nature Protection Society of Sweden, the Svenska Naturskyddsforeningen, is doing its best to convince the Lapps that the golden eagle is not so harmful as they imagine.

Professor Holger Holgersen of Stavanger Museum, Norway, tells me that in no part of Norway is the golden eagle protected.

Any municipality may put a bounty on its head and the county parliaments may also order its destruction. Holger Holgersen thinks that the unpopularity of the golden eagle is in part due to the widely-believed rumours that the bird carries off young children. The opinion of the professor is that this has never been proved, yet he says that children have been found far from home with their clothes torn, as is inferred, by the eagle. He says truly that if a baby, six months to a year old, is left where a golden eagle can steal it, the parents of the baby are to blame and not the eagle! Nor can it be certain that the culprit was a golden eagle and not a sea-eagle. In the Highlands and Islands of Scotland the sea-eagle is believed to have carried away babies, but never, so far as I know, the golden eagle. The late Miss Frances Tolmie, who lived at Dunvegan in the Isle of Skye, and gathered during her life an invaluable collection of Gaelic songs, told me that her grandfather as a baby was carried off by a sea-eagle. Martin Martin tells of an old man who was called Neil Eagle because he was carried off by an eagle as a baby.

A more recent incident was the broadcast over the Norwegian wireless by a lady who claimed to remember her experiences when being carried off by an eagle. When I asked whether I might quote her experience in my book, the reply came that she might consider it on payment of £25.

Carl Stemmler, who lives in Switzerland and has written two books on the golden eagle in that country, writes to me from his home in Schaffhausen that the golden eagle is protected in some Swiss cantons but not in all. He says, writing in 1952, the golden eagle is given official protection in the cantons of Berne, Wandt, Wallis or Valais, Schwyz and Luzern.

It would seem, however, that the law protecting the eagle is not always enforced. In the canton of Wallis in 1953 I saw an eyrie in which the eaglet a few days previously had been shot by local hunters who for three days had lain in wait unsuccessfully for the parent birds. They hate the eagle there because it preys on the hares and marmots of the district, both of which are hunted by local sportsmen. The canton of Berne since 1936 has decreed that any damage done by the golden eagle must be reported to the local forester, who will examine the claim and forward it in writing to the Directorate of Forests, who in turn will fix the indemnity to be paid if the claim should be substantiated. This canton realises the value of the golden eagle and permits no forester to show a stranger an eyrie, or describe its site, without written permission.

Carl Stemmler tells me that a pair of eagles in 1951 nested in a sycamore tree on a cliff near a famous beauty spot. Visitors came at all hours of the day to admire the view. They innocently kept the parent eagles away so long and so often from the eaglet that it died of starvation.

In the canton of Tessin four golden eagles were officially poisoned by strychnine in the winter of 1949-50.

In Italy Professor Toschi tells me that the hand of man is almost everywhere against the golden eagle. All species of eagle are indiscriminately classed as "vermin" here, and the golden eagle is decreasing but is still able to find refuge in the mountains.

In Spain, Professor Bernis of Madrid tells me man is still the golden eagle's enemy. Here the eagle has been decreasing for the past century, with local or short-time oscillations. The persecution of the eagle has recently been intensified as both

The Golden Eagle's Enemies

State and private hunters have initiated a campaign against all birds of prey without discrimination. For this campaign he blames the recent craze of eagle-owl hunting. Professor Bernis is still urging protection for the golden eagle.

In the National Park of Spain the golden eagle is apparently tolerated, for the professor says that a pair of birds of this species which nested in the high cliffs near Gandeleda in the park between 1940 and 1951 were named goat-eagles by the park keepers because they fed their eaglets on the kids of goats.

The United States of America is a vast country. In certain states the golden eagle is protected. In Texas however an almost fantastic campaign of murder has been waged against the eagle during the past decade and still continues as I write in 1954.

An eagle-killing aviator in the pay of a powerful group of West Texas live-stock farmers has shot from his aeroplane an incredible number of golden eagles. The following extract is quoted from the *American Farm Journal* of January 1947:

Now the light airplane has another job—hunting eagles. J.O. Casparis of Brewster County, Texas, shot down 867 golden eagles from his airplane last year, and more than 1,000 the year before. Casparis hunts the eagles for West Texas sheep men, each of whom pays him one hundred dollars a year to keep the range free of the predatory birds. Casparis does not hunt the bald eagle—the emblem of the U.S. Not only is it protected by law—it does not prey on larger animals. But the golden eagle can make off with a new-born lamb with ease. One rancher lost 500 lambs to eagles in 60 days. Another found the skeletons of 25 antelope fawns in a single nest. Eagle hunting is hazardous. Casparis shoots most of the birds at altitudes of 100 to 300 feet after putting his plane into a dive. His weapon is a 12-gauge sawed-off shotgun loaded with No. 4 shot.

The Golden Eagle: King of Birds

The big trick is to pick up the gun, aim and fire (which takes both hands) and then grab the controls of the airplane while it's still in the air.

In his book *Adventures with a Texas Naturalist*, 1950, Roy Bedichek gives us more information of this slaughter—for downright slaughter it is. The golden eagle's superb soaring is his undoing. Immediately a rancher, or one of his employees, sights a golden eagle he telephones to the eagle hunter, who on the instant starts up his plane. In a matter of minutes he reaches the unsuspecting eagle and, manoeuvring his aircraft into position, allows the small plane to fly pilotless while he pours a charge of shot into his victim at close range.

The first golden eagles to be pursued in the air treated the airplane as an enemy and gave battle to it. Indeed it is reported that Casparis had an alarming experience when one eagle dived at his plane, tore through the window, ripped off several feet of the fuselage, and showered the aviator with broken glass. I see no reason to doubt this report, after the experience of the British airman who (vide. Ch. VII, p. 112), one winter during the second world war, was attacked by a pair of golden eagles in the neighbourhood of Ben Wyvis in the Scottish Highlands, and had an anxious few minutes avoiding their dives.

Roy Bedichek thinks that this systematic slaughter of the golden eagle is likely to exterminate the species over a large area. Since reading his account of the systematic killing of large numbers of golden eagles in Texas I have been in correspondence with Roy Bedichek, and he has been good enough to give me additional and more recent information on this subject.

Writing in October 1952, he says that the killing continues, and gives further details of the eagle "bags" of Casparis. He says that he averages about 1,000 golden eagles a year. Begin-

Female eagle feeds her chick.　(*C. E. Palmar*)

ning in 1945, he killed 1,008 golden eagles that year. Since then he has brought his total up to 8,300 birds. When he began his activities he was paid 300 dollars a month by the Eagle and Coyote Club. My correspondent believes that since then his remuneration has been changed to a royalty basis.

This formidable bag of golden eagles is made throughout the whole year in a limited area. With the town of Alpine as centre, the eagle killer's range is not much more than 100 miles. The Eagle and Coyote Club, which pays Casparis his royalties, is formed of ranchmen. A member of this club declares that prior to the engagement of Casparis to kill eagles and coyotes he lost in one season 1,150 lambs out of 1,500 which he had marked. Other ranchmen report similar losses, and all agree that the killing of the golden eagles and coyotes has reduced their losses in lambs. They are backed by the Texas State Game Fish and Oyster Commission: this body assures the public that it is only by killing eagles and coyotes that it has been able to reinstate the antelope as a game animal in the Alpine region and in the great pastures around Maria. Sportsmen are pleased to hear this, for they reason that the fewer the eagles and coyotes the more antelopes they will have to shoot at.

Since Casparis began his campaign against the Texas golden eagles, two other aviators have been attacking them in the same state, one at Kent, the other at Marathon. I wrote to the Marathon aviator, William W. Hargus, about his experiences, and he supplied me with interesting notes. He tells me that his bag is around two hundred eagles a year. He estimates that a pair of nesting eagles will kill up to four to six lambs a day.

The highest eagle he pursued was at 11,500 feet but he believes they reach a height of 20,000 feet without much trouble; the height they rise to depends, he says, on the thermals and mountain air currents. The golden eagle, he writes, is known in Texas as the Mexican eagle.

The Golden Eagle: King of Birds

Roy Bedichek considers that, judging by the number of golden eagles killed by aviators, these birds must come from great distances, probably from the mountains of Mexico to the south. In Mexico the golden eagle is the national emblem but it is not protected anywhere in that country. The region where the killing is done in Texas is the only district in many miles of arid mountains adapted to the growing of sheep and goats, and thus, as Roy Bedichek says, it invites in predators, making an unnatural concentration of them in this marginal area of rich grassy slopes and rather luxuriant inter-montane valleys. In his book *Adventures with a Texas Naturalist,* already referred to, my correspondent very fairly states that when man with his immense herds invaded this fertile region, and when the predators multiplied, the ranching business could not have been carried on unless means had been devised to check the enemies of the sheep which now in great flocks pasture here. But now, by killing this fantastic number of golden eagles, man has upset the balance of nature, and jack-rabbits have greatly increased. Thus in Marfa in or about the year 1950 Roy Bedichek saw a man come in who had killed with a 22-calibre rifle, 81 jack-rabbits in a few hours while driving from Presidio to Marfa, a distance of less than 100 miles. He says that it is estimated 50 jack-rabbits eat as much grass as a steer, and since their enemy the golden eagle has been almost exterminated they now increase at an alarming rate. Thus, he says, killing begets killing.

For bird-lovers, especially for golden eagle-lovers, these reports make sad reading, yet it is obvious that sheep farmers would not go to the expense of employing a special aircraft and aviator unless their losses had been heavy. Roy Bedichek ends his most recent letter to me on a note of hope, by saying that a vast National Park of 700,000 acres, Big Bend National Park, has been formed at the heart of the golden eagle's territory in

Texas. Here both golden eagle and coyote are given protection, but if the Eagle flies beyond the park boundary (and surely this must often happen?) it is legitimate prey.

On this subject Maurice Broun, another distinguished American naturalist, writes to me in words impressive because of their deep truth:

> Here in America we squander our animal and bird resources and then, when a few individuals remain, we pitch into deep lamentations and place the species concerned on a pedestal, as an object lesson.

Even before the airman eagle hunter in Texas was making his record bags the golden eagle was being hunted by airplane in California. The American paper *Outdoor Life* of December 1936 describes "an unusual and exciting new sport, that of hunting eagles by airplane." It says that for years ranchers in the sheep and turkey-raising regions of Tehama County, California, had no satisfactory method of destroying these lamb-killing, turkey-killing eagles. The idea of using an airplane against the eagles came from the manager of a local airport and the killing of the eagles, so says the report, quickly brought about a lessening of lamb losses. The 36 members of the two associations who employed the eagle hunter reckoned that before the campaign against the eagles started each farmer lost a lamb a day. This loss was soon reduced to a lamb in ten days. The slaughter of eagles here was not nearly so heavy as in Texas, only 38 birds being killed during the first season.

The war against the golden eagle in the United States continues. An article entitled *I fly Against Eagles*, by F. "Mike" McMichael, appeared in the March 1954 issue of *Cavalier*, a magazine published by Fawcett Publications, Inc., Greenwich,

Conn. In 2,800 "eagle flying hours" the author shot down 512 golden eagles in Texas. He killed nine in one day.

I quote from the article:

> "Pretty soon we saw two eagles, killed one of them quickly, then turned to the second one before he could get away. He was an evasive bird, turning off whenever I got behind him. After a dozen passes I got in close but it was a fast shot and the eagle was only lightly hit. He set his wings, sailed down to a draw . . . and landed on a ledge. We could see him sitting there and decided to finish him off."

Although in Britain the golden eagle has inveterate human enemies who would be glad to see it disappear, it has more friends here than anywhere else in the world. It is also, I think, true to say that in the whole of Europe the headquarters of the race are now in the Highlands of Scotland. Although we have lost the sea-eagle we have become bird-minded in time to save the golden eagle from a similar fate.

We must not relax our vigilance. More and more land in the Scottish Highlands is being utilised for sheep-farming, and large areas of the Highlands are already, or will be shortly, National Parks. Neither in sheep country nor in a National Park can a golden eagle live so undisturbed a life as in a deer forest. On 22 April 1952, the Secreatry of State for Scotland gave the latest figures for red deer in Scotland. In 1951 there were 196 deer forests, with a total acreage of 3,100,000. Of this great area, 1,000,000 acres is capable of grazing cattle and sheep. The red deer population in 1951 was estimated at 100,000.

To sum up, certain mammals and birds have for the eagle a considerable "nuisance value." Fox, raven, grey crow and buzzard are in this category, but I do not think that any of them could cause the golden eagle to change its territory. Only

138

the buzzard and the fox really compete with the eagle for food. No bird or beast attacks it seriously, neither do they compete with it effectively for space.

One can say that, in Europe at all events, probably throughout the world, Man is the golden eagle's only serious enemy.

CHAPTER IX

A Tree Eyrie

A N ACCOUNT of this eyrie was published in *Days with the Golden Eagle*. That book is now out of print and I therefore give here some of our more important observations.

The eyrie was built on the crown of a Scots fir at an elevation of approximately 1,800 feet above the sea. A birch grew so near the fir that its crown mingled with the crown of the fir. Although the tree was old, it was of no great size and the eyrie was so large that it covered the whole crown of the tree. The nest was eight feet in diameter, and its depth may be judged by the fact that when I climbed the tree and stood (I am six feet one inch in height) on a branch at the base of the nest I was unable to see into the cup. Yet the height of this eyrie was small compared to that great nest visited by Edward Preble in British Columbia, which was nearly twenty feet from base to crown and exceeded by five feet the highest eyrie I have visited in the Scottish Highlands.

At the foot of the fir lay another eyrie, so ancient that the sticks of which it had been built had partly disintegrated into fine earth. In the eyrie now in use the crown was composed almost entirely of green branches of Scots fir and the cup was lined with the great wood-rush. The two eggs in the shallow cup could be seen without climbing the tree, for the hill slope was so steep that by walking a few yards higher up the hill the observer stood level with the tree-top. Here, at a horizontal distance of some thirty feet from the eyrie, a hide was built, and was covered with fir branches and heather. In this hide either I myself or my wife spent altogether thirty-one days, spread over a period of eleven weeks, our watches in all totalling one hundred and sixty seven hours.

We were soon to realize that there was one great advantage and saving of time and energy in the recording of the home life of this pair of golden eagles. If a nest is in the open, it is necessary for two persons to approach the hide together. After the observer has crept into the place of concealment, his companion at once leaves the neighbourhood as ostentatiously as possible and the bird, unaware that one person has been left near the nest, soon returns to it. But here the forest of old firs was thick, and the eagle, with her wide view from the crown of the tree, saw the approach of the observer and left the eyrie while he or she was the best part of a mile away, before the forest zone had been entered. After two visits to the eyrie we discovered that the eagle could not see us when we were near the nest, and that the observer could therefore approach the hide alone and, provided the eagle was not actually on the eyrie at the time, could leave the hide unknown to the bird. Since it took nearly two hours to walk from our base to the hide, this was a great help.

Our introduction to the eaglets in early May coincided with the first of many attacks we were to see made by one eaglet on the other. On 13 May, the day on which I took the first watch in the hide, the larger eaglet, then approximately twelve days old, felled the smaller with two or three well-aimed blows, and on two other occasions that day made deliberate attacks.

Two days later, the larger eaglet mercilessly attacked the smaller, several times driving it to the edge of the nest and, when the victim seemed about to fall to the ground, seizing it and throwing it back into the nesting cup. This the aggressor was able to do because of its greater size and strength. The larger eaglet habitually pushed the smaller out of the way at meal-times and the mother bird never seemed to notice the smaller of her two children cowering dejectedly in the eyrie, at a respectful distance from the bully. It was indeed remarkable that the small eaglet survived its ill-usage. Large billfuls of down were torn from its back, and the eyrie in time became powdered with white from this down. By this time the eaglet was half naked: the fact that it was half-starved and able to run faster than its over-fed companion in the nest undoubtedly saved its life.

The aggressor from the start was considerably the larger of the two and this difference in size remained when the pair were feathered. As in the adult golden eagle the female is the larger in a pair, we presumed that the aggressor eaglet was a female. Although this could not be proved, I shall hereafter in this chapter refer to the larger of the eaglets as "she" and the smaller as "he." We called them Cain and Abel, however ! The down torn from the back of his neck and his back by the aggressor sometimes adhered to her bill and she had difficulty in removing it, yet she continued her fierce attacks. Many a time she chased him round and round the eyrie, but preferred to attack while he slept and to aim a vicious blow at head, neck or back. After one particularly fierce attack she did an astonishing thing. Walking unsteadily to the centre of the eyrie she rose (she was as yet an indifferent walker) unsteadily to her full height and as she flapped her downy stumps of wings uttered a shrill scream of triumph, so strange and weird that it might have been the voice of a spirit.

When the eaglets were about four weeks old, the young male, if I might suggest that he was a male eaglet, began to receive larger amounts of food and, perhaps as a result, his courage increased. One day when his sister began to bully him as was her habit, he retaliated with such good effect that she was obliged to run to the far side of the eyrie to escape him. Yet she continued her attack for some time after this. The parent eagles, like those in the rock eyrie described in the next chapter, from time to time carried in nesting material during the fledgling period of the eaglets.

One day the mother arrived with a branch of Scots fir, fresh and green-needled; scarcely had she left when the male arrived with a branch. On windy days the exposed eyrie swayed violently: one day the mother eagle was seen to balance herself skilfully as a seaman might do on the deck of his ship. She had brought heather to the nest, but it was blown away before her eyes. She then left, but quickly returned with a fir branch, fresh and green. This was heavier than the heather and was not blown away. Within five minutes she returned, carrying a second living fir branch. When the male came in with a grouse one of the eaglets was carrying the branch across the nest; the father seemed to watch with interest this sign of the eaglet's increase in strength.

On May 30 I witnessed a fierce attack by the larger eaglet on the smaller. The feathers by then had begun to sprout, and she actually pulled out one of the growing quills—she had much difficulty in freeing her bill of it.

The mother eagle was now giving both eaglets equal shares of the food brought. This was usually red grouse or mountain hare.

Sometimes the eaglets lunched well on a first course of grouse and a second of hare. On 1 June a willow-warbler during my watch was daintily searching for insects on the outer platform of the eyrie. Willow-warbler and golden eagle are sometimes neighbours, and in a birch tree in which a neighbouring pair of golden eagles nested a willow-warbler used to sing his soft, musical song only a few feet from the eyrie. I once saw a willow-warbler gathering feathers for its nest from a disused eyrie of a pair of eagles. This morning of the first day of June there were in the eyrie two red grouse and part of a mountain hare. That day, the larger of the eaglets was in a bad temper. She tore billfuls of down from her brother and even small growing feathers. He ran to the edge of the nest and lay there sullenly. His sister then uttered several wild, piercing yells. They were strange, even terrifying cries. Much of her brother's down adhered to her bill as she shrieked in triumph.

On 2 June, swifts were wheeling in the air above the eyrie, and a cock redstart, his fiery tail aquiver, was perched on a neighbouring fir. The eaglets were now between four and five weeks old, and their father was bringing red grouse and ptarmigan unplucked to the eyrie—until now they had been carefully plucked. On this day the bully made the most determined attack on the smaller eaglet I had yet seen. The mother was standing on the eyrie at the beginning of this unprovoked aggression, but she did not intervene on the side of the attacked, and almost at once took wing. With wild cries the young female pursued her brother round and round the eyrie, aiming blow upon blow on head, neck and body.

When the mother returned, the victim was down-and-out; the parent therefore fed the bully for half an hour before giving nourishment to the ill-treated child.

By 3 June, the down on the thighs of the smaller eaglet was golden, although on the wings and back it was pure white, except where the small black feather-quills had begun to show.

During the next fifteen days circumstances prevented us from visiting the eyrie; when we returned we found a great change in the eaglets. The larger eaglet on 19 June was well-feathered; the smaller had still much down on head and body but the feathers were growing fast. In the nest lay a green fir branch and a plant of green heather; on the heather the remains of a mountain hare were lying. The carrying in of living branches at this time was an almost daily routine. That evening as I walked down from the eyrie to the low ground beside a sandpiper-haunted loch, the father eagle was sailing high above me in the deep blue sky, the sun shining so brightly on his golden head that it seemed almost white. Behind the eagle, his wings stiff and motionless, rose the Cairngorm Hills, the winter snow still almost unbroken on their slopes.

The next watch, on 21 June, was a red-letter day. The father arrived with a red squirrel and the eaglets were almost as thrilled by this new prey as the observer in the hide. They cheeped excitedly, the call of the larger eaglet being now deeper-pitched than that of the smaller. Both eaglets that day lunched off a grouse, and left the squirrel alone. The feathers on the head of the larger eaglet were now golden; the rest of her plumage was a rich, dark brown although a certain amount of white down remained on neck, breast and legs. There were as yet few feathers on the neck of the smaller eaglet.

On 26 June another squirrel was brought to the eyrie. The smaller eaglet attempted to pluck the prey and, failing in this, lifted the squirrel and walked angrily about the eyrie with the victim. The larger eaglet then took the squirrel and was more successful in tearing it up than he had been. On this day the eaglets fondled each other with their bills—a noteworthy event after their stormy childhood.

We were never to see an open quarrel between them after this, the first day of wing-exercises. That afternoon was memorable because of the spectacular descent of the father eagle from the high hills. He carried a ptarmigan in one foot, and was travelling so fast that he was unable to alight at the eyrie; he continued his downward rush beyond it, swung round, and with his impetus sailed up to the nest, making a perfect landing on the platform. The speed of that slant was breath-taking and must have been in the neighbourhood of two miles a minute. That afternoon the female eagle three times removed prey from the eyrie, perhaps carrying it to some cache out of my sight. The eaglets watched with alarm this depletion of the larder; the sight stimulated the larger eaglet to seize and swallow the squirrel's tail, fur and all.

During the weeks we had watched, the mother eagle had been careful not to feed the eaglets on the entrails of red grouse, hare or rabbit. The entrails of grouse she herself swallowed with relish, gobbling them up as though they had been macaroni. On 25 June, several fresh fir branches and pieces of heather were brought by both parents to the eyrie; the eaglets played with the branches, tossing them into the air and carrying them about. On 28 June a ptarmigan, a red grouse, and part of a rabbit were in the eyrie. My wife reached the eyrie at 5-40 a.m. The eaglets were awake, but soon went to sleep. At 7 a.m. they awoke, and the larger eaglet did wing exercises. She again went to sleep and on awakening threw up a large pellet. Midges that morning pestered the eaglets, attacking their eyes, which they rubbed against their necks. At 10 a.m. both eaglets became excited, calling loudly as they peered over the edge of the eyrie towards the fir trees lower down the hill. One of the parents was evidently there, and my wife wondered why it did not come to the eyrie. When the eagle (the father of the family) did at last arrive the cause of his slow progress from the glen below was apparent. In one foot he carried a heavy burden—the fawn of a roe-deer. The fawn's head, and also the entrails, had been removed, yet the carcase must have been a great weight. The slope of the hill was steep, and the eagle had evidently been flying from tree to tree, with frequent rests, during the period when the eaglets had been watching him. Exhausted by his effort, and panting for breath, the eagle threw down the prey in the eyrie and stalked majestically across the broad nest, ignoring the eaglets' shrieks of joy and excitement. With yells of triumph similar to those she had uttered after an assault on her small brother, the larger eaglet pounced on the carcase and unsuccessfully attempted to tear the flesh from it. The smaller eaglet seized a feather lying in the nest and, carrying it in his bill, dashed backwards and forwards across the eyrie.

Their disappointment was obvious when the father, instead of feeding them on the new and exciting prey, offered them pieces of old grouse! Later that day the eaglets called excitedly to a gull soaring overhead, evidently under the impression that it was one of their parents.

On 3 July the remains of two more roe-deer calves were in the eyrie, in addition to the bones of the first, now picked clean. The eyrie swarmed with house and blue-bottle flies and the eaglets were attacked by biting sand-flies and also by midges. The attacks were so fierce that the young eagles kept their eyes closed and repeatedly rubbed them against their shoulders. The eyrie had become dirty and untidy, and was probably infested by maggots. Fir branches and heather were no longer brought. On 4 July the father eagle lifted some remnants of the intestines of one of the roe-deer fawns: he held them in his bill, but did not eat them. Most of both carcases had now been eaten. The male eagle several times brought prey that day. He had scarcely laid a red grouse in the nest when the larger eaglet seized it and half-flew across the eyrie, gripping the grouse in one foot. On neither 5 nor 6 July did the eagles come to the eyrie during our watches. The fly pest continued and the eyes of the eaglets were swollen from innumerable bites of sand-fly and midge. The head of the smaller eaglet was now feathered, and it was now less easy to distinguish the two young birds. On 7 July 1 was the witness of a rather alarming event. The larger eaglet was standing at the edge of the eyrie, near the remains of a roe-calf skeleton. The combined weight was such that the side of the eyrie gave way, and the eaglet fell, about thirty feet, to the ground. The bird was alarmed but apparently unharmed by the fall. She (her size was such that I am convinced the sex was female) walked with a scared look through the heather out of my sight, nor did I see her again. At the end of my watch in the hide I walked across to the place where she had touched the ground and found the remains of a roe-deer fawn and a red grouse, both of which had accompanied her in her fall. The second eaglet, asleep at the time, was unaware of her precipitate departure, but his future was profoundly affected by it. On the day of the mishap both eaglets had been making periodic rushes across the eyrie, in practise for their first flight, and when the parents returned and found the larger eaglet gone they imagined that she had flown, and thought that the smaller eaglet was also ready to fly. They therefore proceeded gradually to starve him. No food was brought to the eyrie after 11 July, and that last week in the eyrie must have been a time of extreme discomfort, even torture, for the unfortunate eaglet. All moisture assimilated by the young eagle in the nest must come from flesh it eats and as the weather remained hot and dry the eaglet must have suffered severely from thirst. The midsummer sun beat down daily upon him and he was latterly a pitiable object.

On 8 July the remains of a rabbit, brought the previous day, and an unplucked cock grouse were in the nest. The following afternoon the eaglet ate most of the grouse except some of the intestines. The rectum or large intestine he devoured at the end of the meal. He found the grouse's gizzard difficult to hold with his feet but when he succeeded in gripping it he wolfed it with relish. The eyrie had become evil-smelling, for the parent eagles no longer troubled to remove the carcases.

On 10 July, two half-plucked ptarmigan lay in the eyrie. That morning the eaglet slept until 10-45 a.m. when a wren

There are several eyries in this old Scots pine. This tree had been in use for at least fifty years to the author's knowledge. *(Seton Gordon)*

singing near the eyrie aroused him. Twice the parent eagle flew high over the eyrie; the eaglet followed the flight of the bird intently, calling loudly, and when his cries produced no response he leaped with outspread wings upon one of the ptarmigan and ate the carcase ravenously. This done, he made sudden, fierce snatches at the dried-up remnants of the roe-deer fawns, shooting out his talons with a wild, angry look. A course of strenuous wing-excercises followed. In the early afternoon he slept or played with sticks in the eyrie; in the late afternoon wing-exercises, jumping, and snatching were noted by the observer in the hide.

On 11 July, a brilliant summer day, one small rabbit was in the eyrie; when this had been eaten the cupboard was indeed bare and for the next five days he fasted. That afternoon he played with the living fir branches which the wind swayed; as they moved backwards and forwards, almost touching the eyrie, the eaglet attempted to catch them in his bill and occasionally succeeded. That afternoon on visiting an unoccupied eyrie in the neighbourhood I found near it a casting three inches long and five inches in circumference.

No food was in the eyrie on 13 July. The eaglet was ravenous. He attempted, and failed, to swallow the dried-up remains of the rabbit, and later carried about the eyrie the still more desiccated carcase of one of the roe-deer calves. He spent most of his time in searching the heavens for his undutiful parents, who had now no further interest in him. He was tormented by sand-flies, which bit his eyes. On 15 July he was still there, famished and miserable: when we arrived at the eyrie on the early morning of 16 July he had gone. Subsequently we saw neither of the eaglets; they no doubt found shelter in the broad zone of firs, and would have been extremely difficult to locate once they moved away from the vicinity of the eyrie.

The larger eaglet was approximately sixty-seven days old

when it fell from the eyrie; the smaller seventy-six days old when the first flight was made.

Most golden eagles' eyries in Scotland are known, but this nest, situated as it was in a thick forest zone, had escaped detection. We found it by accident. It was an April day of unusual warmth and we were walking beneath the forest when an eagle sailing high above the trees in the warm sunshine suddenly went into a dive and disappeared into the thickest part of the firs. It was a steep climb to where she had disappeared, and the place was difficult to mark, but we had the satisfaction of seeing the eagle rise from her nest. She had felt it safe to leave her eggs on that unusually warm afternoon, and we had been fortunate enough to see her return to them.

Since they were nesting in an old forest of Scots firs, this pair of golden eagles brought to the eyrie rather different prey to the food carried in by the pair described in the next chapter. They evidently hunted both in woodlands and in open country.

Red squirrel as prey is, I think, unusual in Scotland, but not in Switzerland, or in Estonia. This pair of eagles were not tidy at the nest like the pair in the next chapter, and allowed the eyrie to become filthy. The nesting materials brought by them during the fledgeing period consisted of fir branches and an occasional spray of heather, whereas the eagles described in the next chapter brought growing branches of mountain ash, dead sticks of considerable thickness, and many pieces of heather.

Both pairs had certain habits in common. It was exceptional for the male to brood or feed the eaglets, and it was exceptional for both parents to stand on the eyrie at the same time.

The pair of eagles of the old fir must, themselves or their ancestors, have nested in the tree for many years. The eyrie then in use must, from its depth, have been an old one, but it was the successor of that lying beneath the tree, a nest so old that even the large branches of the foundation had disintegrated into dust. The layer of green-needled fir branches woven into the crown of the eyrie before the laying of the eggs followed the common pattern of forest-nesting golden eagles. The extreme bullying of one eaglet by the other also followed a common pattern, and, as usual, no attacks were made after the eaglets became feathered.

A point worthy of notice was the fact that the eaglets were not immune from the attacks of biting flies, and suffered extreme discomfort from them.

CHAPTER X

A Rock Eyrie

MY WIFE and I have taken watch and watch about at five golden eagles' eyries from "hides." Four of these eyries were rock eyries, the other was the tree eyrie described in the last chapter. At one of the rock nesting sites we made observations during several seasons, and our total watching hours exceeded 500.

The rock at which we made observations during five seasons held two eyries, built at no great height above the ground, in a glen where there was only one house—the stalker's.

During the first season only did the eagles occupy the upper eyrie. Here the eaglets were already large before we made a hide and began observations. The following four seasons we watched at the lower eyrie. Both eyries are only 700 feet above sea level, but spring is late in the glen, and one receives the impression of a much greater height.

It was 4 July when the first watch was taken at the upper eyrie. The times given are all GMT but as the eyrie was in 4 degrees 50 minutes west longitude the actual sun's time is about ten minutes earlier. The two eaglets were then well feathered. That season was a very late one, and the rowan tree beside the eyrie was only now in blossom. At 11 o'clock the male eagle arrived with a grouse. He was a light-plumaged bird; his plumage was bleached, and the head so light that it was almost cream-coloured. He threw down the grouse with an impetuous gesture and one of the eaglets seized it and carried it off to a rocky "overhang" near the eyrie. An hour later a second grouse was brought, but neither eaglet showed much interest in the prey.

Near the nest a wren was in song, and I recalled the Celtic legend, that wren and golden eagle contended for the Kingship of Birds, which the wren by a subterfuge gained.

In the early afternoon the sky darkened, thunder pealed. and rain fell in torrents. The hide, excellently built by the stalker though it was, ran with water: in a steady stream it poured down my neck and into my boots: I sat in a miniature river. Thunder rattled overhead and lightning flickered; a cold, damp wind blew through the hide. The eaglets, alarmed and bedraggled, stared moodily at the warring elements. My peep-hole gave me little view, but as the rain eased slightly I looked out of the back of the hide, just at the right moment, to see a memorable and awesome sight. When I had crossed the river that morning, a mere trickle of water flowed down its channel, and it was possible to cross almost anywhere dry-shod. Even as I looked from my eyrie, a wall of water, turgid and menacing, roared down the river-bed, and in a few seconds a shallow, meandering stream was transformed into a raging torrent. When I had entered the hide that hot July morning a great herd of deer were grazing on the slopes of the hill beyond the river. As, soaked to the skin, I emerged when the storm spent itself, the deer had gone, or were invisible in the gloom, and the thunder of the water filled the strath. With difficulty I forded the river, being several times almost swept off my feet.

Next morning at 8-40 another grouse was brought. One of the eaglets from its retreat a few yards from the eyrie ran to the grouse, seized it, and hurried back to its lair. Its behaviour reminded me of a spider when it sees a fly enter its web. The adult golden eagle has a striking habit of half-opening and then re-folding each wing separately; during my watch both eaglets did this more than once. These eaglets lived in harmony, and sometimes played together. On one occasion the larger, presumably female eaglet stepped down to the eyrie, where her brother was lying, and gently tweaked the feathers of his tail. He responded by nibbling at her toes. At 2-10 the parent eagle brought a rabbit. The smaller eaglet immediately covered it with his wings, and practised pouncing exercises on the carcase. In his excitement he had moved the rabbit a little way, and just as he leaped with it, wings outspread, into the eyrie, the male eagle arrived with a grouse, alighting actually on the eaglet's back and almost knocking the youngster over. The eaglet, in the midst of plenty, could not make up his mind which to eat first—the rabbit or the grouse—and rushed excitedly from one to the other.

On this day the mother eagle brought a grouse and a rabbit, and the father eagle brought a grouse. The bringing of prey by the female bird should be emphasised, as in subsequent seasons at this eyrie, and at the tree eyrie, it was the male that did all the hunting.

On the following day my wife during her watch recorded that the eagle's neighbours in this glen were wheatear, wren, meadow pipit and snipe. All these were heard from the hide. Below the eyrie, near the river, were many sandpipers and golden plover, and a few dippers.

On 7 July the male brought a large black vole to the eyrie. My wife, whose watch it was, recorded that the smaller eaglet shrieked with joy over this tit-bit, and in three minutes had eaten it—not a trace was left. Later the mother eagle brought the hinder end of a rabbit, and the watcher records in her diary "she is a light FAWN colour all over."

A curious "yapping" cry that afternoon intrigued both my wife and the eaglets, and my wife from the peep-hole in her hide saw a red deer hind, followed by her calf, trotting along

Six weeks old eaglet. (*Lea MacNally*)

the hillside close under the eyrie and then up the hill beyond it. On this day the eaglets slept a good deal, their heads tucked beneath their wings in orthodox avian fashion and not, as we were to discover the next season, in the position in which the mother eagle sometimes sleeps on the nest. That day, while my wife kept watch, I climbed the small hill behind the eyrie. The air was clear, and although July was already a week old. I could see, across many intervening miles of hill and moor, the Cairngorm mountain range rising on the horizon. The great snowfield near the summit of Cairngorm was still unbroken. That snowfield is one of the few in Scotland having a name. It is Cuithe Crom, Bent or Crooked Snow Wreath, and in clear weather may be seen from a distance of almost 100 miles.

Next year, we had word from the stalker that the eagles had repaired and laid in the eyrie (the alternative site) rather lower down the rock face. He said, he had already made the foundations of a hide. We had told him that any hide that was made should be constructed slowly, in order that the birds might have time to become used to it, and on 20 May we arrived at the lodge. Early the following morning we started for the eagle's rock, accompanied by our friend the stalker, and cautiously approached the nesting ledge. The hide was perfectly camouflaged—so much so that I should have unwittingly put my foot through the roof had not the stalker uttered a warning shout. The sides of the hide were built of turfs, with a thatching of heather; the top, of turfs laid upon boards. The door at the back was of wire netting, with heather drawn through the meshes. In the front of the hide a small recess had been fashioned for the camera and, to the left of it, a small peep-hole. That hide was indeed a masterpiece and, as we were to find, the eagles had no fear of it. On our way up to the eyrie, we had heard from the stalker how one of the eagles early that spring had coursed a mountain hare. There was no snow on the ground, and the hare, in her white winter fur, was conspicuous. The eagle swooped down on the hare, lifted it, dropped it again, and the hare, still unhurt, ran on at her best speed. Again the eagle playfully picked up the hare, and again dropped her. This time the terrified hare doubled back, and each time the eagle stooped, she quickly turned. Finally she ran between two large stones, where she remained without visible movement. The mystified eagle flew low, backwards and forwards, and, apparently failing to sight her, gave up the search and flew away.

That year spring was late. As we walked up the glen, golden plover were still in flocks near the small river. The sweet, wild notes of a ring-ouzel came from a rocky slope not far from the eagles' eyrie. When the female eagle left her nest she was mobbed by a lapwing, which was apparently a visitor to the glen and was not nesting here.

We climbed to the rock, and found in the eyrie one eaglet, about a fortnight old. I took the first watch, the camera in position and the lens well-shaded in the recess in the front of the hide. I had not been left long before I watched the eaglet fall asleep, its downy white head laid comically on a tuft of wood-rush as a pillow. After sleeping for half an hour the eaglet awoke, flapped its small stumpy down-clad wings, then preened its down.

At 9-30 in the morning (G.M.T.) the female eagle came in. She was magnificent in bright sunshine as she stood only twelve feet from me, entirely at her ease. She fed the eaglet on the carcase of a red grouse lying in the eyrie. Her behaviour then became almost human, for she arranged tiny heather twigs over the eaglet, working very gently and carefully; then stepped back to admire the effect. At 11 a.m. she brooded the eaglet for an hour, flying away at noon and returning with her mate, who carried a heather plant.

A Rock Eyrie

On 22 May we made an early start, reaching the eyrie at 5-30 a.m. G.M.T. I left my wife in the hide at 5-40. The wind was then bitterly cold. Half an hour later the eagle arrived and brooded the eaglet, which had been calling softly. The mother eagle was drowsy; she sat low and kept closing her eyes. At 9 a.m. I took the next watch. When the eagle returned she fed herself and the eaglet on one of the grouse in the nest, then seized a second grouse and flew off with it in her *bill*. Almost at once, she returned. I watched her, like a great aeroplane, approaching the eyrie (and the hide) at the same level, her broad wings held motionless and rigid—a magnificent sight. During the last seconds, I realised that she was returning with the grouse, this time held *in one foot*.

On 25 May, there was nothing of special interest to record, except that the mother eagle took a long time in arranging to her satisfaction fresh green plants of great wood-rush, brought that day.

26 May was a beautiful morning, the air scented with young hill growth. When I entered the hide I saw that there were small flower-buds on the rowan tree which supported the nest. In the eyrie lay the remains of a rabbit and a grouse. A willow-warbler arrived at the rowan, and sang vigorously, but a meadow-pipit, apparently considering the tree part of his territory, drove the stranger away. At 8 a.m. the mother eagle arrived carrying a heather branch; almost at once she flew off, carrying in her bill the remains of one of the grouse. When she returned the second time, the sunlight was brilliant and she looked magnificent as she alighted and stood in a stately attitude. Her eyes gleamed, and the feathers of her neck were almost white in the strong light. For a time she continued to stand rigidly, as though fashioned of bronze.

On 27 May, we began a 30 hour continuous watch at the eyrie. I took the first watch, beginning at 6 a.m. and lasting

157

for seven hours. The stalker relieved me at 1 p.m., remaining in the hide until 9 p.m. My wife then began an all-night watch in the hide, from 9 p.m. until 7-15 a.m. I then took over, remaining until noon. I imagine that this is the longest continuous watch ever kept at a golden eagle's eyrie, and it may be of interest to record the notes taken during the watches.

As we approached the eyrie in the early morning one of the eagles flew over, pursued by a flock of common gulls: like white midgets they darted angrily at her but she did not heed them. She had probably trespassed over their territory, a hill loch near. This morning there was no food in the eyrie and the eaglet slept until 7 a.m. when the mother eagle brought in a heather. branch. Thirty seconds later, the male also came in, throwing down the hind-quarters of a hare as he alighted. In the rowan tree a ring-ouzel serenaded the eaglet, and me, with his long song notes, repeated many times. Both eagles by then had left the eyrie, but a little later the female arrived and fed the eaglet, which we had now christened Francis, from its fancied resemblance to a human neighbour in Skye, on the hare. Francis loved it, and she gave him quite large pieces. She often rooted in the eyrie, picking up and swallowing what she found, and once fell over Francis ! A little later she made a wonderful picture as, opening her great wings, she stood protectingly over the eaglet. Drops of water, glistening in sunshine, dripped on to the wing nearer to the rock, from the wing to the tail, and from the tail to the ground. On three occasions she very, very gently massaged the downy head of the eaglet with her terrible bill.

During the afternoon watch, taken by the stalker, the male eagle came in with a grouse, plucked and partly eaten, and a little later the female, who had come in, tried to coax Francis to eat some of it, but he refused the small tit-bits she offered.

At 9 p.m. when my wife entered the hide for the all-night

158

vigil, the weather was mild and the sky clouded. The cuckoo had just arrived in the glen, and on her walk up to the eyrie my wife heard its soft notes for the first time. The ring-ouzel was also in song. Francis was asleep, nor did he waken when the stalker left the hide and my wife commenced her watch. At 9-33 p.m. the mother eagle came in very quietly. She stood with wee Francis between her legs, her feathers just touching him, on the leeward side of him. She fondled him with her bill, then went to sleep, standing thus over him, but not actually brooding. At 9-42 p.m., perhaps aroused by the calling of a snipe, she awoke and preened herself. At 9-45 p.m. she fell asleep, this time with her head beneath her wing. All through the night hours golden plover were calling, or were in song-flight. They were heard at 10-4 p.m., 11-40 p.m. and at 1-15 a.m. They therefore appear to have no definite roosting hour during the summer night. Snipe were also calling throughout the night. At 1-35 a.m. red grouse began to call; at 2-15 a meadow-pipit was in song, and a wren sang at 2-55. At 2-45 a.m. the mother eagle and Francis awoke. She preened her feathers, then fondled Francis. The sky in the north east was now flushed with pink and the small birds were in full song, but the mother eagle went to sleep once more. At 3-10, an incident of considerable interest was recorded by the watcher. Two miles down the glen, a blackbird lived near the stalker's house. Perhaps encouraged by the fine morning, this blackbird (for it was the only one in the glen) arrived at the rowan tree, and began to sing. His song awoke the eagle. She looked toward him, her head on one side, and listened just like a person trying a gramophone record. The local meadow-pipit (I had the previous day found its nest at the foot of the rock) arrived then with food in its bill for the family and furiously attacked the blackbird. Despite this un-provoked aggression, the blackbird attempted to continue his song, although the meadow pipit fluttered over him and endeavoured to push him off his perch. It took five minutes for the meadow pipit to drive the musical blackbird from the tree. What a subject this would have been for a bird artist— the golden eagle, sheltering her young, watching with mild interest the furious attacks of the meadow-pipit on the blackbird less than six feet from her eyrie ! At 3-30 the dawn chorus was over, but ten minutes after the departure of the blackbird visitor the local ring-ouzel arrived and sang in the rowan. The meadow-pipit, acting the part of sentry on duty, permitted him to sing unmolested, recognising in him a firm resident of this part of the glen. At 3-27 a.m. an early bumble-bee visited the rowan tree, although the flowers would not open for some weeks. Five o'clock in the morning came, and now the small birds, having breakfasted, again saluted the young day in song. The mother eagle and Francis, having sunk into slumber after the routing of the blackbird, continued to sleep until 5-35, when the mother awoke, looked up the glen, and took wing. Francis, cold and hungry, called miserably. Without moving, the female eagle had stood in the same position for eight hours, sheltering Francis from the cold of the night but not actually brooding him.

When I arrived at the rock at 7-15 a.m. I found my wife so stiff after her ten hour watch through the night that I had to help her out of the hide. She told me that she had been extremely cold, and had deeply sympathised with the eaglet's plaintive appeals to his mother to cover him up.

During the morning watch, which I then took, the mother eagle arrived with a small branch of rowan in leaf. This she carefully laid on the back of her child, and surveyed the effect with a pleased look. She evidently believed in decorating the nursery—and its inmate! This was the only day on which we saw human life (except ourselves) in this lonely glen. From the hide I watched two men driving several cows and a pony slowly along the old track beside the river. Later I heard that their destination was Loch Eriboll, many miles distant. The mother eagle left the eyrie as the travellers passed, but soon returned, carrying a branch of heather. She fed Francis on a hare which lay in the eyrie; he was reluctant to be fed, until he saw with alarm that his mother was swallowing most of the carcase herself! Donald Mackay the stalker had watched from the hide the previous day from 3-30 p.m. until 9 p.m.; my wife had then watched throughout the night and early morning, and all that time the eaglet had not been fed. It was surprising therefore that after a fast of over 16 hours Francis had not more appetite.

Our last watch of this series was on 31 May. That morning the father eagle arrived with a green-leaved rowan branch. He later seized the fresh carcase of a grouse which lay in the eyrie and flew off with it. My wife noted that he was more golden on the under-parts and thighs than his mate, who came in shortly afterwards, carrying what seemed to be the carcase of the same grouse. We noticed that the male was more tightly-feathered than the female, and this seems to be the general rule. As the mother fed Francis he called all the time softly, and called louder when a larger piece than usual was offered him. His mother later swallowed entire one of the grouse's legs then, carrying in her bill the gory neck of the grouse, she left the eyrie. This pair of eagles were tidy birds.

She in particular was a good housewife. All carcases and bones of prey were removed from the eyrie. Their only child, Francis, was fed approximately every five hours, but had no regular mealtimes, as witness his long fast during our 30 hours' watch. Each day the parent eagles brought to the eyrie fresh branches or twigs of rowan, or pieces of heather, and also their favourite plant, the great wood-rush.

That year we returned to the eyrie on 22 June, and found a

great change in Francis, who was by now well-feathered and almost grown up. When I entered the hide at 10 a.m. that morning a north west gale was blowing. The wind moaned through the small rowan tree, breaking off the young leaves. The blossom was not yet out, although the flower buds had shown more than three weeks before.

The young eagle spread its tail wide in the sun, and I could count the 12 feathers or rectrices. The parent eagles were much less interested in the eaglet than they had been three weeks before, and indeed seemed to be rather bored by it. The male came in once that morning, bringing a small indistinguishable animal; as usual he moved his head quickly from side to side during his short stay at the eyrie. That day when I was near the hide I saw one of the eagles stoop at a common gull. The gull was flying down the glen, and the eagle planed at it at tremendous speed. The gull was terrified, but the eagle was playing and did not attack. The gull climbed in circles to a great height, driving its wings hard; when last I saw it, the fugitive was still climbing.

During our four days' watch at this time we recorded nothing of special interest. That season we watched in all 88 hours from the hide.

The following season the same eyrie was occupied, and we took our first watch in the hide on 8 May. There was again only one eaglet and it was about a week old. We christened it Francis II. There was also one addled egg in the nest. Four red grouse lay in the eyrie. There was a snowstorm that day, and no watches were taken.

9 May was a morning of hard frost, dull and November-like in character. At 6-30 a.m. I took the first watch. The eaglet was hatched approximately seven days earlier than the previous year's bird. In half an hour the mother eagle returned to the nest and rearranged the heather surrounding the eaglet to her

A rare photograph of a male feeding its eaglet.   (*Seton Gordon*)

A Rock Eyrie

liking. She then brooded Francis II as snow began to fall. Darkness settled over the glen, and over the eyrie. Snow began to lie on the eagle's back and on her gold head. The flakes eddied and whirled, and inside the hide a desperately cold air stream played upon me, through the peephole and through the opening for the camera. At eight o'clock the snow lessened, and the eagle rose to her feet. Walking to one of the grouse carcases, she tore from it a small morsel of flesh, advancing one step, and very carefully and gently offering the food to Francis II. She then retreated a step, tore off another morsel, and advanced as before. Francis watched her with attention. His breakfast over, he was brooded once more. The mother eagle on these occasions is most careful to close her great claws before standing over the eaglet to brood, for she realises their danger to a small downy chick. The snow fell softly; a wren sang from the rowan tree.

An hour later the snow ceased and the sun shone. The mother eagle rose from her brooding, preened herself, and gave Francis a second meal. This done, she picked up the grouse carcase and stood motionless, holding it in her bill, then flew up the glen carrying the carcase with her. The following morning my wife took the watch. In the eyrie was part of a young hare. The eagle spent some time that morning placing heather around, and over the eaglet. A greenshank in the glen uttered repeatedly his deep-toned whistle, and the eagle listened as though this to her was an unusual call. For some time she slept, her head sunk on her breast, her bill almost resting on the eyrie.

The following morning I entered the hide at six o'clock. There was one fresh grouse in the eyrie. Five minutes after my two companions had left me a meadow-pipit alighted on the eyrie. The bird seemed tiny, standing on that huge nest. Its mate joined it, and they flew off. They were perhaps the same pair which had nested below the rock the previous season.

The Golden Eagle: King of Birds

In twenty minutes the mother eagle arrived and brooded the eaglet. She had brooded him for 50 minutes when the male arrived. The sun now shone brightly, and he stood motionless, a glorious bird. He brought in a grouse, and at once left. The mother eagle, brooding Francis II, seemed surprised at the shortness of his visit, and half rose in alarm. She fed the eaglet on the grouse, then flew from the nest. Five minutes later the male came in, and his attempts to feed the eaglet were ludicrous —so like a father! Earlier that day his wife had fed Francis II with minute portions of grouse, chiefly tit-bits from the liver, and now he picked up the entire grouse, which was larger than the eaglet, and offered it! The response of Francis was naturally not what his father had expected—or hoped. He therefore replaced the grouse in the eyrie, again picked it up, and a second time held it out to the tiny eaglet. The response was no better than before. The father eagle again laid down the grouse. You could almost hear him saying to himself, "What ails the child?" Again a third, and a fourth time, he proffered the grouse and then, perhaps fortunately, his mate arrived at the eyrie.

She brought heather with her, and at once busied herself arranging it to her liking. This morning I chronicled a noteworthy occurrence—the male brooding the eaglet. He sat for 15 minutes, during the absence of his mate. His smaller size was at once apparent, and his expression was different—nor was he so exceedingly gentle in his brooding of the eaglet as his mate. His eyes were noticeably larger.

The following day was dark and misty, but 13 May was mild and sunny and at 6-25 a.m. G.M.T. I left my wife in the hide to take a watch. The only prey in the eyrie was a baby rabbit. At 7-05 the male eagle alighted at the eyrie, and in her notes my wife recorded that his movements were quicker, and his eyes, besides being larger, seemed redder than those of his mate. He hastily swallowed a grouse's leg for breakfast, and watched the female's arrival, leaving immediately she alighted at the eyrie. At 8-30 the male returned and brooded the eaglet for 15 minutes, when his mate flew in with a large spray of heather. That morning when we arrived at the eyrie for my wife's watch, I found that each time I bent over Francis II and whistled to him, he replied at once in baby language. The stalker and I climbed to a hill loch near, and watched a pair of black-throated divers swimming in the peaty water, but not apparently nesting. The sun was warm, and the air clear, but a thunder cloud descended on the high hill near us, and from it came, with awe-inspiring effect, a vivid lightning flash. Rain soon fell in torrents, and there was no more watch-keeping that day. On 14 May an all-day watch in the hide produced nothing of especial interest.

When we reached the eyrie on 15 May the eaglet for the first time was outside the cup of the nest, and was sleeping so soundly on the rim of the cup that when I lifted a wing he did not awake.

Both eagles were perched on the rock and were unceasingly mobbed by a pair of common gulls. At 8-30 Francis II had his hair brushed—or the equivalent in the golden eagle world. The mother eagle was still occasionally brooding the addled egg and listening intently for any sound of life in it. As she now took a spell of brooding on it, still hoping that a second eaglet might even now arrive in the world, she bent her golden head towards Francis and, beginning at the back of his small downy head, very gently massaged his head and neck with her strong bill. The satisfied expression on the eaglet's face during this operation I was able to record on the camera (see Plate 9b, p. 119). He was a spoilt only child, and, resenting being tidied up, aimed peevish pecks at his mother. Later the parent eagle brooded the addled egg in several different positions, for the day was fine, and the eaglet did not need her attention. From my peep-hole I could see distant Clibreck, a majestic snow-covered cone: behind the summit of that hill towered a great thunder cloud, primrose-tinted and wonderful. As I crossed the moor that day I saw a cock red grouse carrying a bill-ful of grass—an unusual sight.

16 May was a day of rain, and the next morning there were many large earthworms in the eagle's eyrie. It is possible that when the eagle as she brooded rummaged with her bill in the eyrie (this she did frequently) she was searching for earthworms. On this day we did not take a watch in the hide, but observed the dunlin which were courting on the heathery tussocks near the hill loch. 18 May was sunny. After accompanying my wife to the hide and leaving her to take the morning watch, I returned to the lodge. The light was so good that from the house I could see, through my stalking glass, the eagle perched on the rock. Even as I watched, she took wing and sailed into the eyrie, where I could see her moving about—this at a distance of nearly two miles.

My wife recorded that the male eagle that morning brought a grouse, and attempted to feed the eaglet on small pieces of its entrails. His mate would certainly not have approved of this, and when Francis II refused to take the proffered food, the father left in disgust. The mother eagle when she arrived looked long and lovingly at her child, but would not feed him, although he called lustily for attention.

19 May was the last day of our watch that season. When we reached the eyrie at 6-20 a robin and a cock stonechat were near the nest; the robin, especially, it was unexpected to see. Francis II was growing fast. His eyes were dark and beady and he now appeared to have pencilled eyebrows. For the first two and a half hours of my watch nothing happened, then the mother eagle flew in with heather, which she laid carefully on Francis. Reproachful and hungry, Francis II pecked hard at her, fast and often, until she fed him on a rabbit. He was now

able to take quite large pieces, and was much quicker in swallowing, and more "on the spot." The mother now stood over him, using one wing as a parasol to shield him from the sun. I have seen no bird show the same love and affection for her young as the fierce golden eagle; the change in her stern expression to mother love as she looked at him was very remarkable.

The following season no observations were made, but two years later I was in the same hide. It was so firmly constructed that it had stood up to the winter storms of rain and snow. The narrowest escape it had was one day when a stag was shot, and fell over the rock. The stalker knew that the stag had fallen very close to the hide, and was therefore relieved to see, when he looked over the rock, that the deer in its fall had just missed the shelter.

It was 3 May when we arrived at the glen that year. An April blizzard, almost unprecedented in its severity, had swept the district and even the stalker, familiar with the ground as he was, had more difficulty than he cared to relate in reaching home on the afternoon when the snowstorm was at its height. Many red deer were smothered by the drifting snow, which swept over them as they slept and suffocated them. One hind had been overwhelmed in soft ground. Her fore feet were sunk deep in the moss, showing that she had desperately tried to force herself through the great weight of snow which held her fast until death came to her release. On the morning of 4 May, Francis III was chipping the egg and calling feebly. The second egg this year again did not hatch, and we found later that it was addled. The next morning we found that Francis III was hatched, and the eggshells had gone. There was one grouse, half-eaten, in the eyrie. The male eagle arrived shortly afterwards. His head was bleached almost white. He brooded the eaglet for an hour, and when his mate arrived, I recognised her at once after two years. Her gentle expression contrasted with his wild look. She stood quietly behind her mate as he brooded the tiny eaglet; in her eyes was a look of mother love. I photographed the pair—the male brooding, the female listening intently to Francis III, who continually cheeped beneath the covering of warm feathers. Then she walked slowly forward, the male rose and sprang into the air, and she settled down to brood the eaglet. At 12-30 she rose and fed Francis who, less than a day old, refused any morsel of grouse that was not very small and tender. At 1-20 the male dropped from the heavens like a thunderbolt, but swept past the eyrie without alighting.

Two days later there were two red grouse in the eyrie. Before entering the hide we covered Francis III with heather to keep him warm, and when the mother bird arrived she carefully removed the heather, then settled down to brood Francis and the addled egg. She later fed herself on the grouse, swallowing a leg with a certain discomfort. Francis was given minute helpings.

On 9 May a hen grouse, carefully cleaned and plucked, lay in the eyrie. When the mother eagle arrived she often fondled the eaglet's head. Francis III wished to sleep, and this display of affection annoyed him. The day was warm, and she did not all the time brood him: she stood protectingly over him and he blissfully slept, his head pillowed on the eyrie, his small body on its side. He was just five days old.

Next year May was almost as wintry as April had been the previous season. For the first time, both the eagle's eggs had hatched, and when we arrived at the eyrie on 9 May, the eaglets were less than a week old. They celebrated our arrival by a boxing bout, hammering at one another with their small bills with surprising ferocity. In the eyrie were the hindquarters of a stoat: it had a goat-like smell. My wife that morning took a watch, and I went on to the hill loch, above which flew three drake goosanders, very white, very eager, very fast, in single line away from the loch, where they had perhaps had their breakfast of trout. A number of pairs of widgeon were on the loch, and greenshanks stood on its shores, or in the shallows, thigh-deep. The weather soon changed, and by mid-May winter had returned to the glen. At 6-30 on the morning of 16 May the ground was hard-frozen, and snow wreaths were forming outside the stalker's house. The snow continued to fall until afternoon, when the landscape might have been that of a January day. At nine o'clock in the evening we might have been beyond the Arctic Circle. There was little lessening in the daylight: snowy wastes stretched as far as the eye could see. Wheatears stood cowering in the culverts: in the snow golden plover were asleep, patiently awaiting better weather. A curlew strode restlessly across the frozen, snow-covered marsh near the river; a second curlew sheltered behind the peat stack at the lodge. Only the dipper, searching the river bed for food for its feathered young, was cheery. The snow lay so deep and soft that golden plover could not walk over it without fluttering their wings to reduce their weight and keep themselves partly air-borne. There were now three feet of snow on the Hill of Heroes, and the evening sun shone on that hill with Polar effect—there was no single dark speck upon it. Needless to say, we did not disturb the eagles that day.

The following morning at six o'clock the snow was drifting furiously. 17 May—little more than a month until the Longest Day! That morning we climbed to the eagles' eyrie. Icicles hung from the inside of the hide; larger icicles hung from the rock. We found Hitler and Mussolini (for so we had named the eaglets) damp and miserable. In the eyrie were six baby rabbits, two baby hares, the hind-legs of an adult blue hare, and a red grouse. I offered Hitler a piece of rabbit. He took it readily, then

169

went to sleep with his head beneath Mussolini. That year we had no opportunity of returning to the eyrie, but Hitler and Mussolini both lived to make their first flight.

I have mentioned that the parent eagles at this eyrie were in the habit of leaving the district after their young were on the wing before the opening of the grouse shooting on 12 August. In this respect they behaved quite differently from the pair I have described in Chapters XI, XII and XIII.

Two years after the end of our observations the parents of Hitler and Mussolini failed to return to the eyrie. The stalker thought that one of the pair had been shot, trapped or poisoned at its autumn or winter quarters. For several years the two eyries on the rock were deserted. One winter day when the stalker was passing the old hide he heard the sound of scratching inside it. A wild cat then jumped through the hole in the front of the hide which had originally been made for the camera. The cat, which had evidently been using the hide as a winter shelter, made off across the snow and the stalker followed its tracks to rocky ground more than a mile away.

There are once more eagles nesting on the ancestral rock, and in the summer of 1952 Niall Rankin took a number of remarkable pictures of the pair (See Plates 1 (frontispiece) and 13, 14-pp.187, 194). At his suggestion we have compared them with our photographs and it is evident from the expression of the birds that they are not the pair which used to nest on the rock: they may be two of their children.

In conclusion, the pair of eagles observed by us for five seasons were typical of most pairs of Scottish golden eagles. The female eagle did most of the brooding of the young, and did most of the feeding of the eaglet. The male did most, or perhaps all, of the hunting. For the first week, the eaglet was fed upon tiny morsels, usually of red grouse liver, or tender bits of grouse flesh. After ten days or a fortnight any prey was given, but no bones were fed the eaglet until, at the age of six weeks or thereabouts, it could tear up food for itself.

This pair of golden eagles were wary, and left the eyrie when they saw us approaching up the glen and when we were at least a mile away. They were exceptionally tidy birds, and kept their eyrie very clean. Both birds often brought nesting and decorating material to the eyrie after the young were hatched, and even feathered. This material was invariably carried in the beak. The prey, even if small, was brought held in the talons of one foot. Carcases, consisting mostly of bones and legs, were usually carried away in the bill. The eaglet was always carefully protected from hot sunshine up to the time of feathering. It seemed to be purposely hardened to cold and to rain.

Both parent eagles were fairly often at the eyrie together, but never stayed long. This reluctance to remain together at the eyrie did not extend to the rock above it, where they might be seen perched close together for long intervals.

CHAPTER XI

Eight Years' Observations
at a Golden Eagle's Eyrie : Part I

DURING the past eight years I have watched and recorded the home life of a pair of golden eagles. Many hours of watching during frost and snow, bitter winter gales and days of storms of stinging hail have been off-set by hours of brilliant sunshine and warmth. I have expended much energy in reaching my observation post, and during the eight years I calculate I have walked upwards of 1,500 miles, during almost all of them accompanied by my collie Dugie, who passed to his rest as these chapters were being written.

It was in the summer of 1942 that the eagles were first seen. They had not as yet taken over a territory, but were watched, by different observers, at different parts of a hill range. The golden eagle is usually a silent bird, and these youngsters became celebrated because, when they played in the air like children (as indeed they were) they called repeatedly and excitedly, advertising their presence by shrill yelps and barks. That first summer and early autumn they moved from cliff to cliff.

In the early spring of 1943 they took up their quarters on a high cliff which faces north. They were still immature birds, showing large white areas on the tail, and were not ready to produce a family, but they were nevertheless paired, and had chosen their nesting territory. There was an old eyrie on the rock: this they gradually repaired, taking more than one season, but did not actually lay in it.

They were later, in adult life, to become devoted to each other, and ideal parents.

These eagles were almost certainly the children of a pair which nested on a neighbouring hill for 20 years. As eaglets in their large eyrie in a recess in the cliff they may have watched fox cubs play on the rocky ground beneath. From their early days they were familiar with the ravens which nested on a neighbouring cliff, and which furiously attacked the parent eagles when they crossed their territory. They heard the calling of the cuckoo, and the song of the ring-ouzel, and may have watched with interest the comings and goings of industrious starlings which were feeding their families in crannies of the rock near the eyrie.

Golden eagle and fox, cuckoo, ring-ouzel and starling, lived together in harmony.

When these young eagles did decide to make their home on the high cliff above the dark loch which is the reputed home of the "each uisge" or water-horse, they lived here for three years before they nested. They showed their inexperience by alighting at times on the low ground, which they later flew over always at a height. During these three years they were often in company, but it was not apparently until the spring of 1946 that they thought of nesting, and I therefore begin to count my eight years' watching from 1946. That spring, one soft afternoon of sunshine and unusual warmth, I was sitting near the loch when I saw one of the eagles attempting to tear grass from a ledge of the cliff. When the eagle took wing it dropped what it carried, evidently thinking that the small amount of grass it had torn out was not worth transporting as nesting material. The eagle returned, and this time seized a large stick. In the field of my stalking glass I followed the line of flight, and had the satisfaction of seeing the great bird alight on the nest. Later, a second eyrie was made, and the eagles have used the two eyries regularly in alternate years. The eagles rightly considered their eyries secure on that great cliff. For golden eagles, they were unusually tame, and soon became used to the shepherd and his dogs. When I reached the loch with Dugie the collie they associated us with the shepherd, and were never alarmed by us.

Without a stalking telescope, the distance would have been too great for accurate observations, but the telescope, one of 26 magnifications, brought the eagles and their eyrie sufficiently near to enable me to make accurate observations during eight seasons. I was also sufficiently far from the rock to observe the birds without causing them uneasiness.

During those eight seasons I have got to know the eagles well, and may even call them old friends: their devotion for one another has been pleasant to watch and record. One day early in my observations I recall, when the sky was blue except for a single white cumulus cloud at the zenith. Stillness and silence prevailed, then the husky, far-carrying notes of a raven were heard. After a time he was seen, a black speck perhaps 2,000 feet above the loch, in hot pursuit of a golden eagle. The eagle was descending from a still greater altitude, and the raven was forced to drive his wings at their hardest in order to keep in touch. The eagle arrived at the cliff top, and was joined by his mate. For the next half hour I watched as fine a display of soaring and stunt diving as I have ever seen. The eagles were at least 4,000 feet above the cliff when one of them closed its wings and dropped, faster and faster, earthward. The second eagle by now had disappeared. The first eagle fell headlong at giddy speed until it had descended to an altitude of approximately 1,000 feet when it performed a sudden evolution, so quick that the eye could not follow it. The great bird now no longer dropped headlong, but feet-first, its legs outstretched as

174

though about to alight. Although I did not immediately realise it, this eagle was rushing in mock attack at its mate, which then appeared from behind a hill. The raven had by now literally been flown to a standstill, and took no further part in the aerial tourney for the next 20 minutes. The two golden eagles sailed around the cliff, then climbed again on the warm uprising air current. Without effort they reached a great height, when they darted here and there at incredible speed, evidently utilising the uprising air just below the cumulus cloud. In their flight they reminded me of a pair of swifts, and indeed at that height they appeared no larger than swifts. After a time the raven, now rested, reappeared, and one of the eagles alighted on a rocky spur, where it carefully preened itself. I saw one feather float away, and drift down over the cliff.

In early summer, when the cliff beside the eyrie is red with flowers of lychnis, yellow with rose-root, and white with scurvy-grass, and when high on the cliff the cushion pink is bright with clustered flowers; when the small rowan trees (whose dead branches the eagles use for their eyrie) scent the clear air with the perfume of their white blooms, so heavy that the branches bend with the weight, the country of this pair of golden eagles is a pleasant place. Yet in early March, when the eagles begin to brood, the scene is very different. Winter gales may still be raging, and heavy snowflakes may drift in on the north wind, covering the cliff and the shores of the loch, and making the dark tarn more grim by contrast. No sunlight reaches the loch from October until mid-March: for the best part of six months it is shadowed, even at noon, by the high cliff to the south. The eyrie itself, since it faces due north (the second eyrie, later constructed, faces north west) is always in shadow, except at mid-summer for half an hour after sunrise, and again just before sunset when the dark walls of the rock lose their austerity in that mystic light of softest pink.

The Golden Eagle: King of Birds

This pair of golden eagle, are I think, unusual in more than
one respect, but chiefly in their devotion. Nowhere have I seen
recorded the almost hourly "change-over" between male and
female, before hatching-time, and also when the eaglet is small
and downy. These "change-overs" have often cheered the
human observer during an otherwise uneventful watch.

Unusual, too, may be the choosing of the new eyrie in early
November, and the nest-building which I watched during the
short days of November and December.

Characteristic of this pair is the behaviour when the eaglet
is small, and when the brooding bird, relieved by its mate,
sets out to hunt. One might think that, on leaving the eyrie,
it would fly at once in the desired direction. On the contrary,
if the conditions are favourable for soaring, the eagle begins to
climb in spirals, as though it was care-free and in a position to
enjoy itself. Climbing higher and higher, it reaches an altitude
which will permit it to fly to its hunting ground in one long
glide.

The height to which the golden eagle soars before going into
this glide is evidently determined by the distance of the hunting
ground it has decided to travel to. When it rises to a height of
5,000 feet and more, as it sometimes does, the hunting ground
is some distance away. I have reason to believe from my own
observations that the pair of eagles I have watched fly on
occasion more than 20 miles. My own observations are con-
firmed by those of J. C. Leitch, who watched, in 1952, an eyrie
on the Mull of Kintyre, and has on occasion seen the eagle set
out over the sea toward Northern Ireland, the best part of
20 miles away, and also at times toward Islay, more than
25 miles away, although usually the eagle's hunting is done
on the Mull of Kintyre.

By first rising to the height from which a long glide to its
destination can be made, the eagle is then able to travel there

Eight week old eaglet on its lofty eyrie site. (*Lea MacNally*)

without effort, gliding through the still air, or even against a strong breeze, without a movement of its bent-back wings. It has achieved complete mastery of the air. There are exceptions to this rule. I shall long remember the departure of the male bird from the eyrie one stormy evening. On being relieved from his brooding he at once moved across the face of the cliff, down-wind, at tremendous speed. His wings were driven with great power, and in the brief moments while he remained in my field of vision he embodied the spirit of the storm.

In this pair of golden eagles the devotion of the male bird is, as I have said, remarkable. When he grandly alights on the eyrie where his mate broods, and he is anxious that she should take a rest from her brooding, he sometimes finds that she is in no mood to leave. On these occasions he remains quietly beside her, obviously talking to her in eagle language until she reluctantly rises from her brooding position, takes a few steps to the edge of the nest and throws herself into the air. As she sails out over the cliff, and sets off to hunt, or to find relaxation in soaring and diving, he escorts her a little way, then swings round and glides swiftly back to the eyrie. Now come the moments when his extreme care of the egg is seen. He walks forward gingerly to the nesting cup and, once in position, lowers himself slowly over the precious egg which takes six weeks' of brooding to hatch—through storm and calm, through rain, snow, hail and fine weather. But there are occasions when the female refuses to leave, and then the male after a time flies away, to return hopefully a little later.

It may be asked, how I am sure, at a distance, which is the male and which the female eagle ? The male, as is well-known, is the smaller bird—unmistakably smaller when they are seen together. The male golden eagle always has "tighter" plumage than the female. In this particular pair he is a much darker bird. Even in flight there are certain things which now tell me which is which. His wings, for example, are relatively longer than hers. The pair have different habits. Thus, if I see a golden eagle perched on the post which is all that remains of an old fence running along the top of the rock, I know it is the female. Here she may rest, almost motionless, for long periods. Her mate does not use the post, but perches, it would seem more comfortably, on a rocky spur, or on a grassy ledge almost at the cliff-top.

Being a devoted couple, it is natural that these eagles should keep their young with them longer than is usual with the species. Late in December I have seen father, mother, and eaglet still together, nearly five months after the latter's fledging. It seems indeed as if the eaglet remains with the parents until the first repairs to the eyrie to be used the following spring occupy the thoughts of the adult birds.

It is said that birds of prey, the golden eagle among them, drive their young from their territory when they are able to hunt for themselves, but the young bird of this pair is apparently in the habit of visiting its parents from time to time, in the same way as our sons and daughters do after they have left the parental roof. To take two instances. One afternoon in mid-April, after watching the "change-over" between male and female eagle on the eyrie, I saw an immature eagle, conspicuous by reason of the white area on the tail, soaring above the nesting cliff. This eagle rose so high that at last it entered the clouds, which I estimated to be at 6,000 feet. On another occasion—we must now go forward to February 1952—three golden eagles appeared near the nesting site. One of them, as I could see by the white areas on the wings as it spiralled, was a bird of the previous year. A strange golden eagle flying over the nesting-place in early spring would not have been tolerated, yet here were three golden eagles sailing together high above the hillside, in friendship. I have no doubt the immature bird was the child of the pair. In 1952, when some mischance overtook either the egg, or the baby eaglet, and the parents thereafter deserted the rock for some months, the eaglet reared in 1951 haunted the neighbourhood of the nesting site throughout the summer.

During the first month of the brooding, one of the "change-overs" occurs regularly around 6 p.m. G.M.T. On one occasion the relieving bird made a spectacular arrival, escorted by an irate pair of ravens. His mate flew from the eyrie to welcome him, the ravens at the last moment sheered off, and the "change-over" took place, the male eagle escorting his mate to the far end of the cliff before he returned to brood. One afternoon at the beginning of May I saw the male eagle visit his mate on the nest three times in an hour. On one of these visits he appeared, with one raven in attendance, soaring grandly against the breeze. In his talons he carried a rabbit, which he deposited in the eyrie. The brooding eagle was now sitting higher as she watched his arrival, and the eaglet had probably hatched. In thirty minutes the male returned, this time without prey. He was intercepted, in true fighter fashion, above the cliff by the pair of ravens. The three birds swung together over the precipice in a glorious tumult of speed, the eagle leading as he shot, with half-closed wings, over the abyss. He then sailed along the cliff face, legs held stiffly extended earthward; attempted to land on a crag; missed his footing; endeavoured, with wildly-flapping wings, to secure a foot-hold on the rock; failed to effect a landing; opened wide his great wings, and resumed his effortless sailing. It is not often that the golden eagle makes a bad landing, although I have seen him pitch heavily on the short grass on the top of the cliff.

On the occasion when on 24 June 1946, I flew in a Sunderland flying boat to Rockall, I passed on my flight close to the eagles' rock. It was exciting to see the eagles' home from the air, and I hoped the birds themselves would be visible, but if they were at home they did not appear; they may have been surprised and alarmed to see an aircraft the size of a Sunderland flying scarcely above the level of the cliff.

Although I have seen the eagles standing, times without number, on the top of their rock in fine sunny weather, I have seen a bird sun-bathe here on one occasion only. I have seen the sun-bathing of another family of golden eagles early in August, and also a brooding eagle leaving her eyrie in full exposure to a cold east wind, to sun-bathe on a heather-covered knoll above it. It might have been expected, therefore, that having seen two instances of sun-bathing during casual observations, I should have seen, during extended observations over eight seasons, more instances of sun-bathing than one in the pair of eagles whose home-life I now describe.

It was on an afternoon at the end of April. The eagle had alighted on the short grass immediately above the cliff. It stood there a short time, then sank to the ground, having just before spread out its great wings to their full extent. As the eagle lay there, it spread wide, with a quick movement, its tail also: the sudden spreading of the tail reminded me of the opening of a fan. With outspread wings resting on the ground and tail spread fan-wise, it remained without movement for the space of three minutes. A cloud obscured the sun, and the eagle half-closed its tail, but continued to lie on the grass with wings outspread—and then suddenly, literally out of the blue, a raven appeared and rudely stooped at the sun-bather, so that it was obliged to get on its feet and close its wings. The eagle later rose into the air, with the pestering raven still in close attendance, and both birds climbed until they had entered a cloud which hung above the rock at a height of some 4,500 feet.

The single eaglet (only one is reared by this pair) left the eyrie in the second week of July.

My observations for the year 1947 began early. On 13

January, a day of north wind, I watched the male eagle rising and then falling with closed wings as he passed high above the nesting rock. He later alighted on a pinnacle (his legs had been held stiffly towards the ground during the last 100 feet of the descent). He soon rose, to meet his mate at some distance from the rock. She sailed in, carrying a rabbit which, from the direction of her flight, she had probably captured on a promontory across a wide sea loch. If so, she must have carried her prey the best part of ten miles. I could see the red flesh of the rabbit, and the intestine hanging down like a tube. She alighted on the top of the rock but, still grasping the rabbit, almost at once took off again and flew to a high grassy slope, where she was joined by her mate. Again she rose, still with the carcase, and the two birds disappeared from view.

On 24 January, a flock of snow-buntings were feeding in the heather not far from the eagles' rock: their small white wings flashed in the winter sunlight as they rose. One of the golden eagles was standing on the rock. A pair of impudent grey crows were running round the eagle, baiting him and shouting rude remarks. The eagle kept his temper and later joined his mate in the air. After carrying out flying manoeuvres, both eagles alighted on the top of the rock and stood there, feathers touching, in the January sunshine. Thus they remained for over an hour until, just after the sun had set, first one, then the other rose and flew down to the roosting ledge before frost and darkness brooded over their cold country. That year, although the eagles left their rock during the severe weather of February, by early March the female was tearing up greater wood-rush to line her eyrie with, and at the end of the month she was brooding. On 2 April there was an interesting "Change over." The male was brooding at 5-20 p.m. G.M.T. when she arrived back at the eyrie, just an hour and five minutes after the male had relieved her. She waited patiently at the edge of the nest for him to rise, but, since he was reluctant to move, she bent down and almost touched him. Undoubtedly they held converse, and he then rose from the egg so that she might take his place. On 14 April that year I witnessed the only attack made by the eagles on a trespasser of their own species. The female eagle was brooding on the eyrie at the time, the male soaring overhead. He suddenly hurled himself earthward, and, with difficulty following him in the field of my telescope, I saw that he was in pursuit of a passing eagle. From the line of the stranger's flight it was, I think, one of the owners of an eyrie about three miles to the south. Both eagles did some stunt flying, but there was no anger in the pursuit of the local bird, and when last I saw the two they were flying almost side by side toward the distant eyrie, the "local" eagle, once his territory had been left, escorting the stranger in a friendly manner—no doubt that stranger was a near relative of his own. I had often watched that eagle at its own eyrie, and once had seen the bird when skimming low above its own rock suddenly shoot out formidable talons towards some starlings perched on the cliff top: the starlings scattered, chattering with fear.

On 9 June the back of the eaglet was well-feathered, but the neck was still in down. That afternoon the mother stood on the top of the nesting rock, close to a cushion of red flowers of the moss-campion, *Silene acaulis*. I wished a specialist among eagle artists, like J. C. Harrison or the late George E. Lodge, had been present to portray golden eagle and red flowers together.

A visit to Norway (where we saw only one golden eagle in three weeks) with J. C. Harrison interrupted my observations: when I again saw the eaglet in mid-July it was well-grown. I did not see the first flight, but on 27 July saw the parents with the eaglet on the cliff some distance from the nest. The eaglet, having received the freedom of the air, was now sure of itself. It fed on a rabbit which had been brought it, then sun-bathed. This was the second and last occasion on which I saw the parent eagle, or the family, indulge in sun-bathing at this eyrie.

In 1948 the eagles again reared one bird. The food provided was, as usual, mainly rabbits, and one day I watched the parent eagle very carefully plucking a rabbit at the edge of the eyrie: the rabbit's down floated over the precipice as it was skilfully removed with quick, jerky movements. That season my notes record no outstanding event. The young eagle flew in mid-July.

In 1949 I saw the first "change-over" on 18 March, and so it was evident that the egg had been laid before that date. Indeed it was only when I saw the change-over that I realized that a new eyrie had been chosen that year. Four days later I had an example of the marvellous eyesight of the golden eagle. The male bird was approaching at a height of at least 1,500 feet. Above a gradual hill slope where grew tussocky grass, whitened by the frosts and snow of winter, he suddenly checked his flight and fell headlong. A couple of minutes later he rose with a small object grasped in one foot. It was, I am almost sure, a field-mouse or vole. Since he had caught his prey at an elevation well above that of the eyrie, he was able to go into a glide when he took wing and made for home. When he had grasped his prey he had torn from the ground some of the long grass in which his small quarry had been hiding: during his subsequent glide, as he moved faster and faster, the grass streamed out rigidly behind him. The picture he then conveyed was one of tremendous speed, and I can still visualise him as he rushed towards his brooding mate. I was unable to see whether, on alighting at the eyrie, he himself ate his small victim, or gave it to her. She then rose from her brooding and they both took wing, but almost at once he returned in a fast glide, and took her place on the eyrie.

The young eagle was well-feathered by the morning of 18

June, when, very early, my wife and I walked along the ridge above the eagles' rock, and was standing outside the eyrie.

The brilliant weather which then prevailed induced me to leave home before four o'clock on the following morning to visit the eyrie of the pair of neighbouring eagles. I had seen the afterglow on the northern horizon strengthen, and as I was climbing a hill pass in the direction of the eyrie watched the rising sun suddenly light up the green grass of the high corries, their green changing to red-gold, glowing and wondrous. At six o'clock as I climbed the ridge the air was already warm, and when I came in sight of the eyrie, I saw that the sun was shining full on it (that eyrie faces east) and the single eaglet, still in down, was white as snow. This eaglet appeared to be at least three weeks later-hatched than that of the pair I had been watching regularly.

I then recalled an earlier visit, when a raven gave one of the parents of this eaglet a bad thirty-five minutes, during which, croaking continuously, he attacked without pause. The raven had then returned to his own rock, about a mile distant, and had shown his satisfaction by turning on his back and flying upside down, not once but many times.

Now, as I looked at the downy eaglet, shining white as a snowball below me, the sun each moment gained strength, and the heated air was scented with alpine plants—the high hills were fragrant and radiant. On that, and the previous morning, I realised the precious hours lost by the sleeping world of man (even the crofters were in bed and presumably still asleep) at mid-summer in fine weather.

Next day, my wife and I left for Switzerland, where for a fortnight we were in apparently ideal golden eagle country in the neighbourhood of Zermatt. During that fortnight we did not once see *Aquila chrysaëtos,* for the eagle is hated here and destroyed whenever possible. When we returned to Scotland

and again saw our golden eagle friends we realised how fortunate Scotland is, to have a considerable resident population of golden eagles, which add life and beauty to otherwise lonely country. No hill scenery, however grand, is completely satisfying to the bird lover if the eagle is absent.

We found the eaglet well-grown and practising wing-exercises with great energy. On the afternoon of 17 July, one of the parent eagles came in with a rabbit and the young eagle immediately hurried to the prey, covering it with its wings. The parent eagle later removed the remains of the rabbit and, while actually in flight, picked off, and no doubt ate, a piece of its flesh.

This was the last occasion I saw the eaglet in the eyrie, but the young bird, and its parents, were in the neighbourhood of the nest until near the end of that year.

CHAPTER XII

Eight Years' Observations
at a Golden Eagle's Eyrie: Part II

DURING the years 1950, 1951, 1952 and also 1953, I
made frequent observations at the eyrie, and there were
few days during these nesting seasons when I did not visit the
neighbourhood when weather permitted observations and when
the hill was free of cloud. Each year the eagles reared one child,
until 1952, when the egg for some reason did not hatch, or the
small eaglet died or was stolen—as I shall later narrate.

I saw little or nothing of the eagles during February 1950,
and indeed was wondering what had happened to them when,
on 7 March, I saw one bird flying along the cliff. It had been a
February of almost continuous storms, and I thought, when I
saw the single bird, that the repairs to the eyrie had not yet
begun. Judge my surprise when, on visiting the neighbourhood
on 9 March, I had been at my observation post only a few
minutes when one of the eagles dropped from a height, on the
keen north east wind which was blowing against the cliff, to a
grassy ledge in the neighbourhood of the nest. The eagle
snatched at some long grass with one foot, tearing it out and
at once flying to the eyrie, to lay the grass carefully at the edge
of the nest. Instead of flying away, as I had expected, she stood
there awhile and then, to my astonishment, I saw the second
eagle rise from the eyrie. The "change-over" now took place,
the incoming bird settling down to brood, the other taking

186

flight. Later, the mate, looking down at the eyrie from a great height, performed some spectacular dives for the benefit of the sitter, then disappeared. This was the earliest brooding I had seen, and it is indeed possible that the eagle was brooding two days before, when I had seen only one bird at the rock. Absence from home prevented me from visiting the site until 28 March, when almost at once I saw the male relieve the female on the nest. That day a cormorant, coming in from the distant sea and flying at a considerable height, was planing down to the loch to feed on its numerous small trout when it caught sight of me and departed in haste—a long flight for nothing. Cormorants make heavy weather of it when flying against a strong wind, and I have seen them, their mouths open and gasping for breath, as they passed over me on a stormy day.

Although the eagles had been brooding for over a fortnight, grass was being carried to the eyrie on this day also. I reckoned the eaglet should hatch on 20 April. On the 22nd, I saw that the eagle was sitting high (a sign that the young had hatched). After a time she left the eyrie, was joined by her mate, and when she returned to a neighbouring ridge, plucked the down off some light-coloured prey, which she then carried to the eyrie. She fed the tiny eaglet, which raised its small downy head unsteadily and snatched with little precision at the small morsels she held out to the baby with loving care. She gave the eaglet two feeds during that afternoon. On 26 April, the male eagle ordered off his territory a passing greater black-backed gull, then carried, in his bill, a long fern frond to the eyrie, afterwards feeding the eaglet for some time.

On 28 April, at 2 p.m. G.M.T. I was at my observation post.

Eagle arrives at nest with a bill full of Common Rush (*Juncus effusus*). (*Niall Rankin*)

187

There was a fresh north west wind blowing. The female eaglet was brooding. The male for a time was not seen; he later came in from the south, and dropped towards his usual perch, where he alighted. The wind was strong there, and his breast feathers were ruffled and blown in disorder. He seemed, nevertheless, indifferent to this and to the cold wind. He later rose and slanted down the cliff, his yellow legs distinct against the dark basaltic rock. He alighted on the steep grassy slope beneath the cliff and gripped an object which lay there. This object I could not at first identify, but gradually I realised that it was a dead lamb. The eagle stood on the lamb, and for half an hour fed upon it. He then began to pluck it, throwing the white down from him with quick jerks. In the ensuing few minutes the grass around the eagle became white with down. A heavy shower of rain and sleet drove in on the wind, and I could barely see the eagle through my telescope. He was soon a bedraggled bird, yet seemed heedless of the rain, and began a second course in his "high-tea" of lamb. The rain passed, the sun shone, and the eagle's plumage quickly dried. When at last he had finished his meal he did not, as I expected, carry the lamb to the eyrie but gripped it savagely, then left it. He rose, sailed along the base of the cliff (throwing a shadow more distinct than himself) then mounted, with no thrust of his wings, above the top of the cliff. He had climbed at least 500 feet of altitude in less than a minute, without a movement of his broad wings. The sky cleared with a shift of wind to the north, and as I walked home that evening the sun shone brightly.

That spring there was a heavy lamb mortality as the result of a severe April snowstorm, with much drifting on the high ground, and on 8 May, I saw one of the eagles pick up a dead lamb from the top of the cliff and carry it to the eyrie.

By 4 June the eaglet was well-feathered, except for the head and neck, yet the two eaglets of a neighbouring pair were still in the white downy stage two days later. That year, as was to be expected from the early laying, the eaglet left the eyrie during the early part of July.

Six weeks later, 13 August, I reached my observation place in the early afternoon. Almost at once I saw an eagle drop to the ridge below the cliff. Foxgloves were in flower on the ridge, on which grew a small rowan or mountain-ash. For some minutes the eagle stood there, looking intently all around. It then began to feed on some object hidden from my view. With the typical golden eagle wrenching motion it tore pieces off the carcase and swallowed them. When the bird moved its position I saw that the tail was almost white, and realised that I had been watching the eaglet, by now of course strong on the wing. It dragged the rabbit (as the object turned out to be) in one foot a short distance uphill, then sprang into the air with its prey. It sailed strongly along the face of the cliff then, rising above the top, sailed into the south-west wind current with masterly flight, the legs of the rabbit hanging down. The eaglet now alighted on a broad heathery ledge, three-quarter way up the cliff. It was evidently full-fed, and stood quietly beside the rabbit.

I had started home when I saw one of the parent eagles sail in fast down-wind. It was carrying a half-grown rabbit. The eagle continued at speed at least a mile beyond the cliff, then swung round and, soaring against the stiff breeze with wings well bent back, came in magnificently in a glide, to alight on the ledge where the young eagle was. The eaglet showed no pleasure at its mother's arrival (I recognised her as the female when she alighted). The mother eagle, receiving no welcome, soon flew off with the rabbit, but quickly returned with it, alighting this time at a different part of the ledge. Again the eaglet gave her no welcome. Again the mother flew away, and again alighted, this time on the 'feeding knoll' on which I had watched the young bird feeding itself. She stood for some time, preening her feathers and oiling them from the oil gland situated beside the tail. She was a superb figure against the black rock and green grass, her tawny plumage much lighter than that of the eaglet. She waited a considerable time on the knoll, then, seizing the prey with a terrific grasp, she once more became air-borne. Again she came in to the eaglet's ledge, and when she alighted the young eagle opened its wings, and there was the flash of a white tail: this time the rabbit *was* accepted. It was noteworthy that the parent would not leave the prey beside the young bird, until it was actually *accepted*. Again the mother eagle swept into space, and when she came in her legs were extended stiffly earthward. She alighted on the ledge, and, following her in the field of the telescope, I was surprised to see that the father eagle had meantime arrived on the ledge. The male in this pair is a very dark bird—in some lights his plumage appears black. The male also may have brought in food—at all events the eaglet was now covering prey with its wings. The parent eagles were showing much more interest in the eaglet, more than a month after its first flight, than they did during its last weeks in the eyrie. It was interesting that the eaglet should have been, in mid-August, within 200 yards of where it was born, although it was by now strong on the wing.

Three days later heavy rain fell during my walk to the territory of the golden eagles. The ling was almost in bloom, and the moors were assuming a purple tint. I had hardly time to sit down when all three golden eagles took the air together. They had evidently been sheltering. The two parent birds sailed along the wall of the cliff, flying westward, perhaps to hunt; the young one, after soaring for a time, alighted on a steep slope three quarters of the way up the cliff, where I could see meadow-sweet in flower. Here it remained for a time, and must have taken wing unseen by me (the midges where I sat were active!) for I saw it later, coming in from the east, and flying with all the assurance of the old birds. Indeed I could not be sure that it was not a mature eagle until it alighted and I saw the white on the tail, and the white circles on the under-sides of the wings. Alighting on the top of the rock, it then ran to the ridge, where it remained for perhaps an hour. It evidently expected its parents to come from the *east*, for it looked all the time in that direction. At 4-24 p.m. it rose, and flew fast down-wind, eastward. Scarcely had it left when I saw the female eagle coming in, from the *west*, with a rabbit. It was, I think, a coincidence that the eaglet had taken flight just then, but it now pursued its parent as fast as it could and when the parent, almost without slackening speed, set down the rabbit on a grassy hill face, the youngster was on it at once, seizing it and for some minutes standing over it quietly. It then rose, carrying the rabbit, and sailed into the breeze, the rabbit being clearly seen. It alighted on a ledge, and as it stood there with the rabbit the parent eagle sailed past it once, as if to assure herself that the young one had the rabbit safely. She then flew west—to hunt again perhaps.

On 28 August I again took a watch. It was a clear and sunny day: white heather was flowering beside the track. Both parent eagles were perched on the top of the rock, the female with legs well-spaced, a large and sturdy bird, the male standing beside her. After a time the female called thrice and walked right up to her mate. They almost touched bills, then stood side by side, their folded wings touching, a picture of happiness. Suddenly the young eagle appeared from nowhere and stood beside them —the family party was complete. The large white area at the base of the young bird's tail, and the darker colour of its plumage, were plain.

The wind died and midges in incredible swarms appeared above the heather; they formed a cloud around Dugie the collie, now fast asleep. Their attacks made it impossible for me to sit still. A black thunder cloud formed behind the eagles' rock and soon came torrential rain, through which the sun slanted. The air remained warm, and before the intensity of the rain blotted out the rock I could see the family group of golden eagles still perched against the sky-line. After the first heavy shower the female ruffled her feathers, and I could see the down floating from them. That evening, when the storm passed, there were salmon-tinted cumulo-nimbus clouds in the blue sky high above the eagles' rock.

On 2 September, the young eagle was happy with the carcase of a rabbit. This it was feeding leisurely on, carrying the prey first to one place, then, after a short meal, taking wing and alighting with it perhaps half a mile away, where it again fed.

This change of scene during a meal may stimulate the appetite, just as we have one course at dinner, and light conversation before our second course is brought us. Later one of the parent eagles came in from the west, "stunting" as it flew. It alighted on a grassy slope and was joined by the young bird: they stood side by side on the grass. The young eagle suddenly rose and made a playful swoop upon a lamb about four months old a hundred yards below it. The lamb, almost as large as its parent, bounded away as though taken aback. The young eagle returned at once to its former station, evidently pleased with itself. The parent eagle now rose and, climbing to a great height, began to perform aerial manoeuvres. Behind him as a background was a white cumulus cloud, which showed off this aerial display. Rising and falling repeatedly with wings closed, the eagle gave me the impression of the rising and falling of a gnat on a warm windless day, although each rise and fall was made more leisurely. The comparison was heightened because the eagle, now at a great distance, seemed no larger than a gnat.

That autumn of 1950 the young eagle must have left its parents earlier than usual, because on 5 November the nesting cycle for the following year had already begun. It was a cloudless day of late autumn, very clear and pleasant, and I was in sight of the eagles' rock at half past two in the afternoon. Both eagles were standing together in the sunshine. The male rose, his yellow legs bright against the dark background of rock, circled for a time, then alighted on a tussock of rough grass on a small and narrow ledge. For five minutes he stood there, and when he rose above the rock I saw that he held in his bill a small object. He rose to a great height, went into a dive so swift that I had difficulty in keeping him in the field of the glass, checked his descent at the cliff, and alighted at the 1949 eyrie. He placed the object in the nest, then worked at the cup of this flattened and weather-beaten eyrie for five minutes, sitting low as he busied himself. His work completed to his satisfaction he rose, stood at the edge of the nest, then flew away over the top of the cliff. I had witnessed the choice of the new home, and the first of the repairs done to it. At this time I did not know that the golden eagle repaired the eyrie in late autumn, for it was not until the following season that my extended observations of late autumn and early winter nest-building were made.

Having been present at the choice of the new home, it was interesting that I saw on 28 January, the mating of the couple in deep snow (vide Chap. IV, pp. 42 and 43).

Three weeks after their mating, I was watching the eagles on 21 February, a day of sun and fresh north west wind. I had just arrived at my observation post at 3-30 p.m., and was spying the nest which I had seen chosen on 5 November, when the female arrived with a piece of heather. Placing it in position she at once left, travelling high and fast down-wind, but first dropped in a cork-screw dive with legs extended, on a grassy ledge, although she did not, as I had expected, gather nesting material here. Half an hour later I fortunately had the eyrie in the field of my glass when she again arrived, carrying in one foot a large tuft of grass or greater wood-rush. She was evidently gathering the nesting material at a considerable distance from the eyrie. Again she disappeared eastward: as she had not come in again by sunset she had probably finished nest-building for the day.

The high hills were deep in snow that afternoon, but the eagles' rock was snow-free. That year, it appeared from the behaviour of the eagles, the egg was laid on, or around 11 March. On 19 March I had scarcely arrived at my station when one of the eagles came in from the south, several times diving with wings tightly closed, then regaining height with a few vigorous wing-thrusts. I was able to identify the stunting bird as the female when I saw, through my glass, that a primary feather was missing from one of the wings, for I had previously taken note of this. When the male appeared the two birds soared, wing-tip to wing-tip, into the wind. When they separated the female made a swift glide to the cliff, falling in a corkscrew dive down the face of the rock. She dropped too far to make a landing at the eyrie; and therefore rose with buoyancy high into the air once more. Again came that swift dive, and at the end of it she spiralled down the face of the cliff, sailed grandly across to the eyrie, and settled on it.

The male appeared again. He sailed, with primaries fully spaced (in thus holding the primaries he could be distinguished from his mate in the air, who did not have them so widely-spread) for a time, then headed out toward the sea, and the Outer Hebrides beyond it. He may have been travelling to

Female eagle in flight illustrating a wingspan of nearly seven feet. (*Lea MacNally*)

Lewis, blue in the distance; he had not returned when I left half an hour later.

There was at this time a large green object on the eyrie. I was puzzled as to what it might be, but later, when the light was good, I identified it as a branch of ivy with its green leaves; it had evidently been carried in as a decoration. This was noteworthy, as there is very little ivy in the district.

On 25 March, before the male flew in to take his turn on the egg he tore up grass and heather with his bill, his movements being similar to those made when prey is being dismembered. His bill quite full, he sailed into the eyrie, placing the material carefully in the great nest. The female had at once risen, and the "change-over" took place.

On 8 April, I watched the male eagle fall in a great dive, and noticed that his tail was held flexed towards vent and even close-pressed to it—perhaps to lessen wind-resistance. While still high in the air, after coming out of the dive, he several times shot out his legs. He alighted on the eyrie and then flew off, carrying in his bill a piece of grass which trailed behind him like the wire of a gin. One of the ravens dived repeatedly at him, giving him little peace, and he set off north east at a height of perhaps 1,500 feet. I then saw, so high as to appear no larger than a kestrel, a second eagle. This bird came from the direction of the eyrie of the next-door neighbours. The local eagle either did not see the passer-by, or else took no notice of it. The stranger was at least 5,000 feet up. It was steering in the direction of the mainland of Scotland, 25 miles distant, and was perhaps going to hunt there.

Winter had returned when I visited the eyrie on 18 April. Four inches of snow had fallen that morning and the strong sun, shining from a deep blue sky, created a dazzling scene on which the eye could scarcely rest. Each burn and rivulet was brim-full of snowy water. A small object flew uncertainly over the snowy expanse—it was a butterfly, the first to appear, that late spring. The eyrie was white, all but the cup where the eagle brooded motionless except for the turning, now and then, of the golden head.

That afternoon the eagle may have been cold on her shadowed eyrie, for when the male came in to relieve her at 3 p.m. G.M.T., she stood up on the nest immediately he had alighted on its edge, and took wing before he had settled. As she left, small avalanches were falling from snow cornices, and the scene was Alpine. A male wheatear, newly arrived, must have thought the country a strange one; not so the snow-bunting which flitted on white wings high across the dark rock.

It was on 25 April of that year that I witnessed an attack, the second I have seen in my life, by one of the eagles on a lamb. The distance was too great for me to be sure whether the bird figuring in the incident was male or female. The eagle was sailing low across a grassy slope. Here a number of sheep, some of them with their small lambs, were feeding. The eagle checked its flight, dropped suddenly, seized a small lamb, and flew about 80 yards with it. It may have then proceeded to kill the prey, but the distance was too great for me to be sure of this. I saw no sign of movement in the lamb afterwards. The ewe did not at once realise what had happened; when she did, she ran down the slope toward eagle and lamb. As she approached the eagle, the bird rose with the lamb and flew to the edge of a small cliff, where it made a leisurely meal off the victim. After feeding for about half an hour, the eagle flew back to the eyrie: it seemed to me that the flight was made in order to acquaint the mate with what had happened, for it left again almost at once and flew very fast to where the lamb was. The idea in the eagle's head was, I am sure, to carry the lamb at once to the eyrie, but before it had reached the lamb, two ravens began to mob it in the air. The eagle's defence against the raven's attacks is to turn on its back and thrust its talons at its adversary. Had it picked up the lamb, that defence would not have been available. The ravens thus deprived me of seeing an unusual sight. By evening the sun had melted some of the snow. A flower of the draw-moss was out; on a sunny bank the first violet showed, and beside a stream the yellow petals of the first marsh marigold had opened.

The eaglet had probably hatched before the lamb was killed on 25 April; at all events it was visible in the eyrie four days later. The carcase of the lamb had then gone from where it lay, and there was now a lamb—presumably that killed on 25 April—lying in the eyrie. That day as the male eagle flew across the cliff face the up-draught was so strong that he flew lightly as a butterfly. He then gained height at tremendous speed.

That year, 30 April was the first warm sunny day and I could see the eaglet, which had been left by its parents unattended because of the warmth of the weather. The eaglet seemed to be taking an intelligent interest in its surroundings; it looked a week old—as it should have been according to my calculations.

The contrast that day between the warmth and strong sunshine near the eagles' rock and the high hills, still spotlessly white, was remarkable.

A visit to Dutch bird sanctuaries kept me away from the eyrie until 7 June. That evening, the eagles steered high above their rock like two aircraft. Their wings were motionless and they were dark specks against the blue of an unclouded summer sky, the sun slowly sinking, their rock bathed in its clear light. One eagle that evening brought in prey to the top of the cliff, but did not carry it to the eyrie. The eaglet had grown fast, and the back was already feathered.

On 3 July, the eaglet, now a large, feathered bird, was asleep in the eyrie when I first arrived, but later awoke, stood up and fed itself on some prey. The mother stood on the cliff top. An old sheep in her feeding approached the eagle, walking nearer and nearer with evident curiosity. The eagle at last reluctantly took wing in order to avoid her attentions, and alighted on the cliff behind the ewe. There is obviously no natural enmity between sheep and eagle.

On 8 July, I watched the eagle remove a rabbit from the eyrie: she carried it on one foot to a pinnacle, where she plucked it, and I could see the rabbit-fur floating away on the breeze. She then returned to the eyrie with the rabbit, on which she fed for some time, the eaglet standing expectantly beside her. When she left, the young bird also made a meal off the rabbit. The parent returned, fed the eaglet herself, then carried away the entrails to the pinnacle and later went off, flying at a great height, eastward.

On 12 July the weather partially cleared after the eagles' rock had been invisible in mist and rain for three days. The eaglet after preening itself walked to the edge of the eyrie, turned slowly so that it faced the rock, and having got carefully into position lowered its head, raised its "behind," and shot out a stream of white, semi-liquid excreta with such force that it was caught on the breeze and carried up the cliff and over the top—a distance of some thirty feet. I have often noticed the tremendous force with which the eagle evacuates itself. This is no doubt in order that the liquid stream should be shot well clear of the eyrie. On this day the eagles when soaring assumed a strange attitude. They suddenly flexed their out-spread wings, yet kept their primaries wide-spaced. With wings thus drawn in, they continued to soar. I have several times seen a golden eagle draw in the wings when soaring, but the primaries have not been wide-spaced, as on this occasion. Still on flexed wings, they mounted into a passing cloud, through which they showed dimly, as though they were phantom eagles, or the shadows of eagles. Side by side, they disappeared into the depths of the white vapour, emerged again, then rose into its shadows, finding evident pleasure in losing sight of the earth and discovering it again beneath them.

On the late evening of 13 July the sun was on the eyrie at nine o'clock. The eaglet now, full-feathered, was petulant, for the parents were keeping it on short commons to induce it to fly.

From the hill-top at ten o'clock that night St. Kilda rose on the far horizon, ninety miles of ocean lying between. Hirta and Boreray, Stac an Armuinn and Stac Lee rose in lonely beauty where sea and sky became one. At midnight the strongest light came from the north, and I saw the rock of the eagles suffused by the midsummer midnight glow, seeming thus a kindly and pleasant place, and not grim and dark as it is when in deep shade during the day. The scent of thyme was in the still air; northward the sky was salmon-pink and the sea beneath it opal. Where sea and sky met, the flashes from a distant lighthouse came at intervals. The eaglet, lonely now without its parents, slept in its eyrie high on the rock.

By 18 July, the eaglet had made it first flight and the nest was empty.

I did not see the young eagle again until 16 September, although I frequently visited the rock. That day I was about to leave my observation post when a golden eagle flew in and alighted on the top of the rock. After a few minutes it rose and sailed half-way down the cliff, alighting on the heather below a rocky face. I then saw that a dead rabbit was lying where it had alighted. The eagle seized the rabbit, sailed off with it, soared along the top of the cliff, then, still holding the rabbit, returned to the exact spot where it had picked it up. A second time it did the same thing; when it laid the prey on the heather it practised "grabbing exercises" on it. A third time it lifted the rabbit, sailed with it on exactly the same flight, and returned to the identical spot! It was only then that it began to pluck its prey. I identified it as the eaglet from the white areas on the wings. That it should have carried back the rabbit each time to precisely the same place was remarkable; it showed that its memory for places was strong, for I am sure that the human observer would have found it almost impossible to find the exact spot each time, even had he been miraculously endowed with the power of flight.

Two days later, the young eagle was practising "grabbing exercises" on the top of the rock. These ended, it sailed across to the far cliff, and as it was nearing the top, shot out its legs, wide-spread, toward the approaching rock; I realized from this action that it had already learned a characteristic habit of the adult birds. I had not noticed that one of the eaglet's parents was perched on this part of the cliff. The eaglet collided with its father, who in disgust rose, then sailed across to a ledge sheltered from the wind. I had seen, near the horizon, an approaching shower, and, knowing how good a weather observer the golden eagle is, was fairly sure that the shower would be a long one. He was quite right to fly to shelter—when it came, the shower lasted for half an hour, and mist later hid the rock. The eaglet had remained on the top of the ridge, and until the mist fell it called repeatedly, for it was hungry.

On 30 September I was seated beside a hill loch when the young eagle appeared. It was sailing down-wind only a few yards above the water's surface and looked enormous. It alighted on the far side of the loch, and began the usual "grabbing exercises" in the grass and heather. It then partly hopped, partly walked, using its wings to aid it, up the steep slope to the rock-foot. There it remained for some time, and I could see the broad white tips of the tail feathers, and the rest of the tail mottled with white. The head was chocolate, and both head and back were darker than in the adult eagle, and the legs a lighter yellow. This clear view of the almost white tail of the young eagle made me understand how easy it is for an untrained observer to mistake the young golden eagle for a sea or white-tailed eagle, as frequently happens.

On the late afternoon of 23 October, I watched the young eagle stand on the top of the cliff for perhaps an hour. The eagle's head when it turned sideways (as it often did) was ruffled by the wind, so that the white bases to the feathers, and the white down, were clearly seen; the breast feathers were also blown aside, exposing much white here also. There had been a heavy shower shortly before, and I came to the conclusion that the eagle was deliberately standing in full exposure to the wind in order that its feathers might be dried before it went to roost: it evidently did not feel the cold.

On 28 October one of the parent eagles was perched on the rock, when it was joined by the young bird. There they re-mained for some time before they went off together—pre-sumably to roost.

On 18 November, I saw the young eagle for the last time. At 3-45 one of the parent eagles was on the rock, and was shortly after joined by its mate. A little later, I saw one of the pair look round, and, following its glance, saw the young eagle soaring a little way off the cliff. It alighted, when I had no difficulty in recognising it by its plumage. For long the young eagle went first to one parent then to the other, yelping and pleading for food. The parents were in no mood to respond, and when the youngster became too much of a nuisance one of the parents would move a few paces away. As the young bird pleaded with plaintive yelps, it sometimes thrust its head close up against the head of the parent. Dusk came early, and when I left the rock one of the parent eagles still remained beside the youngster; the other had gone to roost.

Four days later nest-building had definitely begun. The young bird had presumably been driven off, for I did not see the three at the rock again.

CHAPTER XIII

Eight Years' Observations at a Golden Eagle's Eyrie : Part III

Seasons 1952-3

IT WAS on 22 November 1951 that I first saw the eagles building their eyrie for the following season. The day was fine and sunny. The female eagle came in with green nesting material—I think greater wood-rush—held in one foot. She sailed along the cliff toward the eyrie, but, not satisfied with the line of her approach, swung round, increased her height by soaring in spirals, and planed in at speed, alighting at the 1950 eyrie. For the space of several minutes she assumed a brooding attitude, and occupied herself in placing the nesting material to her satisfaction. I then realised that the eyrie, which before had been flat and delapidated, had been considerably built up, and a cup-shaped hollow formed. Yet only four days previously the young eagle had been pleading for food ·

The eagle later returned, and perched above the cliff. Suddenly she launched out towards the loch at terrific speed. I saw then that a red-breasted merganser was approaching, no doubt with the idea of catching some of the many small trout which were rising that mild afternoon. Seeing the eagle, the merganser wisely increased its speed and did not attempt to alight on the water. The eagle did not pursue. As dusk fell, both eagles arrived above the loch, and one of the birds did the rising and falling display. At 4-25 they flew westward. It was now too dark to use the glass, yet still the eagles were abroad, although in summer they would have gone to roost long before dusk fell. The next morning when I reached the observation post the light was better for "spying," and I was astonished to see how much nesting material had already been brought. The sides of the eyrie had been built up, mostly of heather, and the nest had the appearance of being almost completed. One of the eagles came in, flying low above the loch, quite close to me. In less than 30 seconds it had climbed the 700 feet of almost vertical rock, and now appeared against the sky above it, poised on the breeze, with wings made very broad and primaries well-spaced. The eagle's head could be seen to move this way and that as it calmly surveyed the scene. The eagle seemed to come to a sudden decision, and moved off at great speed, with powerful wing-thrusts, dropping once in a nose-dive. The sweep of the eagle, down-wind, low above the loch was memorable. The bird seemed to embody the spirit of dusk, its broad wings black against the basaltic rocks beneath a clouded sky. At 4-15 p.m. both eagles came in to roost.

On 25 November, both eagles were playing high in the sky, and once the male with outstretched legs almost dropped on the female's back. A few minutes before 4 o'clock a hail squall drove in. The eagles, evidently being able, from their aerial view-point, accurately to judge the speed of the approaching storm, planed in to a sheltered ledge from a distance of half a mile just as the first hail-stones rattled on the rock. A blizzard of snow followed the hail, blotting out the cliff and even the farther shore of the loch, now inky-black. Thus I left the eagles at their roosting ledge.

The weather now became too stormy for nest-repairs. On 27 November when I reached the observation post a westerly gale was blowing. The eagles that afternoon came separately in to roost. The second bird had difficulty in finding a sheltered ledge. He came in, but swung round and flew down-wind for about a mile, travelling with the gale. He then turned, rose higher and higher, and, when he considered that a sufficient altitude had been gained, began a spectacular glide against the gale. The wings were half-closed and made very thin and narrow, and the bird had the appearance of a gigantic peregrine falcon. Slowly and steadily, without movement of the wings, he forged ahead against the gale. When he reached the down-draught from the cliff he rocked and swayed and had a good deal of difficulty in keeping himself under control. He may have taken pleasure in his combat with the gale; at all events he did not alight but again turned, and shot down-wind. This time as he travelled east he passed low and near me—a dark shape travelling at perhaps 100 miles an hour. Again he travelled about a mile eastward, then rose to 3,000 feet or more in a very short time. Again he went into the glide against the gale, the wings made narrow and falcon-like. Again there was the slow and steady approach, the same rocking when the down-draught was reached—then he had dropped below the cliff-top and I was surprised to see him sailing slowly on an *easterly* eddy which evidently prevailed half-way down the cliff. A squall of rain hastened his alighting. As I struggled home, I was almost blown down by the force of the gusts of that severe gale.

Each day was now shorter. On 29 November, one of the eagles came in to roost at 3-30, the other at 3-40. When the second bird arrived the first soared out of the rock, and they staged an aerial tourney, sometimes entering the storm-wrack that drifted swiftly past at a height of 1,400 feet. The ravens came in later to roost, arriving at 4 o'clock, and having a hard struggle to reach the rock.

On 1 December, the eagles at dusk made a spectacular appearance out of a black storm-cloud, diving one after the other to the cliff and the roosting ledges, and reaching them as the storm broke. As the birds soared, the wings of one were rigid, those of the other flexed.

On 7 December there was much to see. After a three days' gale the wind moderated and the light was good. At 3-20 that afternoon the female eagle came in from the east, moving very steadily. She swept grandly round the broken cliff-face, then moved her wings tremblingly, as a gannet sometimes does when climbing a little way above the seas on a passage flight—a delicate, un-eagle-like motion that was almost hovering. She alighted on a ledge and attempted to pull up some moss or grass, but did not succeed. She flew out and came round once more. This time she tried to alight on the white, bleached stump of a dead rowan, but lost her balance. I then missed her in the field of the glass, but in less than a minute she appeared above the ridge, and in one foot she carried heather. She flew swiftly to the eyrie: when she alighted on it the cup was already so deep and well-formed that her legs were hidden and only her head and back were visible. She moved about, arranging the nesting material, then alighted on the cliff-top. At 3-40 she went off eastward, flying very fast; she had perhaps seen her mate and was hurrying to join him. Seeing the eyrie almost completed by early December, I realised why in previous years there had been so little nest-building in February and early March.

In December, 1952, one of the deerstalkers in the Forest of Mar saw a golden eagle lift a fir branch from the ground and carry it towards where, later in the year, an eyrie with three eaglets was found. This I did not hear until later.

On 15 December, when one of the eagles was on the cliff-top at 4 p.m., he sailed out suddenly and, following the line of his flight, I noticed that a passing gaggle of barnacle-geese had brought him into the air to see them off his territory. Five

minutes later the female eagle appeared, flying from the west
down-wind and escorted by the pair of ravens, which had
already taken possession of their last spring's territory farther
along the cliff. When the eagle had reached her own territory
the ravens returned, having hard work in beating home against
the wind. They kept far out from the edge of the cliff, perhaps
because there they would have been more vulnerable to attack
by the eagles.

On 18 December the eagles again invaded raven territory,
and there was a "rough and tumble" above the cliff. Before
going down to roost both eagles stood on the cliff top for a time,
so near together that their feathers touched. From a dove-grey
cumulus cloud to the north came a brilliant lightning flash.
Thunder, this winter evening, pealed, and lightning lighted the
eagles to their roost. On 22 December, the shortest day of the
year—though actually the afternoons begin to draw out a week
before that date—one of the eagles was rising and falling in
display as he approached the rock against the wind. There was
not a single thrust of his wings made; he apparently relied
entirely on the wind currents as he rose and fell, all the time
moving forward against the strong breeze. To-day he was
caught by a hail squall before he arrived, and at times he was
almost hidden in the hail. As I was watching the arrival of the
eagle through the glass I saw, half-unconsciously with my other
eye, a large object fly past me, very close. Later, I was surprised
to see a white-flanked bird swim past me on the loch a little way
off-shore. It dived without splash, and, as the hail squall
lessened in violence, I saw that it was a goosander drake.
Keeping near the lee shore, it swam backward and forward,
now and then diving, its flanks very white in the dim and fading
light. At the passing of the squall both golden eagles appeared.
As they flew west they entered the ravens' territory and both
ravens came out to the attack. One of the eagles then made a

strong attack on one of the ravens, flying at it in a determined manner as though thoroughly exasperated. The second eagle joined in the pursuit, and just as things looked black for the raven he turned the tables by himself attacking one of the pursuing eagles. The second eagle meantime flew down-wind right over me. Apparently it had noticed the goosander and swooped down towards it. The goosander drake had vanished by the time the eagle, looking enormous, and seeming to blot out the sky, was over me, nor did I see him again. The eagles were now definitely going to roost later; they were remaining abroad until it was almost dark, perhaps because the hunting hours of a December day are shorter than they would like. One afternoon as they came in, Jupiter was already shining brightly. By 12 January 1952, the eagles were three quarters of an hour later in coming in to roost. That afternoon one of the birds went into a rosy cumulus cloud, then returned to engage the ravens, and, a little later, planed in to roost at 4-35 p.m. Two minutes afterwards, the tip of the moon rose silver from a line of cumulus clouds on the horizon.

On 20 January a large, bleached branch was in the eyrie. That afternoon flights of fieldfares at sunset flew from the low country towards the eagles' rock. The snowy rock was apparently their roosting place and they flew down to the snow-free country to feed during the day.

The weather now became severe, and on 27 January I was surprised to see a pair of whooper swans on the small loch, which was half frozen over. The swans were feeding in shallow water, "up-ending" and tearing out the water weed: as they slowly swam, long pieces of weed trailed from their bills. When one of the eagles came in to roost, the white swans and the dark eagle soaring above them made an unusual and beautiful picture. The fieldfares that afternoon were coming in singly to roost.

Eight Years' Observations at a Golden Eagle's Eyrie: III

On 10 February, one of the eagles alighted on a small rowan tree, where it rested a little while before attempting to break off a branch with its bill, but the branch resisted the bird's efforts. It then took a short flight, returned to the tree, and made more determined efforts to tear off the branch. Its bright yellow legs were distinct against the dark background. Its efforts were so vigorous that it suddenly lost its balance, and immediately spread its wings to steady itself. When a little later it took wing and rose above the line of the cliff I saw that it carried a small rowan branch in one foot. The eagle did not take the branch at once to the eyrie but flew down-wind, turned back about a mile from the cliff, and came in against the wind, soaring high and steadily. Alighting gently on the eyrie, it then carefully arranged the branch. It now sailed out into the wind, using the tail constantly as a rudder to steady itself. The flight ended with a high dive to the rock just before the arrival of a hail squall.

There was nest-building again on 12 February. The light was bad when, in the late afternoon, the female eagle arrived, flew in to the rock, and tore out what seemed to be a small branch of dead juniper. Her first approach to the eyrie with the nesting material did not satisfy her; she swung round, sailed down-wind, then returned at a rather greater height, with an impetus just sufficient for her to rise, still soaring, at the end of her flight and alight gently on the edge of the large nest without pitching forward; a fast and heavy landing would perhaps have damaged the nest. When she had placed the branch in position she returned to the rowan tree, or to one close to it, and again wrenched at a branch. This time she had a still harder struggle to break it off, but in the end succeeded, and flew to the eyrie with it. She placed the branch in position, took wing, gained height by soaring, then made a skilled landing on the top of a post driven into the ground above the rock.

There I left her, a solitary figure, large snow flakes falling lightly on her dark plumage.

On 16 February, the day on which I saw the eagles mate, I held one or other of the birds in the field of my telescope continuously for two hours, and felt the strain of this when I was walking home across the moor in the gathering dusk.

When I visited the rock on 23 February, an assembly of ravens were on a neighbouring hill. There were a score of these birds and they were behaving in an unusual manner. They were flying, or were hovering on the breeze, over the highest part of the hill. Sometimes they would alight for a few seconds, then rise into the air, where they would somersault and roll, and perform aerial stunts. It is possible that a dead or dying sheep had attracted them; if so, they seldom alighted to feed, but it was afternoon, and they may have been there since early morning and were therefore already well-fed. At 4 p.m. the ravens left, all but two travelling north east and those two south west.

On 25 February, a calm, mild day, frogs had begun to spawn on the peaty pools below the eagles' rock: numbers of excited frogs stuck their heads out of the water as I passed. That afternoon I watched one of the eagles standing on the gentle slopes of a hill. The eagle carefully preened and oiled its feathers, then strode quickly through the heather, as though it were a gigantic red grouse. When it found a spot sheltered and sunny, the eagle stood quite still, enjoying the warmth until the sun was sinking, when it rose, soared awhile, flexed its wings while soaring, then made a fast slant towards the place where the ravens had earlier been seen.

On 4 March, both ravens of the rock in turn dive-bombed the female eagle in the air. She parried these attacks with claws and bill, but latterly became flustered: one of the ravens pursued her well into her own territory. On 10 March there was a "change-over" on the eyrie at 3 p.m.; the egg must therefore have been laid by then.

Repairs and additions to the eyrie continued, as usual, after the birds had begun to brood. Thus on 31 March, I watched the male eagle alight on a dead, up-rooted rowan which may have fallen many years ago from its root-hold in the cliff. The eagle stood on the tree, then sprang down to the short, green grass beside it, examined some of the branches which rested on the ground, and with considerable effort broke off one of them with his bill and carried it to the eyrie, where it remained beside his brooding mate for about three minutes. Two days later, when I "spied" the eyrie I saw that the brooding bird had an unusual appearance. I was puzzling over this, when I realised that, for the first time during all the years I had watched, I was seeing the eagle brooding with her head facing the rock, her tail spread out over the edge of the nest. When the male arrived at 3-45 to "change-over" they both faced the same way. There was much flapping of wings before the "change-over" took place.

On 13 April, the male eagle was on watch above the cliff when he became suddenly air-borne; following the line of his flight I saw a gaggle of pink-footed geese flying high and fast toward the north-west. These were perhaps some of the great colony discovered in the interior of Iceland by Peter Scott and his party in the summer of 1951, for their flight was north west and in the direction of Iceland. The eagle shepherded the geese off his territory, then returned to his look-out station.

Eagles carry prey to the neighbourhood of the eyrie before the young are hatched. This was evident when, on 15 April, the male bird planed down and alighted on a buttress beside the carcase of a rabbit which must have been carried there previously. For some time he had a meal off this, rapidly and skilfully plucking each portion before tearing it off and swallowing it—a quick jerk of his head sent the fur off his bill-tip, to float away in the air. After feeding, he sprang down to the heather below the buttress, seized some heather in one foot and, after rising to the correct altitude, planed in with it to the nest. His mate rose, arranged the heather, and stretched one wing, but there was no immediate "change-over." Yet scarcely had he alighted on the top of the rock when the female joined him. He then took wing, sailed in to the eyrie, and took his turn at brooding.

The female eagle now preened herself carefully and flew down to the sunniest part of the cliff. She stood motionless, evidently enjoying the warmth and sunlight after her cold home. The day was a brilliant one. Bumble bees for the first time were abroad, and dog violets were opening on sunny banks.

On 17 April, another warm day, trout were rising for the first time that spring on the loch. A ring-ouzel was in the rowans high on the cliff. The male eagle slanted down, legs outstretched, towards him. If he meant to grab the ouzel he failed. He then alighted, pulled up heather in his bill, and in his bill carried it to the eyrie. A little later a herring or perhaps a lesser black-backed gull was sailing in spirals above the loch. The eagle on guard flew menacingly towards the gull which, alarmed, gained height as rapidly as possible, then made the best of its speed from so unhealthy a neighbourhood.

On 19 April, when a high wind was blowing, the male eagle, attacked by two ravens, flew down-wind at tremendous speed, then returned in a glide with wings bent so far back that they were almost pressed against his side. He alighted on a spur, and as the wind ruffled the feathers of head, neck and breast, an old ewe fed fearlessly up to him. He later planed down to a ledge on which prey of some kind was lying, making a hearty meal off the animal: I could see the entrails being swallowed although I was unable to identify the animal itself. The female eagle was brooding closely, for the egg should have been near hatching.

At four o'clock G.M.T. on the afternoon of 21 April when the male eagle came in to relieve his mate, she was anxious to be off, and stood up in the eyrie even before he had alighted. When she took wing he convoyed her as far as the east buttress before returning to brood. I now witnessed a display of stunt flying by the female for thirty minutes. Time and again she rose at her fastest speed almost vertically, driving her wings hard. Then, while travelling in a fast climb, she closed her wings. Her impetus carried her forward in this position, and when the impetus was almost exhausted, she tilted over and, still without opening the wings, began to fall, using the tail as a rudder during the tilt over. These dives were magnificent to watch and followed each other in rapid succession. In her excitement she fired off excreta in the air, white and flashing against the blue sky.

After this joy stunt she returned, exactly thirty minutes after she had left the nest, and settled down again to brood, moving with her bill some of the nesting material so that it lay more to her liking around the nesting cup. The male, freed from family responsibilities, instantly began his own aerial display, rising and falling like the female. I noticed that his neck seemed thinner than the female's and that the wings were larger in proportion to the body. That both eagles should have displayed in rapid succession seemed to show that the eaglet had hatched, but I avoided disturbing the pair by going to the top of the rock. The next day, too, the male eagle as he set out on what seemed to be a long hunting-flight, made a single joy dive, when flying high above the low-lying moor.

On 24 April, the male was brooding when I "spied" the nest. His mate flew down to a grassy hollow in the cliff, where she very thoroughly preened one dappled wing, and her tail: she drew her bill carefully through the tail feathers. She then flew to the eyrie. There was no sign of the brooding male, but in a second or two I saw a slight movement, and I realised that she was holding her golden head close to his. The "change-over" was at 6 p.m. G.M.T. When the male rose and stood at the eyrie, his darker plumage and slimmer build were plain. When he took wing he was buffeted by the ravens, and even after he had returned to his territory and had alighted on a ledge above the eyrie, one of the angry ravens continued to "dive-bomb" him, then, alighting on a ledge about 12 feet above him, tore up grass in fury and every few seconds swooped down very fast upon the eagle, who seemed bewildered. The black fissures of the basaltic rock were bright with primroses, that day.

On 27 April, a summer day, the female eagle was kept off her nest by two shepherds who came along the top of the rock. When she returned she came in to the eyrie with her legs held stiffly out in front of her—the first time I had seen her do this. It was not until 6-35 p.m. G.M.T. that the male arrived. He brought no food, and slanted down to a warm sunny rock—facing west and so in sunlight. There he stood, the sun shining full on his dark plumage, a carpet of rich yellow lesser celandine flowers and paler primroses beside him, and deep-green grass around him. Just before he flew in, a male sandpiper arrived at the loch; his mate had already arrived and he flew to her as she stood on some half-submerged stones, where he daintily mated her.

On 30 April a strong east wind was blowing. The female eagle came in at 5-45 p.m. Her tail as she flew was up-tilted and her legs stretched earthward. As she sailed along the face of the cliff, perhaps half-way down it, the up-draught was sufficiently strong to neutralise her weight and she hung there, motionless. For the moment she had taken to herself the light-

214

In Mongolia the golden eagle is used for hunting foxes. Here the eagle
perches hooded on its master's wrist. (*G. Dement'ev*)

ness, airiness, and grace of a fulmar. She then alighted and brooded. Her mate also alighted at the eyrie and stood beside her for half an hour, hiding her entirely from me.

On 6 May the male eagle twice rose from his brooding and flew away, but on neither occasion did the female brood, although she came in to the rock. Later they flew away together and he did falling stunts before coming in down-wind to the eyrie, faster than I had ever seen him fly. The female later arrived, and when about 100 yards from the eyrie shot out her legs. The evening sun-glow was full upon her and she looked magnificent. Two incidents not without significance, had occurred that afternoon—the male was taking more than his share of the brooding and the female once alighted on the previous year's eyrie, a thing I had never seen her do in the nesting season before. But at the time I had no doubt that the eaglet had hatched. It was significant too, that on 15 May, when they should have been busy looking after the young eaglet, both birds were sailing idly backward and forward across the sunny part of the cliff. So near to the rock did they fly that their shadows were as life-like as they themselves; there seemed to be four eagles on the wing and not two. One of the eagles snatched at heather with one foot, but the heather did not come away: the golden hackles crowning head and neck were well seen as he did this.

On 20 May, both eagles were perched on the top of the cliff, the female standing on the old fence post. A ewe and her lamb came close, and the lamb ran about playfully near the eagle, who showed no interest in it. Later a solitary ewe arrived. She looked with interest at the eagle on the post and almost, so it seemed through the glass, touched the eagle's tail. The eagle looked embarrassed, and it was interesting that the lamb showed no fear, nor the ewe, as in the somewhat similar incident the previous year, any hostility toward her.

The Golden Eagle: King of Birds

During the last three visits I had not been near the eyrie, but on 23 May, when the light was exceedingly good—the sky was almost cloudless and beside the evening sun two mock-suns shone—I spied it carefully, and for the first time realized that there was neither any sign of the eaglet, nor any "whitewash" below the eyrie, as there should have been if it had hatched. The ravens' nest, on the other hand, held four full-fledged young birds, which were busily practising wing exercises: the evening sun shone full on their shiny plumage, soot-grey rather than black.

In order not to disturb the eagles I had always avoided approaching their eyrie too closely, but since I realised that the eyrie was probably empty I climbed the eagles' hill on 8 June, and walked round the top of their rock. Even on the top of the cliff, although the eyrie itself can be seen clearly, the observer cannot without considerable difficulty see the eggs or egg, although he can see the young bird even when it is quite small and in down. When I looked across at the eyrie it was obvious that either the egg had not hatched (only one young bird had until then ever been reared at this eyrie) or some mischance had befallen the eaglet while it was still very young: it is possible that it was carried off by one of the ravens during the absence of its parents. It seems more likely that the egg never hatched—there is a golden eagle in Sutherland which lays infertile eggs each season, and there are frequent instances of one infertile egg in an eyrie, where the other has hatched. Carl Stemmler tells me that in one Swiss eyrie, in the Canton of Berne, a pair of golden eagles often have infertile eggs.

On this day of early June there were plants of moss-campion, the cushion-pink, still in flower on the north face of the rock, and the delicate stems and white flowers of *Saxifraga hypnoides* swayed in the breeze on sheltered ledges. The raven brood were soaring on the up-rising wind current, but the golden eagles

216

had gone, and for the first time in seven years the June sky was empty of those dark forms which usually sailed so steadily above the human observer. The marks of the female eagle's claws on the wood of her perching post, and a breast-feather, downy and delicate on the grass below, recalled to me her dignified and stately presence. At the edge of the cliff lay the dried remains of a rabbit; on a knoll near it were castings of the eagles. I then realised how much the eagles meant to me, and how much pleasure they had given me during seven years' watching, and I hoped that they might avoid poison, trap and gun, and next season might return and nest once more on their dark rock.

And they did !

After an absence of almost four months the eagles were seen again on their rock in October of that year, 1952, and once more took up residence. This time, there was little or no winter nest-building. On 26 December I did indeed see at the side of the eyrie a new tuft of dried greater wood-rush. That afternoon the female made an impressive arrival at her roosting ledge. It was dusk when she appeared—a dark, shadowy bird, darker than the dusk-enshrouded rock. On 24 January 1953, the male arrived from the east in a skilled, corkscrew dive, alighted half-way down the cliff, pulled up heather, and flew with it to the 1951 eyrie, which I then saw was already well repaired and built up. The female now came in, and closely inspected his work. Together they remained at the nest for a short time. The weather for a week had been spring-like.

On 19 February I witnessed an incident which I had not previously seen, and which I do not think has been recorded in print. The female as she stood on the top of the cliff, plucked a rabbit which was lying there (the male had previously been standing near the prey and had probably brought it in). After a time the female, grasping the rabbit in one foot, took wing and sailed around with it. She again alighted, and for the space of half an hour continued to pluck the rabbit carefully. To my surprise, she again seized it firmly in one foot, launched out over the precipice, and disappeared over the far hill top, a distance of two miles as she flew. She did not again appear. She evidently believed, like many of us, in the advantages of carrying a good lunch with her on her travels.

On 10 March, I was so fortunate as to witness the laying of the first egg, and also to see the first "change-over" between male and female less than 20 hours later. Three times on 10 March, between 2-30 and 3 p.m.,* the female alighted at the eyrie, on each occasion arranging the lining with care. She then flew out of sight, but at 4 p.m. came in, alighted on the eyrie, and for the first time settled into the laying or brooding position. I left her still sitting closely. The following morning at 12-50 p.m. the male came in, tore up grass on a ledge about 200 yards from the eyrie, let it fall as he rose (I could see the grass stems gyrating as they fell), flew straight to the nest, and as he alighted I saw the golden head of his mate appear. She slowly rose from her brooding, and he at once settled down to brood in her place. The first egg had been laid !

Over three seasons laying has been very regular. In 1951 it took place approximately on 8 March, in 1952 approximately on 11 March, and in 1953 certainly on 10 March.

In 1953 one eaglet was reared. The incidents which I observed during its hatching and rearing were mostly similar to those noted during previous seasons. On 4 May, when the eaglet was approximately a fortnight old, the mother alighted on a broad ledge and first plucked some greater wood-rush with her bill then, holding this in the bill, continued to tear

*I should mention that this eyrie is situated in long. 6° 23′W., and thus the sun's time is approximately sixteen minutes earlier than the times in G.M.T. I have given in these three chapters of observations.

out more of the plant with one foot. I thus had the interesting experience of seeing nesting material gathered in both ways.

When one of the parent eagles went to hunt it was usually away for several hours, but on 7 June the male eagle returned in a quarter of an hour with a rabbit, although the rabbit ground is almost two miles distant. When he sailed out from the nest the intense sunlight, as he passed near the sun's disc, suddenly gave a silver edging to his wings— a beautiful and unusual effect.

I was abroad during the first fortnight of July and on 16 July saw, to my surprise, three eagles soaring above their rock. My first thought was that the third bird must be the 1951 young eagle, but its unskilled landing showed me that it was the young bird of 1953. Disturbed by an old ewe the eaglet took wing and when it again alighted I could see the short tail with much white on it, and the chocolate head of the young bird. In its sailing on the breeze it was already, almost, if not quite, as skilled as its parents and yet it is unlikely that it could have left the eyrie more than a week. The laying date was nearly the same as in 1951, when the eaglet was still in the eyrie on 13 July.

On 2 August the eaglet was flying very low across a steep grassy slope, closely grazed by sheep, below the cliff. The bird checked its flight, dropped to the grass, and seized a small object. As the bird circled low before pouncing I had seen the almost white tail of the young. As I watched the eaglet intently through my stalking glass, I saw that its prey was a mouse. Time after time, the eaglet tossed the mouse into the air with a jerk of the bill, playing with it as a dog might do. The grassy slope was steep and the mouse, no doubt dead by this time, rolled down the slope. The eaglet would then rush after it and pounce upon it, playing with its victim for some time.

On 16 August a kestrel made repeated stoops at the eaglet, both birds being at a considerable height. The young eagle then turned the tables, and made spectacular dives at the kestrel; as it stooped it held its legs stiffly. Later, as the eaglet soared, the white tail and the white on the wings shone as snow in the bright sun.

On 27 September the eaglet was standing on a rocky ridge when one of the parents brought a rabbit to it. The young bird seized and flew from place to place with the rabbit and it was some minutes before it began to pluck the prey, using its wings as brakes when its vigorous plucking threatened to overbalance it. It was remarkable that it was still being fed, more than eleven weeks after its first flight and three weeks after it had caught a mouse for itself. I had frequently seen it mouse-hunting, but it was evidently still unable to catch a rabbit.

When the eaglet had been flying for no more than five weeks I watched it one afternoon amuse itself by stooping at some grazing sheep. During the first stoop the legs were held out rigidly, and the bird went to within inches of the sheep's back but I do not think actually touched her. The eaglet then came back against the wind and stooped at a group of four sheep, not actually striking them but causing them to move off un-easily. I do not think the bird wished to injure the animals, but was playing with them.

During October the parent birds left the rock, but on 28 October, during a southerly gale, I saw one of them leave the cliff and fly north down-wind at tremendous speed. About five minutes later the bird returned, moving into the gale with no effort in a glide and at considerable speed. As it approached the rock, an up-draught caught it and it rose almost vertically into the air in a magnificent up-surge. It seemed to me that the eagle had deliberately flown down-wind in order to have the thrill of pitting its skill in flight against the gale on the return journey.

I have mentioned the curious flexing of the wings sometimes

seen when a golden eagle is soaring, the primaries still being wide-spaced. On 8 November, the wind being fresh from the west, I was interested to see the variation of this wing-flexing. Both eagles were hunting. When, soaring against the wind, they wished to remain quite stationary, they flexed their wings with the tips curved inwards so deeply that they appeared almost to meet. In this exceptional flight position the birds were able to remain quite still. But immediately they stiffened their wings, to the usual soaring attitude, they moved forward although there was no wing thrust of any kind.

In 1953 the shortest afternoon was cloudless and very clear. Both eagles were standing side by side on a pinnacle. The sun had set, and the moon was bright in the east. At four minutes past four the female eagle flew into the cliff. Four minutes later, the male flew in. But at ten minutes past four, I saw for a few seconds one of the eagles flying along the cliff. I think roosting time was approximately ten minutes past four.

POSTSCRIPT (ADDED IN MARCH, 1954)

During the winter 1953-54, this pair of Golden Eagles showed their individuality by again behaving differently. I did not once see the birds together, either at or near their rock. Indeed toward the end of February I reluctantly came to the conclusion that some mischance had happened to the female.

I was therefore glad to see the pair on a day of snow squalls and frost-laden gales moving at speed across the face of the rock, and over the high hill beyond it. Yet I was still uncertain whether the male (I was able to recognise him in the air as my old friend because of his distinctive poise in flight) had not taken a new mate. If so, I thought that a new nesting site, on another cliff, might well be chosen. Thus it was that I made my way to the neighbourhood on the afternoon of 9 March

1954, in no very hopeful frame of mind. That day winter had suddenly made way for spring. The sun was warm, the sky almost cloudless. A great gathering of frogs splashed as they made cold love in the boggy waters of a slow-moving stream just below its source on the moor.

I reached my observation post. There was no sign of either eagle. I first "put my glass" as stalkers say, on the 1953 Eyrie. It was flattened, and had obviously not been used since the young left in July 1953. The 1952 nest seemed built up, but as it is a much larger nest I was unable to decide if the eagles had added to it.

But, as I "spied" the nest, there was a slight movement, and I saw the eagle rise to her feet, stand for perhaps a minute, fly furtively away, keeping close to the cliff, then return and settle to brood. The previous day, from a distance, I had watched *both* eagles sailing near the eyrie. I had therefore now seen the first day's brooding and believe that when the eagle had risen to her feet she had just laid her first egg, and had flown off for a brief rest before returning to brood. She continued to sit closely while I watched. This was exactly one day earlier than that on which she had laid in 1953.

The following day, again in spring-like conditions, I twice saw the "change-over." I had scarcely arrived when the male flew in, and for exactly one hour took the female's place on the nest. The female had soared out of sight, but returned and for a short time perched on the top of the cliff. She then dropped feet-first to the eyrie and slowly walked across it, to settle down deliberately to brood. Her mate, just before her arrival, had taken wing, and already he had risen above the cliff-top and was enjoying a sparring match with the pair of ravens which, as in former years, were nesting in a different part of the cliff. On 14 March another "change-over" was observed by my wife. The extreme regularity of the laying, and the pattern of the "change-over," leaves little doubt in my mind that the birds are the same: perhaps, as the years pass, they no longer are inseparable during the winter months.

*   *   *

These three chapters of my observations at the eyrie of a pair of golden eagles were made possible because I am fortunate in living within walking distance of their territory. It is not often that an eyrie is accessible from one's home, except perhaps from the home of a deer-stalker who may have neither the time nor the interest to make observations. The disadvantages of my eyrie are that the actual nest is inaccessible and that the distance from which observations must be made necessitates the use of a stalking telescope. This entails considerable strain on the eye.

These chapters of observations are *not* intended to be a scientific account of the golden eagle's life history, but rather to give the ordinary reader a picture of the day to day home life of the golden eagle throughout the year. Other naturalists have been able to make only occasional observations of this home life. I believe, therefore, that my watching of these birds is unique in having been made all the year round, during eight years, on one individual pair of these eagles. I have learnt during this long period that this particular pair—but I cannot say that this applies to all golden eagles everywhere—are mated and remain so throughout the year with every sign of devotion towards each other. On one occasion nest-building began in November and continued on and off throughout the winter. The egg is laid regularly from 7 to 11 March and the eaglet hatches around 20–23 April. It leaves the eyrie on its first flight between 7 and 17 July but remains with the parents until November and on one occasion remained until the end of the year. It is able as early as the beginning of August to catch mice, and thus partially feed itself, while still being brought rabbits until the end of September and probably later.

The next year's eyrie may be chosen and nest-building begun only a few days after the eaglet has been importuning its parents for food (during that short time it has been presumably driven from the neighbourhood). I have proved that both male and female help in building the nest, and that the male takes at least an equal share in incubating the eggs. I have seen the nesting cup fashioned and apparently completed before the end of December. I have timed the eagles in their arrival, each afternoon in winter, at their roosting rock as the light of the short afternoon ebbs.

I have proved that the young of this particular pair do not wander far, for they periodically visit their parents in winter, and in the season when no eaglet was reared and the adult birds left the nesting site for some time, the eaglet of the previous season made its home on the cliff during the summer. On the other hand, there is no doubt that some young eagles wander far in winter as there are frequent reports of them in districts where the bird does not nest. I have also heard of seven young eagles wintering in a Highland area where there is no eyrie.

It is my impression that in most eagle territories in the west of Scotland the golden eagle's "cross" is the raven. In these chapters on my eight seasons' observations it will be noticed what a real pest the raven is to the eagle; it is for ever waging a "cold war" upon its big neighbour.

On the vexed question whether the eagle kills lambs the reader will notice that I have not attempted to "white-wash" the bird. My own particular pair *do* take lambs, but only occasionally. Lamb killing is not a golden eagle's habit as long as the bird can obtain rabbits and hares, field-mice and voles. I am sure, too, that they are not averse to eating dead lambs. I have learnt during eight seasons that "my" eagles are con-

tented, stay-at-home birds, remaining near their rock throughout the year, except for an occasional absence of a few weeks.

I have now known this pair of golden eagles for eleven years
—I have seen them grow up and take to family cares and I have
admired their excellence as mates and parents. How can I regard
them as anything but my friends ? I cannot regard them with
the cold scientific eye and consider their hormones, their
glandular reactions, or their behaviour complexes. Readers
may think I am too anthropomorphic—may it not be that I
am becoming aeetomorphic, akuleimorphic, aquilaeform, or
perhaps it should be—just aquiline.

CHAPTER XIV

Pleasures of Eagle Watching

I HAVE often thought it curious that comparatively few naturalists should be eagle-minded. Nature photographers make hurried excursions to golden eagle country; a hide at an eyrie may be prepared already for them, and they take photographs, often excellent in every respect, but they know little of the eagle's habits of life. Yet the golden eagle repays prolonged observation more than most birds. I never grow tired of watching this magnificent soarer and glider—and dive-bomber. Much has been written on the golden eagle's soaring powers, yet there is little in print about its gliding powers— and these are even more remarkable. The reason so little is known of the home life (outside the actual behaviour at the eyrie) of the golden eagle is because of the remoteness of its haunts and, to a lesser extent, the difficulty in knowing what country an eagle will decide to fly over, and hunt over, on any particular day.

It is fortunate for me that I have lived for fifty years in, or within walking distance of, golden eagle's country, first in the Central Highlands of Scotland, and during the last twenty-five years in the Isle of Skye. The chapters on eight years of watching at an eyrie describe my experiences in that misty isle. I have written this book in a room which looks out across the Minch, blue in sunshine, leaden in storm, on to the hills of the Long Island. I can glance up from my writing and see the ocean clouds gather around The Clisham of Harris, a hill which stands

226

out in snow like a peak of Spitsbergen, or rises black against the midnight afterglow in June. I can see Pabbay, Isle of the Anchorite, rise faintly at the west entrance of the Sound of Harris beyond St. Clement's of Rodil, and in my mind's eye I can see the gannets which pass almost continuously through the sound to and from the invisible stacks of Hirta. Almost daily from my room I see buzzard and raven, but it is seldom that the golden eagle is in sight, for it keeps, almost always, to the high, unfrequented moors and rocks. The eagle is not timid, but it is aloof, and always I have a long walk before I can reach its country.

It is not too much to say that a pair of golden eagles change the character of the land which they choose as their territory. Before they chose this high rock for their home, the walk to the rock, and to the dark loch beneath it, was featureless and grim. Tales were told of strange sights seen there, of strange, unearthly cries heard here: the supernatural water-horse was said to haunt the loch. The eagles, since coming to live here, have changed the character of the country; they now dominate the scene and the supernatural has receded.

During many years of golden eagle watching I have learnt much of their habits, yet there is more, far more, to learn, for the eagle is a complete individualist and no two members of its race behave alike. Apart from this, there are many things we still know little about. Here are a few suggestions for future observers.

Is the early winter repair of the eyrie exceptional or not? I do not think that up to now anyone has troubled to watch at an eyrie in November.

Is the passing of prey from male to female in full flight very exceptional?

What is the greatest journey a golden eagle will take to hunt for prey for its young—what is the greatest journey it will take with its mate (in Britain) from its home territory in winter?

Do Norwegian eagles ever cross the North Sea to Scotland, or Scottish eagles to Norway?

What is the greatest distance a golden eagle will cover in a glide?

What height above the ground may the golden eagle at times reach during prolonged upward spiralling?

What is the eagle's life-span? Is the 93 years, recorded in another chapter, often exceeded?

How will the Hydro-electric schemes in the Scottish Highlands and elsewhere effect its status? These schemes are altering a good deal of eagle country. The eagle is indifferent to this, but it now runs an added danger—that of being electrocuted as well as shot, poisoned and trapped. I understand that at least three golden eagles have been electrocuted by alighting on electric pylons.

How will National Parks, now so greatly in favour, affect the future status of the eagle?

These are a few of the questions which may be answered in time. Before this book is published we may expect to see the home-life of the golden eagle televised; we may expect more eagle-watching in National Parks and elsewhere, than in the past. The custodians of the eagle are changing. In the past they were the eagle-minded Highland landowners; the State, it seems, is to be its future custodian.

The tendency among naturalists now is to think of a bird species as though all individuals had the same habits in that species. This may be true with some species but it can never be true with the golden eagle. The eagle has more personality than any other British bird. It leads a more exclusive and solitary life. It does not normally mix with others of its species, nor feed with them, nor does it flock as most species do at some period of their life cycle. Most bird species have to a certain extent and during some periods of the year a "group mind"—the eagle never.

I cannot imagine anyone studying the ways of the eagle without, as an old stalker long ago put it, "admiring the nobility of the bird." There are two creatures which, in my view, add character, beauty and charm to the Scottish Highlands—one is the golden eagle, the other is the red deer. The eagle is the spirit of the hills and lonely glens, and of the air above them.

After a long life of bird-watching, I have no hesitation in saying that the golden eagle has given me more pleasure than any other bird. I have been throughout the year a student of its habits. The more I see of the eagle, the more I admire it. The fulmar, a beautiful flier and soarer, is another of my favourites, but in time I could grow weary of fulmar study. It is the intelligence of the eagle, as well as its wonderful mastery of flight, that draws me to it. Long may it remain in the Highland area, and may it at some future time repopulate its ancestral cliffs on Snowdon, the Eagle Mountain of the early Welsh writers.

Much of my pleasure of eagle watching I owe to the friend who, many years ago, presented me with the best stalking telescope then made. Previous to this I had used binoculars, but no binocular equals a telescope for eagle watching at a distance. Therefore to the Prince of Wales, as he then was, I owe many happy hours spent on the hill with my glass, watching eagles, sometimes near, sometimes at a distance. As recently as the afternoon of the day on which I am finishing this book I watched through this stalking glass a golden eagle set out for the hunting ground. He dived angrily at a kestrel beneath him, then glided for perhaps two miles low over the hill slopes, his shadow racing over the ground ahead of him. Suddenly he dropped into a clump. He emerged from it, not with a hare or rabbit in his talons, but with one foot holding

229

tightly a bunch of rushes, which he carried in a long glide to the eyrie, on which his mate brooded.

The quiet pleasures of eagle-watching have given many happy hours to at least one student of bird life.

APPENDIX: THE GOLDEN EAGLE ABROAD

(a) *Breeding-distribution and systematics* by the Author and James Fisher. Map on p. 8, by James Fisher.

The golden eagle has a wide Holarctic distribution, and being primarily resident (although it wanders a good deal) has evolved regional races, many of which have been named. Much remains to be done on the races of golden eagle from parts of Asia; meanwhile it is probably most useful to recognize no more than six world subspecies, whose approximate breeding-limits are shown on the map (p. 8). These are:

Aquila chrysaëtos chrysaëtos (Linné, 1758)

Some workers separate the British population, and that in S.E. Europe and S.W. Asia, as *A. c. fulva* (Linné, 1758). This group is slightly smaller. G. Dement'ev (1951) would do this; but we think it best to follow Peters (1931) and the latest B.O.U. *Check-List;* Peters thinks the race "very doubtfully distinct." Type locality, Sweden.

Aquila chrysaëtos homeyeri Severtzov, 1888.

Type locality Balearic Islands and Algeria. Darker and slightly smaller than *chrysaëtos.*

Aquila chrysaëtos daphanea Severtzov, 1888.

Original type locality included Mongolia and Transbaikalia, where birds probably *kamtschatika;* should be restricted to Russian Turkestan, Himalayas and perhaps Ala-shan Mountains. Large; more yellow than *chrysaëtos.*

Aquila chrysaëtos kamtschatica Severtzov, 1888.

Peters (1931) recognizes *A. c. obscurior* Sushkin, 1925, from the central Altai, but we follow Dement'ev (1951) in merging this with *kamtschatika,* whose type locality is Kamchatka. Darker and larger than *chrysaëtos.*

Aquila chrysaëtos japonica Severtzov, 1888.

Type locality Japan. The smallest form.

Aquila chrysaëtos canadensis (Linné, 1758).

Type locality Hudson's Bay. The darkest race.

(b) *Brief notes on status in some countries.*

NORWAY. Much persecuted; decreasing.

SWEDEN. Protected. In Swedish Lapland nests as far north as 68° 5′ N. Breeding stock 50—60 pairs.

FINLAND. Protected since 1944. Population estimated in 1953 by Dr. Einari Merikallio to be a maximum of 80 breeding pairs.

DENMARK. Does not breed. An autumn and winter migrant. Protection being sought.

ESTONIA. No very recent news. Nests in Scots firs (*Pinus sylvestris*) in flat, often boggy country.

RUSSIA. Professor Dement'ev in his book *Birds of the U.S.S.R.* gives the only available recent news. Not protected except for falconry. Numbers unknown.

GERMANY. No longer nests. Bred in Bergsau until approximately 1935, and in Bavaria up to 1901.

AUSTRIA. Decreasing. One correspondent places numbers as 10 pairs; another as 45 pairs. Nested in Partenkirchen to 1937. Stronghold now is Austrian Alps.

SWITZERLAND. Slightly decreasing. Carl Stemmler estimates population at 40—50 pairs. Protection half-hearted.

FRANCE. No census of numbers. Nests in the Alps and,

more numerously, in the Pyrenees. Is not protected and there is apparently little interest taken in it.

ITALY, also Sicily and Sardinia. No census. Nests sparingly. Is destroyed even in National Parks, where it is said to prey upon young goats and chamoix.

SPAIN, and North Africa. Professor Bernis of Madrid says all the birds he has examined in Spain are *A. chrysaëtos homeyeri*. No census. Man is hostile to it. Scarce and probably decreasing.

ALASKA, CANADA AND UNITED STATES OF AMERICA. No census. Rare in south-eastern States, except in a few places in Appalachians. Numerous in Texas, where fabulous numbers have been shot by eagle hunters in aeroplanes.

MEXICO. Widely distributed in the mountains as far south as about lat. 20° N. No census. This eagle is the national emblem of Mexico.

INDIA. Placed with *A.C. daphanea,* but racial status not certain. Breeds in Himalayas. Little known of its habits or life history.

JAPAN. Its name in Japanese is Inuwashi. Nests in Honshu and in Hokkaido, also in Korea. Numbers unknown. No protection. This bird is killed in Japan because its tail feathers are still used for the feathers of arrows. This is of interest, as in the Highlands of Scotland eagles' feathers were used for this purpose long ago, the feathers of the eagles of the Loch Treig district in Lochaber being considered especially suitable.

BIBLIOGRAPHY

AMERICAN FARM JOURNAL (1947) January

ARNOLD, L. W. (1948) Eagle attacks boy. *Audubon Mag. N.Y.* *50:* 256

AUSTIN, O. L. Jr. (1932) The Birds of Newfoundland Labrador. *Mem. Nuttall Orn. Cl.* no. 7; 229 pp. (p. 64)

BEDICHEK, R. (1950) *Adventures with a Texas Naturalist.* New York, Doubleday

BENT, A. C. (1937) Life Histories of North American Birds of Prey Part I. *Bull. U.S. Nat. Mus.* no. 167

BERTHET, G. (1936) Un aigle (*Aquila chrysaëtos*) fauve dans les monts du Lyonnais. *Alauda, 8:* 495

BEWICK, T. (1797) *History of British Birds.* Newcastle-on-Tyne, vol. I.

' BRITISH BIRDS ' (1951). Some recent photographic studies of the Golden Eagle. *Brit. Birds, 44:* plates 65-76

BROUN, MAURICE. *Hawks Aloft: the Story of Hawk Mountain*

BUTTIKOFER, J. (1948) The Golden Eagle, we must not let it die. *Pro Natura, Basel, I:* 65-76

CAMBRENSIS, GIRALDUS (1183-86) *Topographica Hibernica.* MS.

CAMERON, E. S. (1905) Nesting of the Golden Eagle (*Aquila chrysaëtos*) in Montana. *Auk, 22:* 158-67

———— (1908) Observations on the Golden Eagle in Montana. *Auk, 25:* 251-68

234

Bibliography

CARNIE, S. K. (1954). Food Habits of Golden Eagles in the Coast Ranges of California. *Condor 56:* 3-12

CATHART, JONES (1929) Letter on flight. *The Times*, 3 August

COLQUHOUN, J. (1888) *The Moor and the Loch*. Edinburgh and London, posthumous ed.

DARLING, F. F. (1947) *Natural History in the Highlands and Islands*. London, Collins, *New Naturalist*

DEMANDT, C. (1939) Der Steinadler als Brutvogel in Vorarlberg. *Beitr. Fortpfl-Biol. Vög. 15:* 14-16

DEMENT'EV G. (1936) Le vol a l'aigle au Turkestan. *Oiseau, 6:* 361-65

———— (1937) Where Eagles Work for Men. *Zoo Mag. 2*, no. 4; 4-9.

DEMENT'EV, G. and others (1951) *Ptitsy Sovetskogo Soyuza*. Moscow, Sovetskaya Nauka, vol. *1:* 267-75

DIXON, J. B. (1937) The Golden Eagle in San Diego County, California. *Condor, 38:* 48-56

FORREST, H. E. (1907) *The Vertebrate Fauna of North Wales*. London, Witherby, pp. 227-28

FITZINGER, L. J. F. J. (1853). Versuch einer Geschichte der Menagerien des Österreichisch-Kaiserlichen Mofes Wien..

FLOWER, S. S. (1938). Further Notes on the Duration of Life in Animals.—IV. Birds. *Proc. Zool. Soc. Lond.* (A) *108:* 195-235.

GHIDINI, A. (1914) Aquile ed Avoltoi nelle Alpi. *Riv. Ital. Orn. 3:* 82-83

GILBERT, H. A. and BROOK, A. (1925) *The Secrets of the Eagle*. London, Arrowsmith

GORDON, SETON (1912) *The Charm of the Hills*. London, Cassell

——— (1915) *Hill Birds of Scotland*. London, Edward Arnold

——— (1926) The Golden Eagle. *Nature, 118:* 377-79

——— (1927) *Days with the Golden Eagle*. London, Williams & Norgate

——— (1933) *Islands of the West*. London, Cassell

——— (1938) *Wild Birds of Britain*. London, Batsford

——— (1941) *In Search of Northern Birds*. London, Eyre and Spottiswoode

——— (1944) *A Highland Year*. London, Eyre and Spottiswoode

——— (1947) A Golden Eagle's roosting time. *Country Life, 97:* 209

——— (1947) Male Golden Eagle incubating. *British Birds, 40:* 181

GORDON, SETON and GORDON, A. (1925) Some Notes taken at the eyrie of a Golden Eagle. *British Birds, 18:* 237-40

GRAY, R. (1871) *Birds of the West of Scotland* . . . Glasgow

GROTE, H. (1923) Zwei junge in Adlerhorst. *Orn. Monatsb. 40:* 85-86

GURNEY, H. (1921) *Early Annals of Ornithology*. London, Witherby

HANNA, W. C. (1930) Notes on the Golden Eagle in Southern California. *Condor, 32:* 121-23

HARRISON, W. (1577) Description of Scotlande. London. Holinshed's *Chronicle*, vol. *1:* no. 1; ch. viii

HARTING, J. E. (1898) *Hints on the Management of Hawks*. London, 2nd ed.

HARVIE-BROWN, J. A. and BUCKLEY, T. E. (1888) *A Vertebrate Fauna of the Outer Hebrides*. Edinburgh, pp. 80-83

——— and MacPHERSON, H. A. (1904) *A Fauna of the Northwest Highlands and Skye*. Edinburgh, David Douglas, pp. 140-49

Bibliography

HOWARD, L. (1952) *Birds as Individuals*. London, Collins

JOLLIE, M. (1947) Plumage changes in the Golden Eagle. *Auk, 64:* 549-76

KENNEDY, C. A. (1948) Golden Eagle kills Bighorn Lamb. *Mammal. 29:* 68-69

KNIGHT, C. W. R. (1927) *The Book of the Golden Eagle*. London, Hodder and Stoughton

LEHTI, R. W. (1947) Golden Eagle attacking Antelope. *Wildlife Manag. 2:* 348-49

LELAND, J. (1906) *The Itinerary in Wales of John Leland in or about 1536-39*. London, Bell, ed. L. Toulmin Smith; and see Pennant, p. 280

LEWIS, E. (1938) *In Search of the Gyr-Falcon*. London, Constable

LØVENSKIÖLD, H. (1947-50) *Håndbok over Norges Fugler*. Oslo, Gyldendal Norsk Forlag, vol. *3:* 427-31 (1948)

MACGILLIVRAY, W. (1842) *A History of British Land Birds*, ... London, vol. *3:* 204-17

———— (1855) *The Natural History of Deeside and Braemar*. London

MACPHERSON, H. B. (1909) *Home Life of a Golden Eagle*. London, Witherby

MANNING, T. H. (1952) Birds of the West James Bay and Southern Hudson Bay Coasts. *Nat. Mus. Canada Bull.* no. 125; 108 pp. (p. 34)

MARTIN, MARTIN (1716) *A Description of the Western Islands of Scotland*. London, 2nd ed.

MAXWELL, G. (1952). *Harpoon at a Venture*. London, Hart-Davis

MENDEL, R. M. and WARNER, D. W. (1948) Golden Eagles in Hidalgo, Mexico. *Wilson Bull. 60:* 122

MERRET, C. (1666). *Pinax Rerum Naturalium Britannicorum*, ... London, p. 170

MILLIGAN, C. J. (1931) Occurrence of the Golden Eagle in Co. Antrim 1926-1930. *Irish Nat. J. 3:* 254-55

NETHERSOLE-THOMPSON, D. (1951) *The Greenshank.* London, Collins *New Naturalist*

NIETHAMMER, G. (1938) *Handbuch der Deutschen Vogelkunde.* Leipzig, vol. *2:* 173-79

OUTDOOR LIFE, U.S.A. (1936) for December

PALMAR, C. E. (1949) Photographing the Golden Eagle. *Country Life, 105:* 246-48

PALMER, R. S. (1949) *Maine Birds.* Cambridge, Mass., Mus. Comp. Zool. Harvard, pp. 144-46

PAYNE-GALLWEY, R. (1882). *The Fowler in Ireland* . . . London, pp. 291-305

PENNANT, T. (1778). *A Tour in Wales. MDCCLXXIII.* London

PETERS, J. L. (1931) *Check-list of Birds of the World.* Cambridge, Mass., Harvard U.P., vol. *1:* 253-54

PETERS, H. S. and BURLEIGH, T. D. (1951). *The Birds of Newfoundland.* St. John's, Dep. Nat. Resources, pp. 136-37

PIERCE, W. M. (1927) Status of the Golden Eagle in Southern California. *Calif. Fish and Game, 13:* 66

RAVEN, C. E. (1942) *John Ray Naturalist his Life and Works.* Cambridge, U.P., p. 332

————— (1947). *English Naturalists from Neckam to Ray.* Cambridge, U.P., pp. 322, 337, 353

RAY, J. (1678) *The Ornithology of Francis Willughby.* London

RICHMOND, C. W. (1902) Early References to Golden Eagle. *Auk, 19:* 79

von RIESENTHAL, D. (1876) *Die Raubvögel Deutchlands und des angrenzenden Mitteleuropas.* Cassel, Fischer, pp. 300-12

ROCHON-DUVIGNEAUD, A. D. (1919) L'Oeil de l'Aigle. *Ann. d'Oculist, 156:* 376-77

————— (1929) Sur l'Oeil de l'Aigle fauve du Maroc. . . . *Bull. Soc. Sci. Nat. Maroc. 8:* 160-61

ROSS, W. M. (1941) Aerial display by a pair of Golden Eagles. *British Birds, 35:* 82-83

SLEVIN, J. R. (1929) A contribution to our knowledge of the nesting habits of the Golden Eagle. *Proc. Calif. Acad. Sci.* (4) *18:* 45-71

STEMMLER, C. (1932) *Die Adler der Schweiz,* Zürich and Leipzig

STEPHEN, D. (1950) *Days with the Golden Eagle.* Glasgow, Donaldson

STONER, D. (1939) The Golden Eagle in Eastern New York. *Univ. State N.Y. Bull. Schools, 25:* 114-17

STUBBS, F. J. (1923) Eagles formerly nesting in Yorkshire. *Naturalist, 1923:* 359-63

————— (1931) Former Nesting of the Eagle in Yorkshire. *Naturalist, 1931:* 135-37

SWANN, H. K. (1925) [on the races of *Aquila chrysaëtos*] *Bull. Brit. Orn. Cl. 45:* 64-73

THORPE, W. H., COTTON, P. T. and HOLMES, P. F. (1936) Notes on the birds of . . . Yugoslavia, Albania, and Greece. *Ibis* (13) *6:* 557-80 (pp. 568-69)

WALLER, H. J. (1942) Eagle attacking hinds. *Field, 180:* 597

WILLUGHBY, F. *see* RAY, J.

WITHERBY, H. F. and others (1941) *The Handbook of British Birds.* London, Witherby, vol. *3:* 38-43

WOODGERD, W. (1952) Food Habits of the Golden Eagle. *Wildlife Manag. 16:* 457-59

WORK, T. H. and WOOL, A. J. (1947) At home with the Golden Eagle. *Nat. Hist. N.Y. 56:* 412-17, 428

YAMASHINA, Y. (1941) *A Natural History of Japanese Birds.* Tokio
YARRELL, W. (1874) *History of British Birds.* London, 4th ed., ed. A. Newton, vol. *1*

ZASTROV, M. (1946) On the distribution and biology of the Golden Eagle in Estonia. *V'r. Fågelv., 5:* 64-80

INDEX

Index

245